Islam,
the West and
the Challenges
of Modernity

Tariq Ramadan

Translated by
Saïd Amghar

THE ISLAMIC FOUNDATION

Published by
THE ISLAMIC FOUNDATION

Markfield Conference Centre, Ratby Lane,
Markfield, Leicester LE67 9SY, UK
E-mail: publications@islamic-foundation.com
Website: www.islamic-foundation.com

Quran House, PO Box 30611, Nairobi, Kenya

PMB 3193, Kano, Nigeria

Distributed by: Kube Publishing Ltd.
Tel.: 0044(01530)249230, fax: 0044(01530)249656
E-mail: info@kubepublishing.com

British library Cataloguing-in-publication data
a catalogue record for this book is available from the British Library

ISBN 978-0-860373-11-7

typeset by: N.A. Qaddoura
cover design: Imtiaze Ahmad Manjra

Contents

Part One
At the Shores of Transcendence
Between God and Man

Part Two
The Horizons of Islam
Between Man and the Community

Part Three
Values and Finalities
The Cultural Dimension of the Civilisational Face to Face

An Entire Life

And that this is My path, straight; so do you follow it, and follow not diverse paths lest they scatter you from His path.
(Qur'ān, 6:153)

I still have the intimate memory of his presence and of his silences. Sometimes, long silences sunk in memory and thoughts and, often, in bitterness. He had a keen eye and a penetrating, profound look that now carried his warmth, kindness and tears, and now armed his determination, commitment and anger. How many times was it difficult for me to cross the expression of his big open, powerful, suggestive and interpolator eyes which accompanied his words up to my heart, that they awakened, troubled and shook. All those who have met him were struck by this trouble, this inward trembling. He had learned the essential and called for the same without re-routing. This, always, with a heart and with such intelligence. He was so afraid of causing harm, wounding or hurting someone's ear. His kindness was behind his hesitations and, sometimes, clumsiness.

Very early, I learned at his side how much the world is nourished by lies, rumours and scandal-mongering. When men lose morality they find the jungle and become wolves. Of this kind there were many around him; those who fought and sullied him for political profit, those who forgot him for professional profit and those who betrayed him for financial profit. So much was said, written and lied about: that he has met him who he never saw, that he spoke to him but he never listened and that he was involved in secret plots which he never dreamt of. In my memory resounds the words of one of his brothers of the road: "He could have been a millionaire, not by flattering kings, but by simply accepting to be quiet and keep silent about what goes on. He refused; he said the truth and re-said it, before God, without fear of losing everything."

I also remember the following story, repeated a thousand times by my elder brother Aymen, a story that made him shed so many tears. He was then 15 years old when he heard it during a travel that found him in the presence of wealthy princes: "The money that you want to give me is put on the palm of my hand; as to myself, by God's command, I do not work except for that which is posited in and penetrates hearts..." Despite his material difficulties, he rejected exorbitant amounts of money in the name of his faith in God, of his exactness of truth and of his love for justice. Aymen has never forgotten the lesson; it has fashioned him and he transmitted it.

He learnt everything from a man who gave him so much, offered him so much and who, from a very early age, trained and protected him. On his subject he was inexhaustible. Hasan al-Banna, through his total devotion to God and His teachings, put light in his heart and showed him the way of his commitment. To those who criticised him, spoke without having even met or heard him, or those who had simply read him, he reminded them how much he had learnt at his side of spirituality, love, fraternity and humility. For hours on end, he brought out of his memory the events and instances that had marked him when he was just like his son; and when he was respectfully called, in the whole of Egypt, "the little Hasan al-Banna". The profound faith of his master, his devotion, intelligence, his knowledge and open-mindedness, his goodness and kindness were all qualities that emanated in a permanent fashion from his description.

Often, he spoke of the determination in his commitment, at all moments, against colonialism and injustice and for the sake of Islam. This determination was though never a sanction for violence, for he rejected violence just as he rejected the idea of "an Islamic revolution". The only exception was Palestine. On this, the message of al-Banna was clear. Armed resistance was incumbent so that the plans of the terrorists of Irgun and of all Zionist colonisers would be faced up to. He had learnt from Hasan al-Banna, as he said it one day: "to put one's forehead on the ground." The real meaning of prayer being giving strength, in humility, to the meaning of an entire life. He also learnt love in God, patience, the importance of work in-depth, education and solidarity. Finally, he learnt to give everything. After the assassination of his master, in 1949, he retained the lesson and sacrificed all in order to make everyone hear the liberating message of Islam. History is written by the powerful; the worst calumnies were said about *Imām* Hasan al-Banna. He never ceased to write about and say the truths from which he was nourished. But the despots' love of power caused death and spread much blood as well as so much torture.

Already, when he was barely 20 years old, al-Banna had entrusted him with the editorship of his magazine *al-Shihāb*. Then he volunteered to fight in Palestine, at the age of 21, participating in the defence of Jerusalem. In 1948, aged 22, he went to Pakistan where he was approached about taking the post of General Secretary of the World Islamic Congress. His determination scared the "diplomats". He remained in Pakistan for several months. He took part in the debates about constitutional questions and directed a weekly radio programme on Islam and the Muslim world which made him very popular among the youth and intellectuals. Returning to Egypt, he engaged himself in mobilisation for social and political reform. Then he travelled across the country, gave lectures, and directed encounters. In 1952, he launched, on the model of *al-Shihāb*, a monthly magazine called *al-Muslimūn* in which were to write some of the greatest Muslim scholars and, which was going to be distributed from Morocco to Indonesia in both Arabic and English. But Hasan al-Banna, well before his assassination, warned them: the road will be long, marked out with pain, sadness and adversity. He knew, himself and all those who accompanied him, that they would be subjected to lies, humiliation, torture, exile and death.

For him it was exile, because Nasser deceived them. He had to leave the country in 1954, never to return, except on 8th August 1995 in his coffin – 41 years of exile, suffering, commitment and sacrifice for God and justice and against all dictators and hypocrisies. Exile is the exactness of faith. The length of this road, the difficulties and the sorrows were numerous and continuous. This was first experienced in Palestine were he was designated General Secretary of the World Islamic Congress of Jerusalem before being banned from the city by Glubb Pasha, himself subjected to American orders. Then, in Damascus were he restarted the diffusion of *al-Muslimūn* with Mustafa al-Siba'i. Thereafter in Lebanon, before arriving in Geneva in 1958. He obtained his Doctorate in Cologne in 1959, and published his thesis under the title 'Islamic Law: its Scope and Equity' in which he presented the synthesis of the fundamental positions of Hasan al-Banna on the subject of the *Sharīʿa*, law, political organisation and religious pluralism. This was an essential book, without doubt the first in a European language, on the question of the universal Islamic point of reference. One can find therein conviction and determination and at the same time a manifest and permanent open-mindedness; never once the slightest sanction of violence.

He founded the Islamic Centre of Geneva in 1961 with the support and participation of Muhammad Natsir, Muhammad Asad, Muhammad Hamidullah, Zafar Ahmad Ansari and Abu al-Hasan al-Nadwi. All symbolic figures and faithful brothers of the same struggle. This Islamic centre was to serve as a model for the creation of other centres in Munich, London, Washington and, in a general fashion, in the West. The objective being to enable the immigrant Muslims in Europe or the USA to maintain a link with their religion and find a place of welcome and reflection. It was equally a question of producing an absolutely independent activity in order to present Islam, to carry out works of unimpeded publication, and to analyse current questions without constraint. Numerous books and facsimiles were published from Geneva in Arabic, English, French and German, along with the re-publication of the magazine *al-Muslimūn* which later ceased in 1967. Meanwhile he thought out the creation of the Islamic World League of which he wrote its first Statutes. His commitment was total and the Saudi funds that he received, through the intermediary of this same Islamic League which at that time was opposed to Nasser's regime, were never subject to particular conditions of commitment or to political silence. When, at the end of the 1960s, the Islamic World League, which had then become too much under Saudi influence, and who put conditions on their financial support, in particular a requirement to take over the Islamic Centre and its activities, he refused. Then in 1971, all incomes were cut off. Thus was preserved independent thought and action. The road would be long and difficult. This he never doubted, as he always knew what the price of independence and what the price of the word of truth was.

How many are those who have known and appreciated him during these full years. Travelling to the countries of the entire world; expressing himself in Malaysia, staying in England, Austria or in the USA, creating links, spreading profound, analytical thought and always nourished by spirituality and love. Mawdudi even thanked him for having awakened him from his unconsciousness. Muhammad Asad was grateful to him for having made him know, or rather profoundly *feel* the thought of Hasan al-Banna. Malek Shabbaz (Malcolm X) heard in the kitchen of the Islamic Centre of Geneva that no race is chosen and that an Arab, no more than a black person, is not superior to his white brother, if not by piety. Malcolm X retained the lesson, loved it profoundly and his last written words, on the eve of his death in February 1965, were addressed to him. Yusuf Islam (Cat Stevens) paid him numerous visits in his London hostel. He confessed to me of having retained the memory of his fine intelligence and extreme sweetness. In 1993, in Geneva Airport, the scholar Abu al-Hasan al-Nadwi showed him the signs of infinite respect, and during a visit to Lucknow, in India, where is found the *Nadwat al-'Ulamā'*, al-Nadwi recalled with deep emotion one of his visits and the marks that it left on him. In exile, far from his own, exposed to political and financial harassment, and beset by all kinds of problems, he worried and tortured his mind but he preserved the essential: a deep faith, a faithful fraternity, the eyes of kindness and the thirst for exactness.

His work-place was a room, full of documents and magazines. Here a phone, there a radio and a television, there piled-up books, opened or annotated. The world was at the reach of his hand. Whoever entered this universe entered in sympathy with a story, a past, a life, intermingled with sadness and solitude. One thousand and one memories and, at the same time, an incomparable view on the current events of the world. He was in *affective* contact with the most distant of countries. He knew almost everything that was going on in Tadjikistan, Kashmir, Chechnia, Indonesia, Afghanistan, Morocco, Algeria, Tunisia, Egypt and elsewhere. He followed the regional current events of Washington, Los Angeles, Harlem, London, Munich, Paris, Geneva, right up to Karachi. A horizon burgeoning with information. He suffered so much and with such intensity in his room, from the state of the world, from the lies, massacres, imprisonings and tortures. His political intuition was fearsome; one understood why he was feared.

He did not content himself with current events, he was interested in everything including the development of techniques, medicine, sciences and ecology. He knew the requirements of a deep Islamic reform. His curiosity was without limit, always awakened and particularly lucid. He had travelled across the world; and from then on the world lived in this room. There used to be crowds, scholars, presidents and kings; there remained, henceforth, nothing but observation, analysis and a deep sadness. In solitude, though, there was the Qur'ān; and in isolation, there were invocations. Invocations and tears. He gave his children symbolic names, names from the history of all persecutions and infinite determinations. With each one, he had the cord of complicity, the space of attention, the sensitivity of relation and love. With Aymen, his success and wounds; with Bilāl, his potential and heartbreak; with Yasser, his presence, his generous devotion and his waiting; with Arwa, his complicity and silences; with Hani, his commitment and determination. To each one, he reminded that he made us a gift of the best of mothers. She is, with the quality of her heart, his most beautiful present.

After more than 40 years of exile, an entire life for God, faith and justice, he knew that his last hour was coming. In the most profound hours, he spoke and he spoke so much of love, fraternity and affection. A few months before returning to God, he said to me, with the strength of his sad, drowned look: "Our problem is one of spirituality. If a man comes to speak to me about the reforms to be undertaken in the Muslim world, about political strategies and of great geo-strategic plans, my first question to him would be whether he performed the dawn prayer (*fajr*) in its time." He observed the agitation of each and everyone, including my own. He reminded me so much not to forget the essential, to be with God in order to know how to be with men. An entire life in struggle, the hair turned grey by time, and a reminder: "Power is not our objective; what have we to do with it? Our goal is love of the Creator, the fraternity and justice of Islam. This is our message to dictators." Late at night, in that famous room, he spoke and entreated. The link with God is the way, and spirituality is the light of the road. One day, when having a look at his life, he said to me: "Our ethical behaviour and conscience of good and evil is an arm that is used against us by despots, lovers of titles, power and money. They do that which we cannot do; they lie as we cannot lie, they betray as we cannot betray and kill as we cannot kill. Our exactness before God is, in their eyes, our weakness. This apparent weakness is our real strength."

This strength was his energy up to his last days. He remained deeply faithful to the message. I owe him the understanding that to speak of God is, before anything else, to speak about love, the heart and fraternity. I owe him my learning that solitude with God is better than neglect with men. I owe him the feeling that deep sadness never exhausts one's faith in God. His generosity, his kindness and knowledge were as many presents. I thank God for giving me the gift that is this father, at whose side I discovered that faith is love. Love of God and men in the face of all trials and adversities.

Hasan al-Banna taught: "Be like a fruit tree. They attack you with stones, and you respond with fruits." This he himself learnt very well; he made it his own in the most intimate sense of the word. Observer of the world, distant from the crowds, in the solitude of his place, after years of fighting without respite for God's sake, against treachery and corruption, his words had the energy of the sources and of the *rabbāniyya* (of the essential link with the Creator). He never ceased to speak about God, the heart and about the intimacy of this Presence. He had learnt the essential, and he called for the essential without re-routing.

He was laid to rest next to the one who taught him the way, Hasan al-Banna. May God have mercy on them both. A return from exile in death because despots fear the words of the living. The silence of the dead is nonetheless heavy of meaning, just like the supplications of those who are subjected to injustice. One must, nonetheless, say this word of truth even if it is bitter. Thus have we been commanded by the Prophet (pbuh): "We are to God and to Him we shall return." God called to him a man, on the 4th August 1995, a Friday, just before dusk. A man, a son, a husband, a brother, a father-in-law, a grandfather, my father. The sole merit of those that remain will be to testify, day after day, their faithfulness to his memory and teaching. To love God, respond to His call, accompany men, live and learn how to die, live in order to learn how to die. This against all the odds.

Said Ramadan spent 41 years in exile, almost an entire lifetime. What remains are his words, his outlook and his determination. This life is not the Life. May God receive him in His mercy, forgive him his sins and open for him the gates of Peace in the company of the Prophets, the pious and the just. I ask God to enable me to be for my children as my father was for me.

Tariq Ramadan

Foreword

A man, a woman
at the heart of modernity

To observe and understand it, our world seems inaccessible. The days pass and confirm the folly of men. Carried, here, by technique and noise, they live on speed, computer science, music and cinema. Burdened, over there, by hunger and weariness, they survive on expectation, hope and in silence. Modern times have, for our memories, a concern for image, and also the infinite neglect of reality and meaning.

In the East as in the West, our epoch gives rise to the greatest famine ever noticed on earth. Tortured bodies echo the suffering of minds. Bodies and hearts are thirsty for humanity. Poverty, straying, dictatorships and wars stifle and stammer the dignity of several billions of men and women every day. Solitude, individualism, moral misery, and lack of love eats into the being of all those whom comfort should have made content. Where is the way? Where are we going? How to be a woman, how to be a man today?

So how, at the heart of this agony, do we respond to our hearts and protect the spirituality which makes us be? How, on the precipice of so much imbalances, do we bring forth the balance and harmony that will appease our hearts? How do we remain faithful to the pact of origin when modernity renders us so unfaithful to our humanity?

Memory of the first morning:

> *And when thy Lord took from the Children of Adam, from their loins, their seed, and made them testify touching themselves, 'Am I not your Lord?' They said, 'Yes, we testify...'* (Qur'ān, 7:172)

This testimony lives in the depths of hearts; it speaks and calls to us. Our heart is our hope; spirituality is our way:

> *It is not the eyes that are blind, but blind are the hearts within the breast.* (Qur'ān, 22:46)

This is looking, in one's depth, for strength of sight, real sight. It is being with God in order to read the signs, live with His remembrance in order to fill oneself with humility, to give the night its light and pray loudly in infinite silence:

> *Behold We shall cast upon thee a weighty word; surely the first part of the night is heavier in tread, more upright in speech, surely in the day thou hast long business. And remember the Name of thy Lord, and devote thyself unto Him very devoutly. Lord of the East and the West; there is no God but He...* (Qur'ān, 73:5–9)

To give life to one's heart is so difficult. The daily running of the world steals us from ourselves, to the point, sometimes, of rendering our personality double and tearing us apart. I have this memory, so present in my eyes; an image in Tunisia, Egypt, India, the USA, Europe, in the East as in the West. Friday and all days of the week: the tearing apart of the Muslim world is there.

The crowd, the community, the fervour, the hope and the best of intentions. The most beautiful day of the week, the day of all symbols. The sermon, the reminder to meaning, the wet eyes, the tears of the heart. The world of Islam is vibrating in this end of the twentieth century as it was vibrating at the beginning of the seventh; God is witness of this strength of faith. The mosques open up, the roads are mosques, and the earth is a mosque. The *Umma* is here; the rich and the poor, the computer scientist and the unlettered, witnesses of the same testimony looking to quench the same thirst.

Saturday, Sunday, Monday and the rest. Five hours of the morning, noon, or even four hours. Sleep is so heavy, the jobs so preoccupying. So many silences on Fridays and so many words on other days. So much truth and then so many lies; so many hopes and then so much groaning; so much will and then so much laziness. There was here a memory, what remains is forgetfulness. There was so much, but what remains is so little. During the days of the week, daily life has its excuses that have reason for our faithfulness. Our epoch is one of torture. Spirituality is a trial.

On Friday as on other days of the week, our wounds are deep. There are some who, observing the vanities of this world, will adopt the ways of mysticism. Far from the world, ambitions and conflicts; and nourished by the light of the only Light. In the West, it was even considered that such was "real Islam", "the other Islam"; the one that forces respect, when it is an Islam that attacks minds. One must live far in order to live better; abandoning men in order to come closer to God. Our epoch seems to give reason to the meaning of this exile.

The Sufis, through their contemplation, their inward exile and their shunning of the world have followed and are still following the example of the Prophet (peace be upon him) who used to spend entire nights in prayer, meditation, in beautifying his memory, deepening his gratefulness and perfecting his worship of Him. The tears, born out of meditation, make the signs in the universe appear. The presence of the sacred is revealed:

> *Surely in the creation of the heavens and of the earth and in the alternation of night and day there are signs for men possessed of minds who remember God, standing and sitting and on their sides, and reflect upon the creation of the heavens and earth...* (Qur'ān, 3:190–1)

At the heart of our daily existence, which is agitated and drowned in the most overwhelming occupations, this is tantamount to taking a step backwards, exiling oneself to one's centre, looking for the strength of one's memory, loving and acknowledging, thanking and praying in the noise, looking for silence and living with strength the meaning of the words "*Be on this earth like a stranger or a passer by.*"[1]

This spirituality, and its requirements, is at the heart of our daily existence. It is a question of denying nothing of our being, neither our body, nor our spirit, nor this life nor the Next. The trial of spirituality is a trial of balance; it is the way of the "just middle" as it is the way of all difficulties. Some want but the life of this world, and thus they lose themselves:

> *Now some men there are who say, 'Our Lord, give to us in this world'; such men shall have no part in the world to come...* (Qur'ān, 2:200)

Others, as much as their humanity allows, want to be here in order to be better over There:

> *And others there are who say, 'Our Lord, give to us in this world good, and good in the world to come'* (Qur'ān, 2:201)

It is living one's daily existence, working and committing oneself; putting one's faith in order to test one's own actions, angers, and deceptions. It is being with God amidst men and giving to what one has the meaning of what one is:

> *... but seek, amidst that which God has given thee, the Last Abode, and forget not thy portion of the present world; and do good, as God has been good to thee. And seek not to work corruption in the earth; surely God loves not the workers of corruption.* (Qur'ān, 28:77)

It is to be with one's whole being in this life, carrying the witness of one's faith through actions of justice and goodness. It is tantamount to rejecting nothing of what one "is" in order to be with one's whole being. This before God and men:

> *The best of men is the one who is most useful to his fellow men.*[2]

Yet, our epoch challenges us. The society of entertainment, excessive consumption and generalised individualism coexists with the most extreme destitution and the most total misery. In front of these fatalities, where is the meaning? Filled with the remembrance of God, at which source, in all this modernity, can we quench our thirst?

Each person knows the re-routing of this life which *kills* something in us: sitting in front of the television, battered by a torrent of information, and paralysed by the scope of fractures. This is tantamount to acknowledging God, but living without a life. It is losing one's mind because one has lost one's heart, and this day in and day out.

One would love nonetheless to know how to be a man, how to be a woman before God, in the mirror of one's own conscience, in the looks of those who surround us. One would so wish to find the strength to beautify one's thoughts and to purify one's heart. It is everyone's hope and expectation to live in serenity and to plod along in transparency: the palms of the hands patiently directed towards heaven, at the heart of all this modernity.

A man, a woman, it is simply a question of being. To be good and do good. Which man has not wished to be for his companion the horizon of his expectations; to walk on the same shore and, out of tenderness and pardon, make of their union a sign. A couple that is for humanity what the sun is for nature, the warmth and sign of creation. Which woman has not wanted, with this same will, to be for her husband the energy of the way, at the heart of this modernity?

Which mother, which father or which parent has not hoped for their children the most harmonious space, the most united family, and the most liberating interior force? Who has never wished to see in the eyes of his son or daughter, in the depths of their heart, the sparkle of thankfulness and conviction that make faith? Which son or daughter has not desired living between two beings, carried by their love, nourished by their values and strong in their coherence, at the heart of this modernity?

Such simple things in so troubled an epoch. To be good and do good, before God, is the meaning of this call, chanted more than 17 times a day, yesterday as it is today, at the heart of this modernity:

Guide us in the straight path... (Qur'ān, 1:6)

Walking along the right path, the path of the just middle, to remember God and keep in one's heart the sense of values and finalities. Always walking along despite the dangers and adversities, despite the injustices and horrors, trusting in God so as not to despair of men and events. Walking along, and walking again, simply trying to be a man and trying to be a woman. In transparency and clarity accepting one's weaknesses and humanity, finding at the heart of forgiveness the strength of one's own humility. To be humble, in order to be at the heart of modernity. As also the remembrance and the reminder:

> Remember thy Lord in thy soul, humbly and fearfully, not loud of voice, at morn and eventide. Be not thou among the heedless. Surely those who are with thy Lord wax not too proud to serve Him; they chant His praise, and to Him they prostrate (Qur'ān, 7:205–6)

This by facing up to all inhuman individualism, all reflexes of consumption, all televisual or cinematographical illusions and all neglects. By rejecting all injustices, by opposition to all exploitation, by fighting against all miseries. By saying and maintaining with determination the strength of this humility and trust in God, in an infinite manner. By finding the road in action; arming oneself with light through patience. In the fraternity of men against the society of individuals, in the union of liberties against the egoism of independence. *The right path*, at the heart of modernity: our spirituality, in our heart, is at the heart of life.

By rejecting neglect and listening, deeply listening from the deepest recesses of ages, listening and hearing, the voice of the ancient slave Bilāl calling the faithful to his faithfulness, five times a day, and for eternity. Looking, in the echo of this voice and in the rhythm of prayers, looking and finding the direction and the way, at the heart of all this modernity.

Notes

1. A *ḥadīth* reported by Bukhārī.
2. A *ḥasan Ḥadīth* reported by al-Dāraquṭnī.

Introduction

The world is constantly moving: man seems to be acceding further every day to greater autonomy, as he also sets out to a greater freedom. Scientific progress and technological discoveries have made of rationalisation and efficiency the two emblems of our time. So much so that one very often confuses the fact of *modernity* with what appears to be, by distortion, the ideology of *modernism* (we shall return to this shift in meaning which is neither harmless nor gratuitous). It remains that the idea of modernisation has today one of the most positive connotations. To make it one's own is by extension to accept the principles of modernity: rationality, change and freedom.

It is indeed a haunting question at the end of this second millennium to know whether Islam and the Muslims will embark on the train of progress. To compare the Western world – which is permanently stirred by scientific and technological effervescence, with the Muslim world, which is invariably stilted in memories of flourishing times, clinging to old traditions which mix local culture with Qur'ānic references – is indeed interesting. For one may ask whether the rejection of progress or modernity is not inherent in Islam itself. Such is the contrast, as some have claimed, that it is incumbent to "modernise Islam" if there is to be any chance of seeing Muslims living in harmony with their time, and in order that they might finally adapt themselves.

The question becomes then, can the Muslim world accede to modernity without denying some of the fundamentals of the Islamic religion? Do we have the means to modify from within the links between a millinery traditionalism and an imperative reform which will turn faces towards the present? Many in the

West propose, in all legitimacy, this reflection to their Muslim interlocutors. This reflection inevitably engages us in a crucial debate, in the course of which it would be possible for us to fix, all at once, the points of convergence and divergence between Western and Muslim concepts. This because it may well be that the sole reference to Western history, viz. events as much as mentalities, cannot be enough to give account of the complexity of the problem. We cannot therefore make the economy of fixing with precision the acceptance of certain words and concepts. And this applies as much to the terminology in usage in the modernised West, so *evident* in appearance, as to that of the Islamic tradition so *foreign* because of the same appearance.

We shall attempt, in this Introduction, to determine what the concept of modernity really covers. By dint of Western history, this notion has taken the flavour of its origin and it is this specificity, which we should keep in mind. In Part One, we shall study the fundamentals of the Islamic religion. We will try to explain, 'At the Shores of Transcendence', the basic elements of Islam's universe of reference (in the sense of *religio*, of the bond between God and man). Then it would be possible to address the social, political and economic questions. Part Two, 'The Horizons of Islam', attempts to set out the trends offered by Islamic sources regarding the management of the collective fact. Here, we shall find out that there exists an important margin for manoeuvre enabling us to carry out the reforms which are impressed upon us and which should allow us to face contemporary challenges. The last part, 'Values and Finalities', tackles the question of encounter, when it is not a question of facing up to or of a conflict between Western and Islamic civilisation. Nonetheless, the end of the century is tense; clashes or "new wars" are constantly announced to us. To guard against slipping, necessitates a return to the respective concepts of the universe, of life and of man. This, in our understanding, is the path imposed by any hope for dialogue, or future collaboration. The differences are as numerous as the misunderstandings. Acknowledged differences may create mutual respect, but hazy misunderstandings bring forth nothing but prejudice and rejection. The latter is our daily lot. A dialogue without prevarication must establish itself, and perhaps it should centre around the question of modernity. This notion has become the banner which is held by all overt progressists, and seems to attract to its ranks only a few Muslims who want to remain loyal to their religion and their culture.

I. History of a Concept

The hold of religious power, the unjust traditional order of feudal society and the numbness of thought are a few ideas which will serve to characterise the European Middle Ages.[1] A "sombre" epoch, thought Victor Hugo; "an obscure" period, pointed out Auguste Comte. Nothing seemed to move; men were as if paralysed by the burden which was imposed by their masters as also the clergy.

The fifteenth century, however, saw the first upheaval. A great movement was set in motion and respectively touched the economic (the birth first of mercantile and then capitalist society), political (the first visible jolts of contest against the hegemony of religious power before the more direct mobilisation of the eighteenth century) and social (access to a greater freedom until the recognition of the primacy of the individual) spheres. This great moment of transformation in European societies shall be identified by a term that conveys the most positive considerations: namely modernisation. To put it plainly, modernisation is a liberation, the breaking of the chains of all intangible dogmas, stilted traditions and evolving societies. It represents accession to progress. Within this, reason, science and technology are set in motion. Finally, it is also man brought back to his humanity, with the duty of facing up to change, to accepting it and mastering it.

From the seventeenth century, and more clearly the eighteenth century, a number of thinkers took strong positions in favour of modernity. Everyone became somehow opposed to traditional society and called for rationalisation and the secularisation of society. They also defended a new status for the individual. This movement, which found its vigour 300 years ago, is still very much alive today and has lost nothing of its legitimacy in the West. Many defend modernity in the name of freedom, progress, the autonomy of reason as also in the name of a certain idea of man and humanism.

Dominique Wolton sums up in a clear fashion what this notion covers today:

"Modernity is characterised by distrust, if not opposition towards tradition; the primacy granted to the individual and the crucial importance of freedom; the belief in reason, progress and science – the three being linked together; the detachment of society with regard to the sacred and religion through the process of secularisation; the enhancement of the value of change and discovery; and, more generally, the primacy granted to self-reflectiveness and self-institution – to speak like C. Castoriadis; finally, in the political level, the emergence of a private sector which is distinct from the public sector, the importance of law and state and finally, the necessity of building and defending public liberties which are the conditions of democracy. We understand, in this quick examination, how modernisation and modernity constitute the foundation of our contemporary history."[2]

Wolton has the merit of placing this rapport of modernity in a historical perspective. In fact, the whole of what this concept covers has been influenced by European history. In its source, it expresses a revolt against the old order; at its peak, it is a real transmutation of the order of values. Alain Touraine explains this phenomenon clearly: "The West has, therefore, lived and thought modernity as a revolution. Reason recognises no gain; it sweeps clean the beliefs, the social and political forms of organisation which do not rest on a demonstration of a scientific type... the idea that society is the source of values, that the good is what is useful to society and evil is what harms its integration and efficiency, is a basic element of the ideology of modernity."[3]

Placing the phenomenon of modernisation on the historical plane allows us to better comprehend the logic which rendered it so positive, so liberating and so human. At the same time, this procedure clarifies to us the principles which will straightaway characterise modernity. These principles are its opposition to any tradition, any established order, against any sacredness or inquisitive clergy, against any revelation or imposed values; it is the affirmation of man as an individual, the claim of freedom, the defence of reason and, by extension, an appeal to science and progress. As Touraine and Castoriadis said, from now it is man – society – which fixes norms and values.

II. The Lessons of History

The great movement born in Europe beginning from the sixteenth century brought about outstanding changes to economic, political and social levels. Economic modernisation was to transform society, becoming synonymous with enrichment and the improvement of the conditions of life. On the political level, one witnessed the creation of the state of law, a recognition of individual and religious liberty within secularisation, and finally to the birth of open democratic societies. The social sphere evidently profited from the whole of these upheavals: the rights of individual and citizen, and his social rights (work, participation, representation) followed this same positive evolution.

Who can deny the contribution of modernisation in Europe when comparing the two models of society – feudal and civil? Who can question the validity of modernity? To consider the facts from this angle, modernity has given everything to man in the West: from liberty to knowledge, from science to technology. In short, it restored him to his humanity and to his responsibilities.

Yet, more and more voices are heard criticising modernisation and the founding principle of modernity. In analysing today's societies, some intellectuals level the reproach of excess (without being able to clearly designate those responsible). By dint of giving privilege to rationality, efficiency and productivity for more progress, our societies are on the edge of an abyss. On the economic plane, we witness a continuous course of growth with the consequence of an incredible fracture between the North and the South. On the political level, the democratic ideal is falling apart; and on the social plane, unemployment and exclusion are the lot of an increasing number of men and women.

We repeat, modernisation was in its origin, a revolution. Being an expression of rejection, it actualised itself against an order, and every barrier stripped away was in itself a liberated stronghold, a gain of liberty. It conveyed, at the same time, an unlimited optimism and a profound faith in man. Without any other authority, except its spirit, and without any other norm except the real, it was apt to establish values and fix limits for the good of humanity. As with all revolutions, this one has not escaped excess. Very often, the means of liberation become ends in themselves in an amnesia of any normative value. Liberty has called for more liberty and change has engendered change. Efficiency and productivity in the production of things are henceforth the measure of the good, growth is self-justified within a process which gives privilege to the most extreme pragmatism, and which makes out of any traditional reference, or reference of identity, a reactionary enemy – that is in love with a past which is fortunately passed by. Rationality has become the truth and progress the meaning and value; with the advent of our century was born a new ideology: modernism. It is clearly a distortion of the first *élan*, but, at the same time, it seems that this is the logical result. Defenders of modernisation, because of historical data, have wanted to cut themselves off from any reference in order to rush forward to the future in all freedom. In the name of this same freedom, the ideologues of modernism have made of this *élan* the reference itself, the only reference. It will have as a name: *growth, progress, science or technology*, but the substratum is the same.

The West is passing today through a crisis which we might render, with Touraine, as "*a crisis of modernity*".[4] The rationalisation which is elevated to the rank of an infallible doctrine marks its own limits, and man, who was supposed at the beginning to become the master of the game, is outrun by the logic which he set in motion. The forces of attraction combined with efficiency, productivity, growth, investment and consumption have dispossessed man of a part of his humanity. Without references, in search of new values (ethic), he is subjected to the meaning of progress and the march towards the future, more than he decides them.

From economic crises to political and social crises, from the imbalance of the North-South divide to ecological imbalances, it is nonetheless imperative that man's gain becomes the subject of his history, that he reinvests in diverse fields of activity in order to fix priorities, limits, meanings; this for lack of being able to determine values.

It is difficult, as we see, to disassociate the positive and negative aspects of modernity. In its origin, it is a claim of liberty, a call for autonomy of reason in an acceptance of change. The evolution, in course from the seventeenth century through to and mainly in the twentieth century, has provoked excesses and given birth to an ideology. It is this that we have attempted to identify, so that the ground is cleared for a more precise usage of terms, and in order to avoid indulging in a hotchpotch. Hotchpotch, for example, would consist in confusing the process of modernisation with its recent excessive rendering, and thus justifying, in the process, all the rejections. In the same fashion, by reinserting the process of access to modernity in its European history, it is possible for us to avoid inoperative comparisons, and so especially, avoid confusing modernity with occidentalism. This because to accept the principles of liberty, autonomy of reason or the primacy of the individual is something, but it is something else to identify these solely with Western history which has seen their accession to the social field being done after a conflict whose extent and consequences on mentalities is still unappreciated. The West has given us a particular form of modernity, it partakes of its history and points of reference. Another civilisation can, from within, fix and determine the stakes in a different fashion. This is the case of Islam at the end of this twentieth century.

Notes

1. We know nowadays how much the Middle Ages were, on the contrary, rich and burgeoning with ideas that have, for many, influenced the form that the Renaissance later took.
2. Dominique Wolton, *La dernière utopie*, Flammarion, 1993, p.71.
3. Alain Touraine, *Critique de la modernité*, Fayard, 1992, pp. 25 and 30.
4. Ibid., title of Part II of his book.

Part One

At the Shores of Transcendence
Between God and Man

At the Shores of Transcendence

In our Introduction we identified that for the women and men of the West, Islam seems to be resistant to any idea of modernity. We read such notions in the first pages of certain American, English and French magazines when they address the rise of Islamism in titles such as *Islam or Modernity,* and *Islam or Democracy.*[1] That is when the formulations are not more exclusivist or sentencing. The backdrop that is drawn is the expression of a kind of face to face between Islam and the West. A face to face whereby the latter is attributed a positive quality, representing the principle of openness and respect for humanist and democratic values. Inversely, Islam seems as negatively marked by archaism and tradition, of being locked up in old dogmatic categories, the denunciation of women, a barbarous penal code (rendered as *Sharī‘a*), and the denial of the freedom of peoples. At the threshold of the third millennium of the Christian era, the terms of the alternative are clear.

When one looks at the state of Muslim societies, it is impossible to annul by a stroke of the pen the critiques made against us. They are well-founded when they evidence certain astonishing reflections and behaviours which we justify in the name of Islam. Among these are the privilege of Kings and Presidents, expedient justice, the illiteracy of women along with a variety of discriminations, each one more painful than the other, the narrow traditionalism of some *‘ulamā’* who decide and resolve questions away from any human reality in an absoluteness which only God knows. The facts are there, one must acknowledge and take account of them. However, one must ask whether the debate on Islam has been launched on clear and sound methodological bases. To consider and take into account only the shocking daily events, or more broadly, the state of Muslim societies in order to conclude, in a definite fashion, that Islam cannot respond to contemporary problems is both erroneous and reductionist. It limits Islamic Studies (Islamology) to the social sciences; it also makes the specialists of the latter the specialists of contemporary Islam.[2] More clearly, this is tantamount to making an in-depth study of the fundamentals of Islam (of which we often know nothing, but which we speak about without having anything of substance to say) which then allows us to measure whether there really exists an incompatibility between Islam and the acceptance of the principles of modernity as they are actualised in the West. Such study, nevertheless, is the means to understand the wealth and abundance of ideas which mobilise people today in Muslim societies. This in order to bring about a society which can live with its time, on economic, political, social and cultural levels, without denying or betraying its points of reference.

I.   The Qur'ān and the *Sunna*[3]

The Qur'ān is, for Muslims, the Word of God revealed in stages to the Prophet Muḥammad (peace be upon him) during the 23 years of his mission through the intermediary of the Angel Gabriel.[4] In this sense, therefore, the Qur'ān represents for them an absolute word that gives and takes meaning beyond the events and contingencies of history. It is, for the believers of Islam, the last message to mankind revealed by God, Who had in the past sent innumerable Prophets and Messengers, among whom were Noah, Abraham, Moses and Jesus. The Qur'ānic text is, before anything else, a reminder[5] to mankind so that they revert back to original faith in God and so that they assume an acceptable moral behaviour. More than a third of the Qur'ān is composed of the expression of "*tawḥīd*": faith in the unicity of the Creator Who does not beget nor has He begotten. We also find mentioned in the Qur'ān the histories of other Prophets whose narrations convey the fact of the unique essence of the different messages and their continuity. All these passages give rise to the *spirituality* which should accompany the believer: their absolute dimension is logical and legitimate in itself. A number of verses in the Qur'ān speak of Creation, the universe and other verses insist on the modes of relation that men should undertake between themselves or towards nature. In fact, the Revelation deals with all spheres of human activity: of the economic order, the social project, and of political representation. It is this specificity which may, if not understood in the context of the Qur'ānic strategy for change, cause some problem. The Word of God is absolute and definitive, its application to given situations is governed by built-in rules and a mechanism that ensures the harmony, the application between the objectives and principles behind the injunctions and their specific application in given situations.

That is how the Prophet Muḥammad (peace be upon him), his Companions and the first jurists have understood it. The Qur'ān came down by instalments and the revealed verses which addressed specific situations to which the community of believers around the Prophet (peace be upon him) had to face up to also had a universal significance. As such, on the one hand these revealed verses were *relative* answers to dated historical facts; they also represented the revealed *absolute*, the eternal meaning of the formulation, the general principle which comes out of the same answer. It is this which was held by the first jurists, after Abū Ḥanīfa and al-Shāfiʿī,[6] as the notion of "*maqāṣid al-sharīʿa*": the objectives and principles of orientation of Islamic legislation.

It is a question of a later conceptualisation of what Muḥammad (peace be upon him) and his Companions naturally understood and applied. When ʿUmar, upon succeeding Abū Bakr as the head of the Muslim community, decided, during the year known as the year of famine, to suspend the punishment of cutting off the hands of thieves, he was following exactly the principle enunciated above. To maintain the application of this punishment would have meant a betrayal of the objective of the Revelation which alone is absolute (even if this could be seen as falling short of the letter of the Qur'ān).[7]

There are in the Qur'ān nearly 228 verses (out of 6,238) which deal with general legislation (constitutional law, penal and civil codes, international relations, economic order, etc.).[8] These injunctions lay the fundamental norms of behaviour and define the four corners within which legislation takes place. Built in is a mechanism for change and evolutionary guidance. General and absolute principles[9] which were hidden behind the specific answers given to the inhabitants of the Arabian peninsula in the seventh century. The Qur'ān, therefore, offers directing principles, principles of orientation. The latter are, in essence, absolute, since for the Muslim, they have come from the Creator Who indicates to man the way (the Sharī'a)[10] is to be followed in order to respect His injunctions. These principles are the point of reference for jurists who have the responsibility, in all places and at all times, of providing answers in tune with their environment without betraying the initial orientation. Thus, it is not a question of rejecting the evolution of societies, the change of modes and mentalities or cultural diversities. On the contrary, the Muslim is obligated to respect the Divine Order which has willed time, history and diversity.

> He brings forth the living from the dead, and brings forth the dead
> from the living, and He revives the earth after it is dead; even so
> you shall be brought forth. And of His signs is that He created you
> of dust; then lo, you are mortals, all scattered abroad. And of His
> signs is that He created for you, of yourselves, spouses, that you
> might repose in them, and He has set between you love and mercy.
> Surely in that are signs for a people who consider. And of His
> signs is the creation of the heaven and earth and the variety of
> your tongues and hues. Surely in that are signs for all living beings.
> (Qur'ān, 30:19–22)

The stages of creation of the heavens, earth and human beings and the diversity of idioms and colours are signs of the divine Presence and should therefore be respected. The interpolation of all human beings follows the same sense:

O mankind, We have created you from a male and a female, and appointed you races and tribes, that you may know one another. (Qur'ān, 49:13)

Thus, man who has faith, has to acknowledge, at the very moment when he is busy with the affairs of humans, the facts of historical evolution as well as the diversity of cultures and worship. To face up to his responsibilities as a believer is to comprehend the horizon of this complexity, and to activate himself to find, for his time and country, the best way of establishing harmony between absolute principles and daily life. The *Sunna* of the Prophet (peace be upon him), the second source of Islamic law, allows one to approach the objective of the Revelation. In fact, by analysing what Muḥammad (peace be upon him) said on such or such an occasion, or how he acted, or again what he approved, we are in a better position to understand the meaning as well as the extent of the Divine injunctions.[11] In the same vein, jurists have exerted themselves to extract from the sayings, deeds and decisions of the Prophet Muḥammad (peace be upon him) the principles which allow Muslims to live with their time and environment while still remaining faithful to his teaching.

At first sight, the constant reference to the Qur'ān and the Prophet (peace be upon him) might seem as an obstacle and as a negation to change, and this is manifested by the will to see applied today a legislation which is 14 centuries old. What we have just said, however, is proof that this understanding is too reductionist and corresponds neither to the teachings of Muḥammad (peace be upon him) nor to the attitude of the 'ulamā' (scholars) of the first era. The establishment of general principles is a fact which is proved in the modalities of juridical readings of the Qur'ān and the traditions, and confirms, if there was need for confirmation, the requirement of "the effort of personal reflection" (*ijtihād*) in situations which neither the Qur'ān nor the *Sunna* mention.[12]

II. *Ijtihād*: Between the Absoluteness of Sources and the Relativity of History

When he had to pronounce a ruling, the first Caliph, Abū Bakr, referred firstly to the Qur'ān, trying to find whether there was an applicable text. If he did not find one there, he would take into consideration the life of the Prophet – according to his memory or that of his Companions – in order to discover a similar situation for which the Prophet (peace be upon him) might have pronounced a specific ruling. If at the end of his enquiry the two sources remained silent on the case in question, he would gather for consultation the representatives of the people and agree with them on a new decision. One which was rationally independent but respectful of the spirit of the first two sources.

This step-by-step procedure received the approbation of Muḥammad (peace be upon him) himself when he sent Muʿādh ibn Jabal to the Yemen to assume the office of Judge. On the eve of his departure, the Prophet (peace be upon him) asked him: "According to what are you going to judge?" "According to the Book of Allah", answered Muʿādh. "And if you don't find the ruling therein." "According to the tradition (*Sunna*) of the Prophet of God." "And if you don't find the ruling therein." "Then I will exert my effort to formulate my own ruling." Upon hearing Muʿādh's answer, the Prophet (peace be upon him) concluded: "Praise be to Allah Who has guided the messenger of the Prophet to what is acceptable to the Prophet."

In fact, things are very clear in legislative matters. Islamic law, which is so much talked about today, is in the first place all the general rules stipulated by the Qur'ān and the *Sunna*. Within a short space of time, as many complex issues and challenges emerged, jurists developed a method and established principles of research in the subject of law. Just as in the example of Muʿādh, they put "all their energies into formulating their own rulings". This duty of reflection is known in Islamic law by the name of *ijtihād*, an Arabic term whose literal meaning is "exerting all one's energy", "making an effort". In the absence of textual references, it is for the jurist to rationally harness a regulation in tune with the time and place but one which does not betray the teachings and spirit of the two fundamental sources.[13] In other words, the answers were adapted to the context. They were themselves, by the force of things, diverse and plural but always "Islamic" when they did not contradict those general principles which are unanimously accepted. Jurists ought to respond to the questions of their time by taking into account the social, economic, and political realities then pertaining. Just as did *Imām* al-Shāfiʿī when he modified the content of his jurisprudence (*fiqh*), following a journey which led him from Baghdad to Cairo. When he was asked about the reason for such modification when Islam is but one, his reply was such that the realities of Baghdad were different to those of Cairo, and that laws which were valid in one place were not necessarily so in the other. In other words, he conveyed the fact that if the letter of the Qur'ān and the *Sunna* are one, their concrete application is plural and supposes an adaptation.

This job of adaptation, which is the work of jurists and is known by the name *fiqh*, regroups the whole of Islamic jurisprudence, as much for that which deals with aspects of worship as for that dealing with social affairs. If the rules which codify worship are never modified, it is not so when it comes to the treatment of social affairs. In the case of the latter, realities fluctuate and *fiqh*, when well understood, is a given answer made in a given moment of history, by a jurist who has "made an effort" to formulate an Islamic legislation. We should salute such a job, but we do not have to sanctify the jurist's decisions or propositions. The issue of resolving the problems of modern life is one of the major problems facing Muslims today.[14] Often, they either mistake the spirit of the Qur'ānic injunctions with the sense that such or such a jurist had given to them in the first period of Islam, or find it very hard to think out a legislation which is drawn from the fundamental sources but which is at the same time really in tune with our time.

We can see explicitly, from the beginning and up to the present time, that Islam has always required its faithful to concretely and rationally think their relation with the world

and with society. Many Orientalists have pointed out that one
of the specificities of Islam is the priority given, from the
beginning, to juridical reflection rather than to theological
consideration, and this because Islam, in its essence, blended
together the private and public spheres and, consequently, the
search for concrete answers was imposed. This blending reveals
a particular conception of man and the universe.

We have tried to show that nothing in Islam is opposed to
the fact of apprehending change or to accepting progress, but it
still remains that we have to put in evidence the specificities of
the Islamic conception of the human being and of the universe.
This is a question, in fact, of analysing some of the most general
and absolute principles, which we have spoken about earlier, in
order to measure how they can convey a certain idea of
modernity, and which will not, nevertheless, be assimilated to
its Western actualisation.

III. God, Creation and Men

1. *The Creator and gerency*

The existence of the One, Creator God is the dogma of Islam.
The principle deriving from this is that the whole universe
belongs to God Who is, by essence, the Owner. We find often
reported in the Qur'ān, the expression:

> To God belongs all that is in the heavens and earth.
> (Qur'ān, 2:284)

It is indeed the idea conveyed in these verses which associates
the Divine ownership of the heavens and earth, the sacred
dimension of beings and the elements of Creation, and lastly,
the recall of the destiny of men:

> Hast thou not seen how that whatsoever is in the heavens and in
> the earth extols God, and the birds spreading their wings? Each –
> He knows its prayer and extolling; and God knows the thing they
> do. To God belongs the Kingdom of the heavens and earth, and to

Him is the homecoming. Hast thou not seen how God drives the
clouds, then composes them, then converts them into a mass, then
thou seest the rain issuing out of the midst of them? And He
sends down out of heaven mountains, wherein is hail, so that He
smites whom He will with it, and turns it aside from whom He
will; well-nigh the gleam of His lightning snatches away the sight.
God turns about the day and the night; surely in that is a lesson
for those who have eyes. (Qur'ān, 24:41–4)

Thus, on recalling this dimension, the believer perceives that
the whole of Creation is sacred and that he should use the
elements with respect and gratitude. He is, as the Qur'ān says,
but the gerent who should give account of his acts:

It is He who has appointed you viceroys in the earth, and has
raised some of you in rank above others, that He may try you in
what He has given you. (Qur'ān, 6:165)

Thus, man lives in a universe whose entire elements are signs
whenever he remembers God. The elements are sacred as soon
as the memory of faith is invoked. They become profane by
forgetfulness and negligence. This shows how great is man's
responsibility. In addition to the trust of faith, he should give
account of his management of the world. Such is the meaning
of the Qur'ānic simile:

We offered the trust to the heavens and the earth and the mountains,
but they refused to carry it and were afraid of it; and man carried
it. Surely he is sinful, very foolish. (Qur'ān, 33:72)

Man is certainly free, but it is a freedom which has its
requirements in the fullest sense of the word.[15]

2. *The original permission*

The whole universe is the work of the Divine Will. In the
absolute, this work is good and reveals good for man. Nature
welcomes him and nature directs him. It is a fundamental rule
in Islam[16] to assert the priority of permission – and thus of

freedom – in our rapport with the world and with men. This original permission (al-ibāḥa al-aṣliyya) ought to be conveyed by a particular comprehension of our being in the world. Freedom and innocence are the first states of man in an open world; more intimately, in a given world:

> *It is He who created for you all that is in the earth...*
> (Qur'ān, 2:29)

> *Have you not seen how that God has subjected to you whatsoever is in the heavens and earth, and He has lavished on you His blessings, outward and inward?* (Qur'ān, 31:20)

Man, thus, conceives of the universe, to which he belongs, as a gift and its elements as given benefits to his presence, and witnesses to his responsibility. The field of prohibition is very restrained in comparison to the horizon of what is possible. It is this that the reading of the Qur'ān confirms and what Muḥammad (peace be upon him) reminded his first Companions with:

"What God has rendered licit in His book is certainly licit; what He has rendered illicit is illicit; and regarding that which He has kept quiet about, it is a bounty from Him. Therefore accept the bounty of God because it is inconceivable that God could have forgotten anything." Then he recited the following verse of the Qur'ān:

> *... And thy Lord is never forgetful...* (Qur'ān, 19:64)[17]

In another tradition, the Prophet (peace be upon him) said: "God has prescribed obligations, do not neglect them; He has set limits, do not trespass them; He prohibited certain things, do not transgress them. He kept quiet about certain things, out of bounty for you, do not try to know them."[18] Adam and Eve, both responsible for disobeying the only prohibition set for them by God, will be forgiven, that is after their act and their life on earth be *a trial which takes its source from innocence and its meaning in responsibility:*

And We said, 'Adam, dwell thou, and thy wife, in the Garden, and eat thereof easefully where you desire; but draw not nigh this tree, lest you be evildoers.' Then Satan caused them to slip therefrom and brought them out of that they were in; and We said, 'Get you all down, each of you an enemy of each; and in the earth a sojourn shall be yours, and enjoyment for a time.' Thereafter Adam received certain words from his Lord. And He turned towards him; truly He turns, and is All-compassionate. (Qur'ān, 2:35–7)

In this place of sojourn which is earth, man is born innocent and successive Revelations come to mark the way (*Sharīʿa*, in the original sense of the term) for him and specify limits. Each, according to his capacity, will be responsible for their respect and each shall account for his actions:

God charges no soul save to its capacity... (Qur'ān, 2:286)

... no soul laden bears the load of another. (Qur'ān, 17:15)

Thus is life, and this trial is the lot of all human beings from the beginning of time:

[He] who created death and life, that He might try you which of you is fairest in works; and He is the All-mighty, the All-forgiving. (Qur'ān, 67:2)

On the juridical plane, this implies an imposed rule in the modality of reading the Qur'ān and the *Sunna* as soon as it is stipulated that permission comes first. Everything that is not clearly prohibited by God is in fact allowed.[19] The prohibition acts both as a limitation as also an orientation. For, by the imposition of limits, the Creator reveals to man the dimension of meaning and points out to him a horizon of values whose respect will build his humanity and dignity. However, the prohibitions, when considered in their entirety, are restrained. What remains for man, in terms of field of action and engagement, is infinitely expanded. In this sense, Yusuf al-Qaradawi is right in clarifying that the original permission does not cover only the natural elements, the different meats and drinks, but also actions, habits, diverse customs, and, therefore, all social affairs. Everything is allowed except that which contradicts a stipulated or known prescription. The dignity of man tends, in its capacity, to blend the two attitudes: to respect the limits and to restore the gift of his humanity.

"That which is lawful is plain, and that which is unlawful is plain. Between the lawful and the unlawful there are matters of doubt which only a few people know. He who steers clear of them has preserved his religion and honour. But he who falls in these doubtful matters will indulge in the unlawful. He will be like the shepherd whose cattle graze around an enclosure in which they risk to fall at any time. Each sovereign possesses a reserved domain; that of God is all of His prohibitions. There is in the body a piece of flesh, which if sound, it renders all the body sound; but if it is corrupted the whole body will become corrupted; this piece of flesh is the heart."[20]

The conscience that the universe is given and wherein are the paths of gift, permission and trust, must come first. There is in a man a nature which is a benediction. It allows him to attain a serenity which is at the source of God's pardon and love. Then, the conscience of limit must act and this in the inward conviction of being responsible before God and not in that of the primacy of his culpability.[21]

3. *The rights of God and the responsibility of men*

The whole conception of man that Islam offers, of his rapport with the universe and with others, derives from the three foundations that we have just presented. The principle of the Creator's ownership, that of gerency, within which enters the idea of original permission are the substratum of the Islamic religion. "Submission" which is the literal translation of the word "Islam", from the very moment when faith is expressed, is the acknowledgement of this essential order: *to submit* is to accept the freedom to be human and responsible before the Creator; it is to make the limits one's own:

Those are God's bounds; keep well within them (do not transgress them). So God makes clear His signs to men; haply they will be godfearing.[22] (Qur'ān, 2:187)

The order of the universe and the sacredness of the elements which ought to be respected, the limits that ought not to be transgressed, are in the consciousness of the faithful *the rights of God* on the whole creation. In Islam this consciousness is marked, from the beginning and beyond any adherence to a specific religion, by the acknowledgement of transcendence. Whosoever makes his way towards the origin will find in himself this natural aspiration (*fiṭra*) towards God:

And when thy Lord took from the Children of Adam, from their loins, their seed, and made them testify touching themselves, 'Am I not your Lord?' They said, 'Yes, we testify' – lest you should say on the Day of Resurrection, 'As for us we were heedless of this.'[23] (Qur'ān, 7:172)

To make one's life and freedom a daily witness of this acknowledgement is the *responsibility of man*. His manner, by memory and gesture, should be to sing the praises of his Creator with the same chanting that frees the flapping of a bird's wings, the succession of days and nights, or a grain when it splits open giving life:

The seven heavens and the earth, and whosoever in them is, extol Him; nothing is, that does not proclaim His praise, but you do not understand their extolling. Surely He is All-clement, All-forgiving. (Qur'ān, 17:44); *It is God who splits the grain and the date-stone, brings forth the living from the dead; He brings forth the dead too from the living. So that then is God; then how are you perverted? He splits the sky into dawn, and has made the night for a repose, and the sun and the moon for a reckoning. That is the ordaining of the All-mighty, the All-knowing. It is He who has appointed for you the stars, that by them you might be guided in the shadows of lands and sea. We have distinguished the signs for a people who know. It is*

> *He who produced you from one living soul, and then a lodging-place, and then a repository. We have distinguished the signs for a people who understand.* (Qur'ān, 6:95–8)

To say that God has rights, is to say that the essence of man is at one and the same time free and responsible. Clearly, man has got the responsibility – the duty – to give an account of his freedom.

This formulation, paradoxical in appearance, conveys well enough the meaning of human life. God willed the order of the world as it is, He decided the diversity of colours and religions; it is the expression of His right. Man, being free, should acknowledge this order and respect, in the other, the right of God. So here we can see the perspectives reversed. There is here no question of *tolerance*[24] that the believer may condescendingly have towards others. The right "to be" is given to all and the duty of each towards God is to acknowledge it. To give oneself the right to tolerate, is transgressing a limit … it is violating, inwardly, the right of God:

> *To every one of you We have appointed a right way and an open road. If God willed, He would have made you one nation; but that He may try you in what has come to you. So be you forward in good works; unto God shall you return, all together; and He will tell you of that whereon you were at variance.* (Qur'ān, 5:48)

The differences of peoples and nations, the specificities of cultures, the particularities of customs are willed by God. It is a richness, but it is also a trial, in that it is difficult for man to conceive of and to live the difference in all its aspects. It is a fact and a challenge. The Qur'ān indicates here that the best way of pointing out and addressing this aspect of terrestrial life is to vie with one another in goodness. And this in all our acts and in the depth of our thoughts; with our gestures, words and hearts. There is no need for tolerance, for there is in everything and before everyone, in all horizons and colours, a need to witness the exigency of truth, goodness and justice.

Notes

1. *The Times* and the French *L'Express* have increased this kind of title.
2. This shift in university specialisation is more and more frequent. The specialists of socio-political Islamic movements have become specialists of contemporary Islam. All this happens as if the Muslims of today do not think any more, do not rethink their sources and points of reference; from now on they are bent on reacting.
3. The *Sunna*, or the reported traditions of the Prophet (peace be upon him) is the whole of what the Prophet Muḥammad (peace be upon him) said, did or approved of during his life. The inventory of these traditions and the verification of their content are, by themselves, the object of a science, the science of the traditions. Its critique today is very refined and allows a classification of texts according to their degrees of authenticity. The traditions confirm, clarify and rarely complete the Qur'ānic obligation, prohibitions and recommendations, which are the first source.
4. Approximately between the years 610 and 632 of the Christian Era, the date of Muḥammad's death (peace be upon him).
5. According to the Qur'ānic verse *It is We who have sent the remembrance, and We watch over it.* (15:9)
6. Who have given both their names, after their death, to juridical schools.
7. The application of this punishment requires very strict conditions, and particularly a social environment which gives to everyone what is vitally necessary. Theft which is motivated by need is not theft in the sense meant by the Qur'ānic verse.
8. Jurists have different opinions on this question. The counting of "legislative verses" depends upon the degree of interpretation made at the time of their reading (some of these count – according to more extensive interpretations – up to 600 verses).
9. The sciences of the Qur'ān (*'Ulūm al-Qur'ān*) are vast. They include a number of domains and require precise types of knowledge: the determination of Makkan and Madinan Revelations, the causes of revelation (for the majority of verses), abrogating and abrogated verses, a perfect mastery of the Arabic language, and so on.
10. In contrast to the usual usage applied in renderings made in the West, the *Sharī'a* cannot be reduced to a penal code. The notion is definitely more vast and conveys, beyond even the legislative formulation, the principle of faithfulness to God, to His Prophet and to His revelation. This faithfulness does not lie in literalism, as we are here trying to show.
11. Muhammad Asad (Leopold Weiss, an Austrian Jew who converted to Islam in the 1920s and author of a number of books on Islam as well as a translation of the Qur'ān into English) reminds us that the best commentary (*tafsīr*) on the Qur'ān is the Prophet's (peace be upon him) own life.

12. How many times have I heard remarks to the effect that constant references to the Qur'ān and the sayings of the Prophet (peace be upon him) amount to a relative fundamentalism, and that there is in this a suspected imprisonment of thought, an impossible autonomy for free thinking. These remarks are sometimes made by committed Christians (Catholics or Protestants) or again by intellectuals, who defend in the most determined way, cultural diversity but find themselves vexed and annoyed by this specificity of Muslim thinkers. However, this is an essential trait of the Islamic concept of the world, history and society. Being a participant in the link which exists between God and man, the points of reference are indispensable for orienting thought (this orientation is indeed a given of faith), but it never imprisons thought. On the contrary, they give account of the necessary concern – of requirement – of the finalities which ought to reside in autonomous reason. It is without doubt one of the fundamental points of divergence between Western and Islamic conceptions of liberty, and, therefore, by extension of modernity. For the former a point of reference is a link, an obstacle and a prison; for the latter it is a link, a recognition and a liberation.

13. In the vast field of *ijtihād*, jurists have made a distinction between types of juridical references and have established priorities. Thus, reasoning by consensus, or *ijmā'*, and reasoning by analogy, *qiyās* (also expressed according to the following expressions, *ijtihād jamā'ī* or "effort of collective reasoning" for *ijmā'*, and *ijtihād fardī* or effort of individual reasoning for *qiyās*) are considered as the most viable sources after the Qur'ān and the *Sunna*. We also have in the domain of enquiry additional references such as consideration of public interest (*istiṣlāḥ*) or the integration of custom (*'urf*). Jurists, if they are unanimous with regard to the priority of the Qur'ān, the *Sunna* and the necessity of *ijtihād*, have, however, different opinions regarding the status and methodological soundness of other references.

14. See Appendix II: The great current problems of Islam and Muslims.

15. The desire conveyed by the philosopher Michel Serres to see nature – the world – being considered as the subject of a natural control to elaborate, finds great echo in the Islamic concept of the rapport of man with the universe and its elements. Cf. below, *Le contrat naturel*, 1988. We shall come back to certain of these considerations (see Part Three).

16. In the science of the principles of jurisprudence (*'ilm uṣūl al-fiqh*) whose first codifier was *Imām* al-Shāfi'ī (767–820).

17. Narrated by al-Ḥākim.

18. Narrated by al-Dāraquṭnī, al-Tirmidhī, Ibn Māja and al-Ḥākim.

19. See on this subject the excellent introduction to these questions in the text of Yusuf al-Qaradawi, *The Lawful and the Prohibited in Islam*, London: Shorouk International, 1985. See also *Uṣūl al-Tashrī' al-Islāmī* (The Principle of Islamic Legislation), Cairo, 1985.

20. Narrated by Bukhārī and Muslim.

21. The idea of original sin is absent in all Islamic references.

22. The added parenthesis is necessary for the translation to get close to the Arabic meaning. The idea of fearingness conveyed in the end of this verse is not a perfect rendering of "*taqwā, yattaqūn*". Here, it is rather a question of intensity of faith when it is marked by humility and love.

23. This verse is the subject of a great number of commentaries. It is also of great interest to the theological discussion concerning *fiṭra* – the natural aspiration of man towards God or the acknowledgement of the natural essence of submission (*Islām*) to the Creator. The Sufis have commented upon this verse abundantly and used it. It is not possible for us to tackle here the whole problematic which is relative to this question. We shall limit ourselves to extracting the fundamental idea that, according to Islam, there is in every man an aspiration, an energy which orientates him towards the Creator. This "tendency" is part of man and of his condition; it is a natural testimony (*shahāda*). This idea joins the expression of the historian of religions, Mircea Eliade when he affirms that the sacred "is an element in the structure of human conscience". *Histoire des croyances et des idées religieuses*, Bibliothèque historique Payot, 1989, Vol.1 [English translation, *A History of Religious Ideas*, tr. Willard R. Trask, The University of Chicago Press]. See also Part Three of this book.

24. Tolerance conveys, by essence, a relationship of strength whose balance is the fact of the free choice of the strongest – or of the majority – and this is tantamount to "suffering" with the presence of the other. It is the reference to the history of mentalities, societies and religion which may allow us to understand the origin of this concept. It was conceived by rationalist philosophy when it was a question of determining the reasonable attitude of *the strongest* or the majority. The pending of this approach as far as *the weakest* – or the minorities – are concerned is the elaboration of their rights. The positive dimension is obvious here if we consider things on the historical plane. But in the absence of a founding principle of obligation (duty), we see that these formulations have not allowed the realisation of a society in a position to manage diversity so much on the legislative as on the cultural plane. This without taking into account that they do not protect us from the excesses of intolerance that are the result of social fractures in the West (cf. below).

Part Two

The Horizons of Islam
Between Man and the Community

The Horizons of Islam

As can easily be seen, social, political and economic life is directly influenced by the fundamentals which we have just analysed. Man, who enjoys a real and fundamental freedom, ought to bear in mind these dimensions of property, law and responsibility. His life is a witnessing. It is in this "landscape of meaning" that the idea of the individual is defined, and wherein the notion of "community" is born. From the latter, the general principles of law take shape. Indeed, it is one of the specificities of Islam to have engendered a mode of thought the essence of which is, before anything else, juridical. This, regardless of whether it is on an individual level, or at a worship, social, political, financial or economic level. The law, insofar as it is the codification of responsibilities, liberties or principles of co-existence, is primal.

Jurists "of the sources of law", following the formulations developed by al-Shāṭibī in his famous book *al-Muwāfaqāt*, have established five principles the respect of which orientates all religious regulations. These principles, *a fortiori*, affect social, political and economic perspectives. The five principles in question are: religion (*al-dīn*), the person (*al-nafs*), the mind (*al-ʿaql*), progeny (*al-nasl*) and property (*al-māl*). All religious obligations and prohibitions derive from a strict observance of these fundamental principles.[1] In fact, the legislation of the different domains of human activity should seek to preserve this basic orientation; i.e. it should act as the point of reference, as a kind of memorandum of finalities, that believers cannot afford to neglect.

I. Social Principles

If there is a domain whereby the fundamental respect of the principles so identified requires vigilance at all times, it is surely that of the social sphere. Whether at the level of worship (al-'Ibādāt, that which relates strictly to the pillars of Islam),[2] or that of daily life, Islam is the carrier of a teaching which is entirely directed towards the collective and social dimension. This, to the extent that we can say that there is no real practice of religion without personal investment in the community. The serenity of our solitude in front of the Creator cannot occur unless it is fed by our relation with our fellow beings, this being something which is renewed daily. We understand, thus, that it is a responsibility which weighs on each individual in front of God. There exists, by extension, a determining requirement addressed to the group and to society. This is the location where the destiny of each of its members is decided. In fact, it is necessary to offer to each individual the optimum conditions which allow him to respond to his moral and spiritual aspirations.

Hence, the social dimension is undoubtedly fundamental, for upon this rests all religious and cultural points of reference. To organise the social space is to give one the means to live fully and serenely one's own identity. Any reflection on a project of society whose aim is to pinpoint the challenges of "modern life", whether in the West or in the East, should, without mediation, articulate itself around this space. When one considers the crises which today face the United States and Europe, whether it be unemployment, exclusion, violence and xenophobia, one realises just how urgent a rethink of "the social fact" is, and this well before any economic or political preoccupations. Let us also be clear that Asian countries, as also the countries of the South do not escape this rule either. If nothing comes "to disturb" actual by-products, the future so announced will be very sombre for all.

If we are to reverse the order of things concrete answers are what is needed, for it is not enough to present a project of a theoretical society based on general and idealistic conceptions. To refer to Islam is to describe a horizon of faith, thought, culture and civilisation. But it is not yet time to elaborate solutions. For, if the expression "Islam is the solution" is a unifying slogan, it, nonetheless, remains a slogan empty of any strategy or planning. To forget this is to come close to a trap which more than one Muslim has already become a victim of. This is often the result of thinking that it is enough to cite the sources in order to convey the dimension of their just applicability in an actual context. History should have taught us, however, that there are two ways of betraying the teachings offered by our sources. To curtail the text is the most common way; but to apply the text outside its context and orientation (qaṣd) is an even more pernicious betrayal. This because, in appearance, everything leads one to believe that one has respected the latter. Islamic window displays are dangerous, and in their superficiality they are outright lies. This formalism is one of the worst enemies of the person, who in all sincerity, wants to respect the Qur'ānic and traditional teachings. For it allows that person to apply them as they are cited, without any effort of research or great cost but with great ensuing harm.

We must warn against this tendency. It is also fitting though not to fall into the other extreme which consists of attaching little importance to points of reference and expect of Muslims – at least those wishing to remain faithful to the orientations of the Qur'ānic Revelation – to render a project outside of any predetermined finality and outside of any cultural or religious dimension. To think modernity requires that we present in a clear fashion the imperatives and priorities of the grand orientations of social action. Once this framework is laid out, it is then possible for us to suggest a perspective of enquiry for contemporary problems.

1. The Individual

As we have already noted, man is a responsible being; not only before God but also before his own fellow men. Building a society requires that one has, beforehand, specified a conception of the individual who constitutes this society. In this, Islam, as indeed have all the spiritualities and religions of the world, has stressed three fundamental principles (which are as such aspirations): the requirement of truth and transparency; the moral dimension (ethics) and the priority of values, and the imperative of respect of men and the norms of balance. Each human being has to try to live, to feed himself and to give sense to that which makes up his humanity; to acquire knowledge in order to draw near to what is truer; to give force to his values in order to achieve good; to listen and participate in order to better respect. The appeal of the Prophet (peace be upon him) to seek knowledge ("Seeking knowledge is an obligation upon every Muslim"); the Qur'ānic requirement for one to get involved in the good vis-à-vis one's person and one's society ("You ought to command good and forbid evil"); and finally all the recommendations for fairness and kindness that we find in the Qur'ān and the *Sunna* ("Speak in the best manners", "Do not forget to treat one another with generosity, goodness, and kindness") clearly leads us in this direction. It is, therefore, impossible to think a society without starting with the individual who should make it his business to reform his own being.

> God changes not what is in a people, until they change what is in themselves. (Qur'ān, 13:11)

The change from the singular of people to the plural of individuals who constitute the former is perfectly clear as far as the extent of the injunction is concerned. The social dimension takes meaning at the source of the conscience of each human being. To the one who is a carrier of faith, this comprehension is made in a perpetual concern for balance.

> ... but seek, amidst that which God has given thee, the Last Abode, and forget not thy portion of the present world; and do good, as God has been good to thee. And seek not to work corruption in the earth; surely God loves not the workers of corruption. (Qur'ān, 28:77)

Thus, society ought to allow each person not to neglect "(his) share of life in this world". Society must be thought of in terms of the function of the individual, and it ought to offer him the possibility of fully living the requirement of his humanity. In other words, it should enable each individual to choose and know the situation well enough. It is, therefore, a question of not being mistaken about the content. To choose in ignorance and illiteracy is not really choosing, to steal while suffering from destitution and misery is not really stealing, and to respect under constraint and repression is not really respecting.

2. The Family

The family remains the constitutive point of reference for everyone. Equally, the modern epoch is characterised by the will for independence, freedom and individualism. One must make oneself on one's own, fly with one's own wings as soon as possible, and in this sense the familial space becomes something of a prison. Yet, to listen to any mother or father, we are persuaded that what everyone wants as best for their children is a balanced, open and serene familial environment. Daily life today, however, makes things increasingly difficult: couples are separating, break-ups are multiplying and imbalances increasing. No one is pleased at this state of affairs, any reading of divorce, and single-parent family statistics can only be accompanied by bitterness and anxiety. Is this the price we have to pay for modernity? Are we facing an irreversible process against which the fight is in vain? Real, answers should be found to these urgent questions. The Islamic point of reference is, in the most clearest of fashions, opposed to this splintering process. If modernity can only be obtained at this price, then we understand why the Qur'ān and the *Sunna* reject the actualisation of such modernisation. Similarly, if the whole world is caught in the rising of this vogue, being ashamed to refer to the family, then the Muslim, wherever he is, should remind others of its importance, its meaning and its finality. The family makes the human being. To ask man to be without family is tantamount to asking an orphan to give birth to his own parents. How can man do it? Do we have the right to give this lie to our children only and then remain passive? The Islamic point of reference requires exactly the opposite attitude from us.

Islam does not depart from the sense of this priority. It is an obligation for all Muslim societies not to spare anything in their effort to preserve those structures which allow for respect of family life. This includes work, education, taxes and allowances and even policies of urbanisation which we know today can have a huge impact on the private lives of city dwellers.

The general orientation within the family is that of complementarity and this should be lived from a starting principle of equality. The Prophet (peace be upon him) had clarified this: "Certainly, women are the sisters of men", and both have the same duties and rights before God and will be rewarded in the same way:

> *And the Lord answers them: 'I waste not the labour of any that labours among you, be you male or female – the one of you is as the other.'* (Qur'ān, 3:195)

In this equality, each will have to give account of his conscience and his life. However, it is together that the first social nucleus must be built, the first home of sociability and the first normative structure. In all this, marriage and the family are of an affective essence. It is love, tenderness and peace which give sense to things.

> *And of His signs is that He created for you, of yourselves, spouses,*
> *that you might repose in them, and He has set between you love*
> *and mercy. Surely in that are signs for a people who consider.*
> (Qur'ān, 30:21)

Between a man and a woman there must be a relation of
consultation, discussion and mutual participation.[3] The Qur'ān
even goes as far as to indicate that the father and the mother
should consult one another as to whether or not the mother
should continue breast-feeding their child.

> *... a mother shall not be pressed for her child, neither a father for*
> *his child. The heir has a like duty. But if the couple desire by*
> *mutual consent and consultation to wean, then it is no fault in*
> *them.* (Qur'ān, 2:233)

If consultation is required in such a precise context, then it is
only to be expected in the larger affairs that concern the couple.
If the man is the respondent of the family, in that he is asked to
respond to its material needs, this has nothing to do with the
notion of "the chief of family" who alone decides for, and
sometimes against, the rest of his family. We shall say later a few
words about those cultural habits of a certain number of countries
with Muslim majorities that attribute to Islam attitudes which
in fact Islam reprobates.

Children's respect for and towards their parents, in light of
Islamic points of reference as also that of the savants (*'ulamā'*), is
one of the fundamentals of religion. This to the extent that the
gratitude of filiation is understood as second condition of the
truthfulness of faith after worship of the Creator. The Qur'ānic
verse in this regard is clear:

> *Thy Lord has decreed you shall not serve any but Him, and to be*
> *good to parents, whether one or both of them attains old age with*
> *thee; say not to them 'Fie' neither chide them, but speak unto*
> *them words respectful, and lower to them the wing of humbleness*
> *out of mercy and say, 'My Lord, have mercy upon them, as they*
> *raised me up when I was little.'* (Qur'ān, 17:23–4)

The Prophet (peace be upon him) never ceased to remind his Companions of the importance of the family, that of parenthood and the gratitude which children should accord them. The following *ḥadīth* is well known by Muslims. Abū Hurayra reported that a man came to the Prophet (peace be upon him) and asked him: "O Messenger of God! Who is most deserving of my company?" He replied: "Your mother." The man again asked: "And then who is next?" "Your mother", came the answer. The man again asked: "Who is next?" He said: "Your mother." "And then who is next?" The Prophet said: "Your father."[4] The recommendation here is explicit and further underlines the threefold role of the mother. The space of this "home" is to be created and society must offer to each one the means of this finality.

We also find in Islamic legislation other general principles which deal with the family. This is, for example, the case with that which deals with marriage[5] and inheritance.[6] Here again, they are to be understood in relation with the whole social order which must allow their respect in justice. So if one of the rules relating to private life provokes an injustice because of the general social order (poverty, shanty towns, etc.) the public powers ought to anticipate appropriate planning. This can either be by the temporary suspension of a rule, or by a compensation – financial or otherwise – until social reform has re-established things.[7]

3.   Social Organisation: The Principle of Justice

We have, above, insisted on the responsibility of the individual, and it is a fact that the organisation of society rests on the degree of consciousness of those individuals who make it up. There is not a single element in Muslim worship, from prayer to pilgrimage to Makka, which does not emphasise and give priority to the dimension of the community. To practise one's religion is to participate in the social order and, thus, there cannot be a religious conscience without social ethics and, nothing is more explicit in Islamic teaching. Yet, to say this is still not to say everything. One must again specify the modalities of social action as well as the place of reference to authority.

In the Islamic conception of human being, what characterises man is the fact of his being able to choose and, in so doing, to be responsible. On the moral plane, human liberty holds in itself the sense of a certain number of obligations. Any society must consequently offer to each individual the possibility of responding to the requirement of these obligations. Thus, it clearly appears that individual duties before God will be conveyed, on the social plane, by as many fundamental and intangible rights. Without making an exhaustive analysis of each of these rights, we can here identify seven which are essential. Any breach of one or the other of these rights requires that measures be taken towards reforming the social sphere:

a. *The right to life and to a vital minimum.* We have pointed out above five principles around which all Islamic obligations revolve. It is clear that the first condition for their applicability is respect for life. Each being must have the right, in any society, to the minimum of nourishment in order to be able to live. This it should be emphasised, is a question of living and not one of solely surviving. All the sources of Islam call the Muslim to live as a practising Muslim in dignity and in respect of himself and others. A social organisation which does not offer its members this minimum, constitutes an infringement of their dignity as created beings, of beings who have to give an account of their persons before the Creator. Being, by essence, responsible, is to necessarily have the means of the responsibility that one conveys. In the absence of this, innocent people are made "guilty".

b. *The right of the family.* Let us specify again that each person has the right to enjoy a family life and that, in this sense, by the intermediary of the politicians in charge, society must offer to all the possibility of living with the family in a sound environment. It is imperative if this is to be achieved that adequate local structures are conceived. To have eight people living in one room is not conducive to sound family life, but is rather akin to running a prison, representing little other than suffocation. This is also conducive to creating future rifts, tomorrow's solitude and marginalisation.

c. *The right to housing.* The expression of this right ensues directly from what we have just said. Housing is the first condition of family life and Islam insists upon the sacredness of private space. A society must give to each one of its members a roof; this is a responsibility which is hugely incumbent upon it. A man without a residence is not a citizen, he is an excluded person and a victim. Dispossessing man from his humanity and making him pay for his essence is doubly unjust. Being before God requires being in oneself and at oneself, both in the literal and figurative senses.

d. *The right to education.* Education must be insisted upon, *a fortiori*, in our times. Being able to read and write, finding in learning the paths of one's identity and human dignity is essential. To be a Muslim, is clearly "to know", and straightaway, almost naturally, to walk towards a greater knowledge. The Qur'ān is a little more explicit on this question, for to know, according to it, is to draw nearer to reading the signs, as also to accede to a greater knowledge of the Creator:

> *Even so only those of His servants fear God who have knowledge, surely God is All-mighty, All-forgiving.* (Qur'ān, 35:28)

It is this that the Prophet (peace be upon him) never ceased to confirm: "Seeking knowledge is an obligation on every Muslim."[8] All types of knowledge are contained within this, but in the first instance, the imperative of basic education and learning does not suffer from lack of discussion. The first Qur'ānic verse revealed is: "Read, in the name of your Lord Who created." This is indeed the specificity of man which gives him prominence over the angel in the story of Creation.[9] A society which does not respond to this right loses its sense of its priority. Even more clearly, a society that produces absolute or functional illiteracy hampers the dignity of its members. Such a society is fundamentally inhuman.

e. *The right to work*. Man should be able to provide for his needs. In this sense, work, just as learning, is part of the inalienable rights of the social being, and each should find his place in the society where he lives. According to Islam, man is by virtue of his action and work.[10] It is clear then that a society that prevents a man from working is one which does not respond to the elementary social contract. We know the words of the Prophet (peace be upon him): "It is better for one of you to take his ropes, go to the mountain and carry a bundle of fire-wood on his back and then sell it, than to beg of people, who will either give him or deny him charity."[11]

Work is a religious claim which goes far beyond the strict framework of the practice of worship; rather it seems more like a duty. This shows how the fight against unemployment must be a political priority; not only is it imperative, but in the broader sense, it is also both religious and humanitarian.

f. *The right for justice*. Justice is the foundation of life in society besides being, for Islam, a major imperative of the modalities of action. We read in the Qur'ān: "Indeed, God commands you justice." This principle of justice applies to all, rich or poor, presidents or citizens, Muslims or non-Muslims. Eight verses from *Sūra al-Nisā'*, "The Women", were revealed to prove innocent a Jew and put the responsibility of action on a Muslim.[12] The verse associating the testimony of faith with the expression of justice makes the subject more explicit.

> *O believers, be you securers of justice, witnesses for God, even though it be against yourselves, or your parents and kinsmen, whether the man be rich or poor; God stands closest to either. Then follow not caprice, so as to swerve; for if you twist or turn, God is aware of the things you do.* (Qur'ān, 4:135)[13]

Social organisation must imperatively guarantee respect to the rights of each individual, and this by the expression of a double preoccupation. It is certainly a question of seeing to it that judicial power applies the laws with equity for each member of the social corpus. But it is equally important that society responds to the whole requirements of organisation which are linked to the fulfilment of the rights that we have noted earlier. To think social justice is to determine a project, to fix priorities, and to elaborate a dynamic current which, in the name of the fundamental points of reference, orientate social, political and economic action.

We should not have any difficulty in considering that the pursuit of this social reform is fundamental. It is part of the condition of intervention in the social sphere. Furthermore, this teaching is manifest in the gradual Revelations of the Qur'ān which lasted 23 years. Any reflection on the *Sharī'a* must take root in the source of this temporality,[14] otherwise one betrays what it came to defend.

g. *The right to solidarity.* It is not possible to apprehend the Islamic religious universe without finding oneself straightaway facing a concept which places the duty of solidarity at the heart of the living expression of faith. Being before God is tantamount to showing solidarity. The third pillar of Islam, the social purifying tax (*zakāt*), is placed exactly at the axis of the religious and social practice. As *duty* before God, it responds to the *right* of human beings. The Qur'ān is clear when it refers to sincere believers:

> ... *and the beggar and the outcast had a share in their wealth.*
> (Qur'ān, 51:19)

The Qur'ānic injunction resonates here with force:

> *You will not attain piety until you expend of what you love...*
> (Qur'ān, 3:92)

The responsibility of each person lies in actively participating in social life. In this, the obligation to pay *zakāt* is but a part of a broader social solidarity. Engagement on personal and familial levels must be accompanied by care towards one's neighbours, life in the neighbourhood as well as towards national and international preoccupations. Certainly, Islam has devised an institutional support for fighting against poverty (by the intermediary of *zakāt*), but it seems clear that the solution is not firstly of a structural nature. It is rather a question of conscience and ethics. The strength of this fraternity and human solidarity is the living source of the fight against social injustice, poverty and misery. Whosoever has faith carries the duty of this engagement; whosoever has faith knows the right to claim it.

The seven rights mentioned above do not cover all the elements that concern the individual and social spheres. However, they give a sufficiently clear idea about what the founding orientations of a Muslim society should be. At the source and heart of reflection one finds, with the acknowledgement of the Creating God, finalities which all revolve around the idea of justice. This justice is basic and primal and all human activity, in all its steps, must maintain this determination. In order to achieve this, it is appropriate to analyse situations rather than apply rules absolutely. This because the context may turn the most legitimate or most logical rules into unjust or obsolete ones, and, thus, betray in practice what they should defend in spirit.

One would be right in pointing out, upon reading the preceding lines, that the picture so described is indeed ideal, but unfortunately nothing that concerns men or their intentions is this marvellous. One would also be right to add that the observation of contemporary Muslim societies – something hardly meticulous – systematically contradicts each point so far put forward. One would also be right that the general orientations of Islam do not have a great deal to do with the daily lot of Muslims at the end of this twentieth century. Nor is it a question of heaping on the West a load of blames and insults, making "the enemy" guilty of all our own shortcomings. This would be to lie, and indeed to lie on two accounts. On the one hand by refusing to assume our own responsibilities, and on the other by demonising, in caricature and without any discernment, a "West" that we do not exactly know.

To think the ideal without preoccupying ourselves with the kind of reality that surrounds us is dangerous. Equally dangerous, is the attitude of some Muslims who think that it is enough to "return to Islam" in order that things be sorted out with one strike. In truth, the danger is twofold:

+ The first is that it tends to present things in too simplistic and crude a manner. We convince ourselves that poverty will be resolved by the imposition of *zakāt*, that the economy will be cleansed by the prohibition of interest (*ribā*) and that society will be united because "the believers are brothers of one another". We are then content with some well-intended speeches, and as far as the rest is concerned we would have to rely on God. As if "reliance on God" means a lack of intelligence or competence in action; as if the Qur'ānic Revelation has not distinguished between orientation and state, between where we should go and where we are; between the actualised foundation of a social project and the well-intended expression of its form. There is no place for such an attitude and "God's tradition" (*sunnat Allah*) throughout the history of humanity shows[15] us that things are more complicated than this, and that the success of a human project is guaranteed, in the light of faith, to whoever knows how to develop the characteristics of his human nature. In other words, drawing near to the Divine recommendations is tantamount to multiplying the qualities of one's humanity. But this does not mean emptying oneself in order to annihilate it in a fatalism which combines mysticism and passivity. This no matter how good our intentions are.

+ The second danger is of a sensibly different nature, but it is nevertheless no less widespread. In fact, we can read today from the pens of certain *'ulamā'* and Muslim intellectuals discourses which transform the profoundness of Islamic teachings in these orientations and objectives (*maqāṣid*) into a literal application of rules called *Islamic* only because they *formally* refer to the Qur'ān and the *Sunna*. Without taking the time to consider the context, the state of society, the modalities of application of laws and regulations, we demand an immediate application of certain measures which are often measures of constraint, as if to be a good Muslim today one must be less free. This formalism has consequences which are properly dramatic, for by wanting to plaster a *façade of Islam* on the problems of contemporary societies we do not go back to the cause of fracture and we, thus, prevent ourselves from finding solutions. The situation, therefore, cannot be improved; and by becoming worse, we intervene in a more coercive manner so as to "apply Islam". Good intention, whether real or presumed, is thus rendered into a daily nightmare, this especially so when making a society more Islamic means prohibiting further, censuring permanently, reprimanding, imprisoning and punishing without respite. It, therefore, remains for us to ask ourselves how is it that a message which, at the source of the original permission, has put so much trust in men for the treatment of their affairs and, which has counted on their responsibility, ends up as the tool of a generalised suspicion which only a totalitarian and police regime can uphold. Formalism here kills the essence of the message, which it pretends to defend. It is indeed this betrayal that we find in the discourses of many a head of state and governments tell us that they want to apply the Islamic *Sharī'a*, and who in order to maintain themselves are equipped with an arsenal of the most repressive laws against their people. Whether military presidents, kings or princes, they *candidly* confuse the project of social reform, which is the real application of the *Sharī'a* today, with the application of a penal code from which they will, at worst, only acquire greater power. It is a display of "Islamisation" used as a cover by dictators and from which many people suffer.[16]

4. What is the *Sharī'a*?

Nowadays reference to the *Sharī'a*, in the West, has the effect of a bugbear. To see it applied is to start the sordid, detailed account of amputated hands, floggings, and so on and so forth. It is further seen as men's moralist repression through which they impose on women the "wearing of the chador" as well as considering them as legal minors. Fed by such imagery, references to the *Sharī'a* appear as obscurantist confinement, medieval stubbornness, and fanaticism. Wherever a discourse raises the notion of the *Sharī'a*, the actors seem to turn their backs on contemporary reality and reject progress and evolution by arming themselves against the perils of the future.

One should also add that some kings and presidents do nothing to facilitate the comprehension of this notion. Repression had not been the way of the Prophet (peace be upon him). That law has a role in the total scheme of reform is not disputed; what should be clearly understood is that moral and social transformation is a multi-dimensional process. The penal sphere is not the be-all and end-all of the *Sharī'a*. It does not consist of adding prohibition to prohibition, and of reprimanding transgressors in the most exemplary manner. The *Sharī'a* aims at the liberation of man and not merely of whittling down liberties. The Islamic model must not be confused with the destruction that has been perpetrated by certain dictators in the name of the *Sharī'a*.

It is appropriate, nonetheless, to take very seriously this interpellation of a central notion of Islamic thought; a notion which today suffers from an incredible misunderstanding, when it is not a question of reprehensible betrayal. To tackle the question of modernity presumes that we have a precise idea of what is entailed in the orientations of Islamic sources. These sources being the essence of what we call, in Islamic law, the *Sharī'a*.

We have identified above[17] the two fundamental sources of Islamic law, and what the role of *ijtihād* is in the formulation of a legislation which is in tune with its time. One must here insist that the *Sharī'a* cannot be reduced to the penal sphere and that, *a fortiori*, such reduction is of a nature that belies its very essence.

"*Al-Sharī'a*" is an Arabic term which literally means 'the way', and more precisely '*the way which leads to a source*'. We understand from this notion, in the domain of juridical reflection, all the prescriptions of worship and social injunctions which are derived from the Qur'ān and the *Sunna*. On the level of acts of worship, the said prescriptions are more often than not precise, and the rules of practice codified and fixed. The domain of "social affairs", however, is more vast and we find in the two sources a certain number of principles and orientations which the jurists (*fuqahā'*) must respect when they formulate laws which are in tune with their time and place. It is indeed *ijtihād*, the third nominal source of Islamic law, which provides a link between the absoluteness of the points of reference and the relativity of history and location. Fed at the source and by the source, the jurist must think his time with a clear conscience of the course which separates him from the ideal of general and oriented prescriptions. He must take into consideration the specific social situation in order to think the stages of his reform.[18] His pragmatism must be permanent.

Thus, only that which is derived from the Qur'ān and the *Sunna* is absolute, and this, as we have noted before, covers the expression of general orientations. Beyond this, reflection is subject to the relativity of human thought and rationality. We can, at the same time, witness in two different locations two different legislations regarding the same question, but both legislations still remain "Islamic". Similarly, we can, in the same place but at two successive epochs, introduce two different regulations, both determined by socio-historical evolution, while still remaining "Islamic" in both applications. *Fiqh*[19] is the way whereby jurists, in light of the Qur'ān and the *Sunna*, have thought out a legislation which is in tune with their times. Their efforts, respectable as they are, remain however only human attempts which cannot be convenient for all stages of history. In fact, each epoch must bring forth its own "comprehension" and make use of the intelligence of the scholars then extant.

Pointing out the confusion between the *Sharī'a* and *fiqh* and reminding that the Qur'ān and the *Sunna* convey expressions of absolute finalities, is not a question of sanctifying the decisions of such or such a jurist of such and such a time. For it is still not enough to respond to what the application of the *Sharīʿa* can cover today. We have said above a few words about the necessity of Muslim jurists' pragmatism, and it is necessary to be particularly precise on this subject. For the Muslim, pronouncing the attestation of faith (there is no deity except God and Muḥammad is His Messenger), praying five times a day, contributing *zakāt*, fasting during the month of Ramaḍān and making the pilgrimage, is already an application of the *Sharīʿa*.[20] It is important to understand this notion from this angle, and one should realise that it is not playing with words or their meanings. The man of faith engages himself in fulfilling the orientation, practice, as well as the individual and collective legislation, whether public or private, from the moment he gives to his actions the sense of acknowledgement of the Creator. When he does so he is clearly on the way of the source.

This application, as much on the personal as on the social level, is the object of tension between the ideal design and the procedure of its daily actualisation. It is the share of each man, just as it is that of humanity in its entirety. Life is this course we take towards closeness of what is better, in the love of the best, while being conscious of insufficiency. Faith, then, must be the conscience of this humility. The Qur'ān, whose revelation was completed in 23 years, itself notes the essence of this tension in that it presents itself truly as a divine pedagogy. It has trained the men of the Arabian peninsula to *rapprochement*. It initiated them, from one revelation to another, and from one phase to another, in the best practice as much on the individual as on the collective level. Once engaged on this path, they never betrayed the meaning of the *Sharīʿa*. Rather, they lived its accomplishment and perfection until the day when this plentitude was achieved:

> *Today I have perfected your religion for you, and I have completed My blessing upon you, and I have approved Islam for your religion.* (Qur'ān, 5:3)

Thus, on the individual plane, each person learned by means of three successive revelations (in the span of nearly nine years) that the consumption of alcohol is forbidden.[21] Similarly, on the collective plane, four revelations progressively confirmed and enhanced the prohibition of interest and usury (al-ribā) before the Prophet (peace be upon him) clarified the imperative scope of this prohibition during his farewell pilgrimage.[22] The 'ulamā' who specialise in the study of the sources of legislation ('ilm uṣūl al-fiqh) have derived from this pedagogical procedure a rule of primal importance for the elaboration of a social project. It consists of thinking and determining the phases of its general actualisation. It is appropriate, therefore, to fix priorities, to plan the phases which create a context within which the application of a rule will remain faithful to the Qur'ānic objective (qaṣd).

Considering the present state of our societies, to apply the Sharī'a from the starting point of an institutional penal code is tantamount to taking the wrong way twice. In the first instance, it is nothing less than starting from the end by not having taken into account a social context which is profoundly different and disrupted. It is, moreover, the height of injustice, for it means transforming the most deprived of victims into guilty people. Above all, it is betraying the scope of the Qur'ānic message which makes social justice the priority of all legislative activity. Hence, from the moment we admit that we are engaged according to our individual and collective abilities in an actualisation of the Sharī'a, it is necessary that we fix the priority of a greater social justice. Any procedure, measure, regulation, or law that moves towards more equity and to the defence of those fundamental rights which we identified above, is a concrete application of the Sharī'a. It is impossible here to be satisfied with a miserable formalism which, in order to appease consciences, is of itself a violation of the Revelation.

The application of the Sharī'a is nowadays the priority given to the actualisation of a social project founded on the principles of justice and collective participation. It entails engaging oneself in eliminating illiteracy, in ensuring training, in managing the distribution of resources, and national and regional development. Legislation must accompany and encourage this dynamic, and power must be a guarantor on all the rungs of political representation. There exists, very explicitly, a contradiction in terms between dictatorship and the application of the *Sharīʿa*.[23]

In fact, the *Sharīʿa* is applied in the immediacy of the daily lot of each practising person, in a more or less complete manner, but always in tension and search; for each person, according to his capabilities, applies it in the hope of always going further in deepening his spirituality and practice. On the social plane, prayer in congregation and *zakāt* are already an engagement in this way, and each step which is carried out towards a better acknowledgement of the rights of people, is a step forward towards the achievement of a model. Therefore, we cannot begin with sanction when everything on the social plane drives us to transgression, theft, lying and delinquency. Such an intervention on the social field dictates that we consider things from the bottom up and also in depth. Legislation becomes here the support of a social reform, and in the interplay of their reaction, the one rests on the other in order to give birth to real change. We may think, at this phase of reflection, that there is here nothing specifically *Islamic*. It remains, in any case, that the orientations we have already spoken about remain the fundamental point of reference and that, in fact, there cannot be a will for Islamic social or political reform without the concrete conveyance of its priorities. In other words, for social action to be *Islamic*, it must, in the first instance, give witness of its respect to ethics; it can never be justified by its formalism.

5.   The Situation of Women

It is within this domain of women, without doubt, that the fight against formalism is one of the most urgent. This is so not because the subject has become the favourite theme of the Western media, but rather because Muslim societies today do not have much to do with what Muslims might wish in terms of faithfulness to Qurʾānic and Prophetic sources. Before God and in conscience, Muslims cannot satisfy themselves by repeating what the texts say and then snap their fingers at daily social realities: that would be to speak of an ideal while at the same time blind themselves as to their daily betrayal.

The tendency which we have denounced above and which consists, from the moment we pretend to apply the *Sharīʿa*, of starting with sanctions, penalties and the restriction of liberties, finds eloquent illustration with regard to women, their status and social role. We always put forward the imperative of wearing the Islamic veil, the limited participation of women in social life, and legislative reforms which codify the domains of marriage, inheritance, and the like. Here again, it is the "*appearance*" of "more Islam" which will be the proof of the *Islamic* quality of procedure. Moreover, it is often in light of permissive Western society that Islamic specificity is justified. If such liberties lead to a Western model, then to restrain them is tantamount to "proving" that we produce the Muslim ideal well. This apparent logic blinds us to the extent of this sophism. It is not more or less liberties, even less a rapport with a real or imagined West, which attests to the Islamic character or to a social or political project. It is, rather, the degree of faithfulness to the principles of the points of reference which alone is credible.

Here, one must also, analyse things in depth. We have said above that Islam offers to the woman, besides absolute equality before God, inalienable rights that all societies must respect.[24] We remember, moreover, that the Qurʾānic revelation produced a progressive reform of mentalities and drove new Muslims to reconsider the status of women in society. In the same manner, during the last 23 years of the Prophet's life, it became possible for women to understand, from within and by means of spirituality, their private and social duties and rights. This parameter of time, of evolution and of accomplishment is inescapable on the personal plane just as it is within social strategy. It is a question of putting in place a long-term process which takes into account actual realities in order to move ahead in respect of Muslim points of reference.

a. *The individual dimension: the example of the veil*

This reflection seems obvious on a personal development level. There still exists, however, many parents who, having understood the Islamic obligation of wearing the veil, impose the same upon their daughters without the latter understanding its meaning and import. Furthermore, very often such children do not practise, pray, nor are open to the inward dimension of faith. They respect an obligation which they do not feel – indeed refuse – but appearances are safer; to whoever *sees them* from the *outside,* they will *look* like good Muslims. Some parents will even obstinately begin the religious education of their daughters by what ought to be its culmination (a desired and voluntary culmination). They forget in all this that the veil was introduced in the fifteenth year of revelation; 15 years which were for the first Muslims as many years of learning, deepening of knowledge and, especially, of intense spiritual life. We find here exactly the same problem we have noted in the application of the *Sharīʿa*, i.e. one of pure "display". To offer women the horizon of an inward message of Islam by beginning with the imposition of the veil is tantamount to committing the same reductionism as that which consists of immediately applying a range of sanctions on the social plane without having undertaken the necessary reforms. It is an act of ignorance in some instances, but above all it is due to intellectual laziness and resignation. Repeating at will that Islam asserts that there is "no constraint in religion" does not change the reality of pressure, and *oppression,* that some Muslim women today are subjected to. Moreover, we reproach those who have refused to submit as having opted for the bad "choice". Yet we have often not presented to them the terms of any real choice. For certain women, it is a question of either blindly obeying amidst discrimination, or revolting amidst transgression. The Qurʾānic verse:

No compulsion is there in religion. (Qurʾān, 2:256)[25]

shines forth in a space which is eminently exigent, and we would be wrong to make the economy of the condition of education that it supposes. It offers human beings a choice; it is giving him, beforehand, sufficient education and knowledge in order to assert himself while possessing full knowledge of the cause. The responsibility of parents, educators, or trainers consists in giving to their children or pupils knowledge and the means to make their own choice of responsibility. Religious education does not go against this rule, even less the education of girls. They have the fundamental right to learn and it is here that is born personal responsibility before God and before society. This responsibility, lastly, has no sense unless women possess a real freedom to determine and choose for themselves.

What we have just said regarding the veil is a good illustration of a disfunctioning still too frequent in Islamic societies. The example of the veil is very vivid, but we can find this same tendency towards formalism in a great number of domains. By making the economy of reforming things in depth, we stop at what is in reality an Islamic varnish, when it is not a question of a social do-it-yourself, whereby we merrily mix restriction, confinement and cultural habit. Such situations are legion in all Arab-Muslim countries, in some Asian regions and in neighbourhoods of Europe and the United States. There is an urgent need for education and training not only of girls and women, but also of fathers and of all men. The worst enemy of the rights of women is not Islam but ignorance and illiteracy, to which we may add the determining role of traditional prejudices.

b. *The social dimension*

To be convinced, in light of the Qur'ān and the *Sunna*, that Islam recognises and defends the fundamental rights of women; to remind ourselves with conviction of our equality before God and of our prescribed social complementarity – for the man as for the woman – within familial priority; to call for a recognition of Muslim identity as the source of a social project which offers to the woman a space for life that returns to her all the rights that Islam bestowed upon her, but which present-day societies daily deny her – to do all this is to hold a very critical view on the contemporary[26] situation and to be engaged in changing things in consequential fashion for the long-term. This patience in action, which is the exact definition of the Arabic word "*ṣabr*",[27] must be armed with the conviction that it is more appropriate to approach a model slowly than to hastily put make-up on the form.

To make any reference to Islam today, on the plane of social identity, is clearly to call for the liberation of women within and by Islam. It will certainly not be the model of liberation which has taken course in the West (this in consequence of its specific history and in which we will be poorly inspired if we do not recognise a certain number of gains), but one which nonetheless takes Muslim societies out of their serious and difficult situations.

It must first involve engaging in a vast enterprise of education and schooling. Great efforts are provided today by caring associations by NGOs and broadly speaking by movements that function on the model of South American based communities, but this cannot be sufficient. It is important that this reform is presented as a priority for states and that it is carried out and defended by a real political will. We know that this is not the case today and that nothing in what the International Monetary Fund (IMF) or the World Bank (WB) do makes this work a priority. For example, the rate of schooling for women in the Maghreb today is the lowest in the world. This situation is inadmissible from the point of view of Islam. The Muslim woman, like the Muslim man, has a right to learning. It is an inalienable right that any social organisation must respect.

The religious education of women should take the form of foundational instruction. For if Islam gives rights to women, it remains that they need to know these rights in order to defend them. The good, theoretical speeches of men have never remedied the daily sufferings of women. Consequently, the latter should have access to a different religious education, one which allows them to contribute in abstracting the essence of the message of Islam from the accidents of its rustic, traditional or

Bedouin reading. This would be a means to facing up to the distortions of such readings. One that requires that we respect the orientations of the Revelation and not the strictly masculine pretensions of such and such a custom, or of any paternal "habit". Women are nowadays more and more engaged in the sense of this education in all Muslim countries. Still we are far from what ought to be achieved. However, the progress, although not spectacular, is tangible. This work of depth is already *an application of the Sharī'a*. Its application is progressive, for the long-term and is fed by the memory of the path of its source. It is with human beings, for the respect of their rights, without ever forgetting God.

At one time women used to trade, and participate in meetings; they were even in-charge of the market at Madina under Caliph 'Umar. Furthermore, they engaged in social life in the seventh century. Is it possible to posit that a process of "Islamisation" at the end of the twentieth century will be rendered by a definitive return to home, house confinement and infantilisation?[28] By what twist of the mind have we managed to disfigure the Islamic message while asserting a willingness to defend it? Undoubtedly, as we have suggested above, it is because nowadays we think Islam more *in contrast* to "Western derivatives" than in function of its proper essence (which indeed has rules to be respected but which has no reactive twist). It is, therefore, necessary to return, serenely we must say, to the original teachings of Islam and allow women, at all levels of social life, to take an active part in the achievement of the reforms that we would like to bring forth. This is the prolongation of the education which they have the right to and which will allow them to run their affairs, to work, to organise themselves, to elect and be elected without any contravention of Islamic ethics or the order of priorities. Women must be able to play a social role. And if Islam clearly stipulates the priority of the family, this has never meant that a woman cannot move out of this space. Priority conveys the idea of a hierarchy but not the expression of an exclusivity.[29] Wearing the veil, in this sense, does not mean the confinement of woman. If it is freely worn,[30] then it must express an exacting and moral presence on the plane of social activity. It marks a limit in the proximity of which man understands that the woman − *a fortiori* one who is socially active − is a being before God. It should instil respect of privacy, before any inclination towards seduction due to her appearance.

The debate on the role of woman drags to its wake a broader reflection on modernity. Is it possible nowadays to defend the idea of a moral presence of men and women in the field of social activity together with a well-defined role for the family? Does wanting to differently apprehend the contemporary world, or the life described as modern, imply rejecting progress or the fact of modernity? One must acknowledge the impressive advancements of industrial societies as one should delight in the progress achieved today. Yet, one must not forget to take account of the dismantling of the social tissue, the profound crisis of values and the generalised doubt which lies at the heart of such. We cannot be so blind as not to notice the consequences of this "very modern" life, which makes out of speed a norm and out of meaning a secondary question. By essence, Islamic civilisation cannot recognise itself in such a strange inversion of priorities. By essence, it measures the evolution of societies by the level of their faithfulness to fundamentals, preferring quality of life (social, spiritual and moral) over quantity of productivity and consumption. There are women nowadays, whose number is constantly increasing, who wish to participate in the construction of a new society, but who at the same time do not want to deny any of their faithfulness to Islam. They defend both access to modernity and the principles of their religious and cultural practices at one and the same time. They are "modern" without being "Western". Those in the West are often incredulous in the face of such a strange "mixture", for it seems hardly possible. The Western media reinforce this dubitative reflex as long as they report with high publicity the words of women from Algeria, Egypt, or Bangladesh who, while opposed to "Islamic obscurantism", think "like over here".

Thus, the trait of these intellectual women is first to have a discourse which is accessible only because it resembles the formulations used in Europe or the United States. They then represent the progressist forces because they claim the same progress and the same modernity as that of the West. This logic does not, however, suffer any discussion: the West is progress, so the one who speaks the "Western language" is progressist. The conclusions are illuminating![31]

These conclusions, if anything, are simple and dangerous. It is not a question here of simple cultural imperialism but, more insidiously, of a kind of thought dictatorship which fixes and determines the "right thinking" by giving itself the air of openness and freedom. Certainly, one acknowledges the difference of belief and cultural relativism as far as difference is limited to folklore and exotism with the condescension that is accorded to beautiful customs, but these are so outmoded. One should one day take an inventory of the measure of real violence that non-Western cultures are today subjected to.

Islam abolishes this hegemony, and Muslim women, who in the name of Islam demand their right status and *freedom* in Islamic society, put their finger exactly where the wound is. In effect, one finds it hard, today, to hear a veiled intellectual who affirms her totally autonomous engagement and her claims for women while rejecting in a determined fashion the Western model. This attitude is more and more frequent in universities. Everywhere from Morocco to Bangladesh, from Norway to South Africa and passing by England, France and even Saudi Arabia, one meets with Muslim women who demand from the societies in which they live faithfulness and respect to, as well as a real application of, the principles of Islam. Against local customs, ancestral traditions, despotic patriarchy and daily alienation, they are convinced that more Islam means more rights and more freedom. In this, their contribution to the profound comprehension of the Qur'ānic message and of the reform of societies is a deciding factor and shall be even more so in the coming decades. Up until now, the West seems to be deaf to the force of this discourse, whereas everything lends itself to believe that it is at its source that tomorrow's Muslim societies will be fashioned. Without considering that there may be some advantages for the West to see itself questioned on the meaning and form of the society which it offers today to its new generations, this external and critical view may be enriching. This because it may lead to relativising the fatality of the unique thought model which drags the world towards more egoism, individualism and finance; this in a great void of meaning and hope.

The presence of such Islam resides, willy-nilly, in the future of the world, and the Muslim woman is a compelling part of it. One must choose responsibly the line of reciprocal questioning and not opt for that of conflict.

6. The Call to *Jihād*

How often has one heard apropos the expressions "the holy war", the fanatic mobilisation of "God's madmen" and this "new flow of rampant fundamentalism". The world of Islam, which is lately haunted by the gangrene of *jihād*, scares and terrorises minds.

How is it, then, that one of the most fundamental notions of Islam has itself come to express one of the most sombre traits? How can a concept, which is loaded with the most intense spirituality, become the most negative symbol of religious expression? The reading of events of recent history certainly has its share of the blame, but the distortion goes far back to an advanced date of the Middle Ages. The understanding of certain Islamic notions was from very early on confined to an exercise of pure comparison. There were the crusades as there were also Muslim expansions; there were holy crusades and, thus, there were also "holy wars", the famous *jihād*. Even if the West has happily gone beyond the initial stage of religious war and crusade, the spectator is indeed forced to notice that the Muslim world is still today lagging behind. This because we see everywhere groups, movements, parties and governments that call for *jihād*, armed struggle and political violence. The symbolical arsenal seems medieval and obscurantist, to say the least. Here also then the question arises, will Islam evolve?

This question seems legitimate and its expression brings up, nonetheless, another misunderstanding which is nowadays undoubtedly upheld voluntarily. But, one must go back to the source of this notion and try to better understand its spiritual and dynamic scope. *Jihād* is the most fulfilled expression of a faith which seeks to express balance and harmony. One must say a word here about its individual scope and its literally "international" dimension, and finally, since it is the subject which interests us here, about its social actualisation.

a. *Peace of heart*

Can any human being assert, from the depth of his heart, that he has never been subject to violence, aggression, hatred, anger and even the excitement of a destructive instinct. Mastery over self, serenity, respect of others and gentleness are not natural, but are acquired by means of a permanent, personal effort. Such is the lot of men. They board the shores of their humanity by means of a long, thoughtful and measured work on the self. Everyone knows this and each heart feels it.

All the world's literature, from the dawn of time, is plain in its representation of this tension. A tension which is sometimes appeased, sometimes agitated and at other times tears apart men's inward focus. From the Baghavad Gita to the Torah and Gospel, from Dostoevsky to Baudelaire, the human horizon remains the same. The Qur'ān, too, confirms the most daily of experiences:

> *By the soul, and That which shaped it and inspired it to lewdness and godfearing! Prosperous is he who purifies it, and failed has he who seduces it.* (Qur'ān, 91:7–10)

The two paths are explicit, at one and the same time, apprehended in the most vivid and moral fashion coupled with remembrance of the life to come. Life is this test of balance for men who are capable of inducing both the best and the worst from themselves.

Here, we are in proximity of the notion of *jihād* which cannot be understood except in regard to the conception of man which implies it. Tension is natural and the conflict of the inward is properly *human*. Moreover, man proceeds and realises himself in and by the effort that he furnishes in order to give force and presence to the inclination of his least violent, irascible and aggressive being. He struggles daily against the most negative forces of his being, as he knows that his humanity will be the price of their mastery. This inward effort and this struggle against the "postulations" of interiority is the most appropriate (literal and figurative) translation of the word "*jihād*".

It is not a question here of reducing *jihād* to a personal dimension (*jihād'l-nafs*), but rather returning to its most immediate reality. *Jihād* is to man's humanity what instinct is to an animal's behaviour. To be, for man, is to be responsible and such responsibility is linked to a choice which always seeks to express the goodness and respect of oneself and others. Choosing, in the reality of inward conflict, is to have a resolve for peace of heart.

We know the words of the Prophet (peace be upon him) in a *ḥadīth* whose chain of transmission is acknowledged as weak (*ḍaʿīf*) but from which we can draw an instruction, since its meaning and scope are confirmed by other traditions. Coming back from an expedition against the Muslims' enemies, the Prophet (peace be upon him) is reported to have described war as "a lesser *jihād*" in comparison to "the greater *jihād*" which is the effort of inward purification and of a human being's spiritualisation before his Creator. More than the simple comparison, what should be retained here is the association of faith with the experience of effort in order to attain harmony and serenity. Life consists of this trial, as spiritual force is signified by the choice of good as well as good action as also oneself and for others.

> ... [He] who created death and life, that He might try you which
> of you is fairest in works. (Qur'ān, 67:2)

The real meaning of Islamic spirituality lies in reforming the
space of one's interiority, appeasing one's heart at the level of
acknowledgement of the Creator and within a generous human
action; it is loving in transparency and living in the light. This
spirituality joins the horizons of all other spiritualities which
require man to be equipped with a force of being rather than
being subjected to the despotic fierceness of a life which is
reduced to instinct. This tension towards the mastery of the self
is conveyed in Arabic by the word *jihād*. Understanding this
dimension is a necessary part of a larger discussion on the
meaning of armed conflict. What needs to be retained in the
first instance, on the individual plane as well as on the
international plane, is that God has willed this tension. He made
it by His management of one of the conditions of access to faith
and to humanity.

"The Prophet (pbuh) exclaimed one day: 'Who is the strongest
among men?' The Companions responded: 'It is him who
overcomes his enemy', and the Prophet (pbuh) responded: 'No,
the strongest is him who keeps his anger in check.' "[32]

b.   The reality of conflict

We have recalled above that Revelations present diversity as
the Creator's choice:

> If God had willed, He would have made you one nation; but that
> He may try you in what has come to you. So be you forward in
> good works...(Qur'ān, 5:48)

Thus, while it is a fact of a choice, diversity nonetheless turns
out to be a trial for men. Management of differences is presented
as a challenge that must be addressed in the same way as inward
tensions must be addressed. The greatness of men is in the
function of their choice, and the Qur'ān orientates the latter, by
aspiration, to a rivalry about good (one finds in another verse

the idea that the finality of the diversity of nations and tribes finds its meaning in the fact of seeking to understand one another). Diversity and pluralism may be the means to an elevation of man – it ought to be. However, it would be naïve not to take account of the reality of conflict. The latter exists, and Revelation informs us, that they are necessary for the preservation of harmony and justice among men:

> Had God not driven back the people, some by the means of others, the earth had surely been corrupted; but God is bounteous unto all beings. (Qur'ān, 2:251)

Thus, diversity and the conflicts which ensue are inherent to Creation. Man addresses the challenge of his humanity not in his rejection of pluralism and differences, but rather in their management. It is man's conscience, nourished by principles of justice and ethics, which must guide him to defend the rights of every community as that of every individual. It is indeed this that the following verse adds to the meaning of the preceding one:

> Had God not driven back the people, some by the means of others, there had been destroyed cloisters and churches, oratories and mosques, wherein God's name is much mentioned. (Qur'ān, 22:40)

Here, we note that monasteries, synagogues and oratories are mentioned before mosques. It is clearly a question of the expression of their inviolability and, at the same time, of the respect due to the adherents of different religions. The formulation cannot be more explicit:

> And if thy Lord had willed, whoever is in the earth would have believed, all of them, all together. Wouldst thou then constrain the people, until they are believers? (Qur'ān, 10:99)

Difference of belief, as of colour and language, are facts which we must live with. Although we have already expressed this, it

is appropriate to forcefully repeat it here. The first principle of
coexistence in diversity is that of respect and justice. Once again,
the Qur'ān is clear:

> O believers, be you securers of justice, witness for God. Let not
> detestation for a people move you not to be equitable; be equitable –
> that is nearer to godfearing. (Qur'ān, 5:8)

In the face of inevitable conflicts of interest and power, true
testimony of faith lies in respect for the rights of each individual.
If the latter is suppressed and if injustice is widespread, then it
is the responsibility of men to oppose such a state of affairs. It is
exactly in these conditions that the first verse calling for *jihād*
and armed resistance was revealed:

> Leave is given to those who fight because they were wronged –
> surely God is able to help them – who were expelled from their
> habitations without right, except that they say 'Our Lord is God.'
> (Qur'ān, 22:39–40)

After 13 years of living in Makka, after almost an
equivalent period of violent persecution and after being
exiled to Madina, this verse allowed the Muslims to defend
themselves in the name of justice and in respect of their
faith. Abū Bakr understood straightaway the scope of this
message and maintained that with the revelation of this verse:
"We understood that it was going to be about armed
struggle." One finds here an explicit expression of what *jihād*
covers on the inter-community or inter-national planes. As
we have pointed out with regard to the inward plane, where
it is a question of struggling against the forces of aggression
and violence which are inherent in all human beings, it is
similarly appropriate to oppose every aggressor, power and
exploitation which are naturally manifest in all human
communities, and which snap at our fundamental rights.

Everything, in the message of Islam, calls for peace and
coexistence between men and nations. In all circumstances,

dialogue must be preferred over silence and peace over war. That is to the exception of one situation which makes of struggle a duty, and of opposition a testimony of faithfulness to the meaning of faith. *Jihād* is the expression of a rejection of all injustice, as also the necessary assertion of balance and harmony in equity. One hopes for a non-violent struggle, far removed from the horrors of armed conflict. One loves that men will have this maturity of spirit which allows for a less bloody management of world affairs. However, history has proven that the human being is bellicose by nature and that war is but one means by which he expresses himself. Resisting the very violent expression of this tendency and trying to implement the necessary balance of forces seem to be the conditions for an order that looks human. The latter being the only situation whereby violence is given legitimacy; situations whereby violence is sustained, repression imposed or rights denied, to the extent that, if one succumbs, one loses one's dignity:[33]

Surely God bids to justice... (Qur'ān, 16:90)

This verse clearly expresses the sense of men's actions. This lies in fighting for good and rejecting injustice with all the force of one's being. To have faith is tantamount to carrying the testimony of this dignity by resistance. The latter is for the community what mastery over anger is to the inward of each person.

One may notice nowadays an effervescence in the Muslim world, and many condemn the violence which accompanies the awakening of a "fanatical, radical and fundamentalist Islam". One must understand this worry, as one must denounce political violence which finds its expression in the assassination of tourists, priests, women, children and in blind bombings and bloody slaughters. Such actions are indefensible, nor do they respect, in the least, the Qur'ānic message. Again, one must also condemn the violence which expresses itself prior to such actions. Such violence is perpetuated by dictatorial powers that are often supported by superpowers. Every day that passes, entire peoples sustain repression, abuse of power, and the most inhumane violations of rights. Until when will these peoples remain silent or see themselves deemed "dangerous", by the West, whenever they dare to express their rejection? Here, it is not a question of defending violence but rather of understanding the circumstances wherein it takes shape. North-South imbalances and the exploitation of men and raw materials, combined with the resignation of the peoples of the North, produce a much more devastating violence than that of armed groups, even if the latter are spectacular. As the end of the twentieth century draws close, can we call all men to mobilise themselves towards more social, political and economic justice, for it seems to us that this is the only way to give back to men the rights that will silence arms? Such an effort would be the literal translation of the word *jihād*. The latter is the testimony of a heart that illuminates faith and the witness of a conscience which fashions responsibility.

c.   *Towards a social jihad*

This brief clarification about the central notions of the Muslim religion allows us to shed new light on the question of social action. All Muslims know and repeat that the practice of Islam does not stop at the exercise of prayer, *zakāt*, fasting and pilgrimage. Every act of daily life which is fulfilled with remembrance of the Divine Presence is, in itself, an act of gratitude and worship. Moreover, we know the close link, which is established in the Qur'ān, between believing and acting through the oft-repeated expression "Those who believe and do good deeds." Thus, to have faith is tantamount to believing and acting, and action here is of a multiple nature. It is the honesty that one imposes on oneself, goodness and generosity towards one's relatives, just as it is the determined engagement in social reform, or even mobilisation against injustice. All these efforts which are deployed in action are part of *jihād* in the sense whereby they are oriented towards that which is more just and more respectful of the revealed principles. The following verse clarifies the same:

> The believers are those who believe in God and His Messenger, then have not doubted, and have struggled with their possessions[34] and their selves in the way of God; those – they are the truthful ones. (Qur'ān, 49:15)

One may read this formulation in the strict sense and maintain that it only addresses the question of armed struggle, and that this armed struggle imposes itself whenever there exists aggression. However, it would be reductionist to draw just that instruction. In a broader sense, a sense which is confirmed by the entire Qur'ānic message and that of the traditions, "fighting in the path of God" means mobilising all our human forces, directing all our efforts and giving of our properties and of our own persons in order to overcome all adversities whether they be injustices, poverty, illiteracy, delinquency or exclusion.

The Qur'ān offers such latitude in the interpretation of the word *jihād*, and this in its first revelation:

> So obey not the unbelievers, but struggle with them thereby mightily. (Qur'ān, 25:52)[35]

There is here mention of a struggle (*jāhid* and *jihādan*) which is of a learned and scientific nature, one which relies on dialogue, discussion and debate. The Qur'ān, in its content and form, appears as an arm in the hands of Muslims. On another level, it is the Prophet (peace be upon him) who presents an extensive interpretation of the word when he asserts, for example, that "Pilgrimage is a *jihād*".[36] One realises that the troubles, efforts and suffering endured by the faithful during a few days in Makka, in order to give strength to their faith and answer the call of the Creator, are a *jihād* in the path of God.

In our daily lives, to live in faith in our societies is tantamount to recognising the sense of effort. Faith involves putting one to the test; it is, in fact, a test itself. In our representation of an ideal of life, respect and coexistence, actual social fractures, misery, illiteracy, unemployment are many elements of the new adversity that the modern epoch has engendered. Mobilisation, as already noted, imposes itself when man's dignity is in peril. But, it is not always a question of an armed appraisal. Nowadays, many women and men see their dignity suppressed, their existence denied and their rights violated. This situation necessitates an urgent response as also a general call for *jihād*. Here, it is about giving from one's own person and property, calling all the forces of all diverse societies and engaging in the work of reform that we have already discussed.

We will not deny that there are struggles wherein circumstances lead us to direct confrontation, in order to oppose a purge here, a military occupation there, or another type of aggression such as the one we have witnessed in Bosnia and Chechnia. However, it cannot simply be a question of focusing our attention on these events alone and forgetting the broader type of fight which occurs daily and is, therefore, so much more urgent. Nowadays, our enemies, in the path of God, are hunger, unemployment, exploitation, delinquency and drug addiction. They require intense efforts, a continuous fight and a complete *jihād* which needs each and everyone's participation.

How many are those Muslims who want to fight beyond their own doorsteps, who want to offer, in the most sincere fashion their own persons for the cause of Islam. But, filled with this intention, they forget and remain blind to the fight that must be carried out here in their own locality, to the cause that ought to be defended in their own neighbourhoods, cities and in every country. To those who sought to assist Palestine in its fight against Zionist colonisation in the 1940s, and who perceived this expedition as representing the fulfilment of their ideal, Hasan al-Banna said: "Dying in the way of God is difficult, but living in the way of God is still more difficult." This *jihād* is a *jihād* for life, in order that every human being is given the rights which are his. The entire message of Islam carries this requirement as well as its necessary achievement.

To think modernity is to reflect on all the strategies and modalities which are apt to change the order of things. Following the example presented by Yusuf al-Qaradawi in his book on the problem of poverty,[37] we should reflect on the sources and on the reality of our societies nowadays. We have spoken briefly already, but we must go still further and think, in a very pragmatic manner, about the strategies which will allow us to find local solutions to the problems identified. Social action has to be a priority and it should mobilise the majority of our energies.

Indeed it is a question of war; for we are at war. This is what Abbot Pierre meant when he forcefully asserted that "I am in war against misery", or when Professor Albert Jacquard and Monsignor Jacques Gaillot said that they "go to war" to shelter those who are homeless. In his social Encyclical, *Centesimus Annus*,[38] the Pope calls for a general mobilisation against poverty and the imbalance of wealth and asserts that it is the duty of Christians to act in this sense. The *jihād* of Muslims is, of course, part of this engagement in the West, but it is equally so in all the countries of the South. It is a wholehearted *jihād* along the line of South American communities who express it in the form of liberation theology, or as it is manifested in the popular and trade unionist forces in the Near East and Asia. Future inter-religious dialogue will undoubtedly find its fulfilment in such strategy and actions. However, we cannot think of the future in terms of political and economic reform without working for the reconstitution of a social tissue which is nowadays torn apart the world over.

Notes

1. We see here how much the orientation of Islamic thought, and the conception which derives from it, is already different from that which gives rise to the formulation of human rights. What is primal here is the responsibility of man *vis-à-vis* the five fundamentals mentioned above. The expression of human rights exists but is included in a more global conception. Thus, it is not a question of claiming a right as a reaction, for example, against a possible

social aggression. Rather, right is a formulation of any humanity from the very moment we are placed on earth and in front of others as "responsible beings", guarantor of the duties of our humanity. It is a question of fixing the terms of balance. Defending rights and fighting for their respect without specifying a field of responsibilities and duties leads to the kind of situation we know of today whereby some states ratify all the declarations relative to rights and, at the same time, light-heartedly violate them.

2. See the second part of *Les Musulmans dans la laïcité*, pp. 42–54, ed. Tawhid, 1994.

3. A *hadīth* reports: "The Prophet declared: 'The most perfect among the believers is the one who has the best character. The best amongst you are those who are best with their wives'", reported by Tirmidhī.

4. Reported by Bukhārī and Muslim.

5. Let us recall that within Islam, a woman has the right to choose her husband, to refuse polygamy, to ask for divorce (the principle of *khul'*), to keep her property (the settlement of separation in marriage), to work and, broadly speaking, to participate in social life. Within this, however, one must establish nuances. For, it is one thing to speak about women in Islam, but it is a completely different thing to analyse the situation of women in actual Muslim societies. We cannot, as has become the habit, prove "the male chauvinist essence in Islam" by means of the discriminations occurring in certain countries. For this conclusion supposes that it is Islam which fashions all behaviour while "forgetting" the role, often primal, of ancestral customs and rural traditions. Thus, everything is Islamic in the Algerian or Egyptian countryside, but it is not exactly Christianity which is at play in Sicily or in the Spanish countryside. We shall return later to the question of women and the actual situation of Muslim societies.

6. We hear a lot of talk about this in the West since inheritance seems to be concrete proof of discrimination against women who receive only half of what men are entitled to. On the private level, man is responsible for his family. Islam imposes on him the fulfilment of the needs of his family and grants a fundamental right to the woman, which consists of not having to spend on the man's needs, whatever the situation may be (it is a question of a right and not of a duty which may stipulate that she cannot work). It is within this context that the differences in inheritance must be understood. The property of a woman is hers and she does not owe anything to anybody. A man, however, is financially linked to all those who are under his charge.

7. This is another principle of Islamic legislation: "Necessity makes law" in a temporary situation and allows by steps resolution (this is what the Qur'ān taught man regarding alcohol and loans by usury, *ribā*). This principle is applicable to all spheres of human activity.

8. The *hadīths* on the question are not lacking, and from among these we quote the following: "Whosoever treads a path of seeking knowledge, God will ease

for him the way of Paradise" (reported by Muslim); "Whosoever leaves to acquire a type of knowledge, is on the path of God until his return" (reported by Tirmidhī); "At his death, the deeds of the son of Adam will cease except for three; a charity whose beneficial consequences last, a type of knowledge from which people derive benefit and a child who always invokes God for him" (reported by Muslim).

9. See, the Qur'ān, *Sūra al-Baqara* 2:30–5.

10. A well understood reading of the famous *ḥadīth*: "Indeed deeds are according to intention" confirms this determination. To say that deeds are measured by the intention does not mean that it is enough to have an intention without acting in order to be judged. On the contrary, the formulation fixes the necessary presence of action and then goes back to the intention which was the agent. It is explicitly said that the appearance or the result of action are not the parameters of judgement. This will be, on God's part, fixed according to the consciousness of the actor. The action, or its project, is the condition of intention.

11. Reported by Bukhārī, we may also quote the following *ḥadīth*: "None has eaten a better provision than that coming from the work of his hand. The Prophet Dāwūd ate from the work of his hands" (Bukhārī). We also know that 'Umar said that it is not appropriate for a Muslim to sit and wait for his needs to be satisfied, for the sky never rains with gold or silver.

12. Qur'ān, *Sūra al-Nisā'* 4:107–15.

13. We find in *Sūra al-Mā'ida* 5:8 which conveys, by inverting the order of words, the dimension of witness: *O believers, be you securers of justice, witnesses for God. Let not detestation for a people move you not to be equitable; be equitable – that is nearer to godfearing. Surely God is aware of the things you do.*

14. See below: *What is the Sharī'a?*

15. As it is also shown to us by the life of the Prophet (peace be upon him) and his way of solving social, political and economic problems.

16. We also find another type of justification of such or such Islamic projects. It is sufficient to encounter the opposition of Western countries, and especially the United States, so that the said project, or such a government, becomes Islamic. The project must be anti-Western or, more explicitly, the West's opposition is sufficient proof for the Islamic character of the project. This is, however, a politicised logic, which leads to serious simplifications. A social project is Islamic on account of its faithfulness to the foundations and points of reference. It is judged from within and one must dispense with such analysis. For otherwise one would continue to shift from are deception to another because of making the mistake of hoping for the reading of the *image* without the slightest analysis of the concrete situation. One must be a believer, but one does not have the right to be naïve.

17. See in Part One, The Qur'ān and the *Sunna*, and *Ijtihād*: Between the Absoluteness of Sources and the Relativity of History.

18. Ibn Qayyim mentions, among the repertoire of qualities expected from a legislator (*mujtahid*): "The knowledge of men, their habits and their time." (Cf. *I'lām al-Muwaqqi'īn.*)

19. *Fiqh* literally means comprehension. In Islamic sciences, this term is employed to cover the field of juridical research. It is indeed of this that it is the question. Between points of reference and the reality of the world, the role of man and his humanity are situated in the fact of comprehending and not in the blind application of rules whose meaning we cannot rationally understand. Reason is to man what instinct is to an animal: making free use of this faculty is part of the same submission (*Islam*) to the order of the world, and it is, therefore, a way of knowing the Creator. Not forgetting though that Revelation is our way of respecting it.

20. We often hear Muslims living in the West say that Islam does not impose upon them the application of the *Sharī'a* while they remain a minority in the West. By saying this, they indeed give a bad definition to the notion. Moreover, they clumsily identify with what their Western interlocutors think to know themselves. By wanting to reassure the latter, they confuse the situation further, and in order to promote calm here, they confirm "barbarity" over there. One must always be precise in one's formulations and specify things well. A Muslim living in Europe and practising his religion (prayers, fasting, etc.) applies the *Sharī'a* in the capacity of his means and in the context whereby he belongs to a minority. With the good understanding of what practice entails, any action in which he engages himself in order to establish more social justice and more acknowledgement of the rights of each individual, in the West as in the East, is an action pertaining to the frame of positive, social action which must characterise the Muslim who is conscious of his responsibilities, wherever he might be. This then is an application of the *Sharī'a* on a broader level, but one which still remains concrete. It is, thus, that one must understand the enterprises of solidarity, school support, the fight against delinquency, drug addiction and so on. It is required from each one of us that we do what we can. In a society where the majority of its members are not related to Islam, it is required of each Muslim to actualise the meaning of the *Sharī'a* in the most positive fashion both in its practice as in its social participation. The message of Islam does not lie in its penalties. Rather, it lies first in its orientation and in its exigency of humanity before God.

21. In chronological order; see Qur'ān, 2:219, then 4:43 and lastly 5:90.

22. In chronological order; see Qur'ān, 30:39, then 4:160–2 and then 3:130–2 and lastly 2:275–81 (see below the chapter on Economic Directives).

23. We shall come back to this question when we address the facts of political orientation in Islam (see the next chapter).

24. See also Appendix IV, The question of woman in the mirror of Revelation.
25. This verse refers to the fact of forcing others to accept Islam, but, by extension, it is legitimate to derive an instruction of what its finality covers.
26. See Appendix II: The great current problems of Islam and Muslims.
27. The Prophet (peace be upon him) reminded us that: "Victory comes with patience..."
28. See the excellent work of research and synthesis undertaken by 'Abd al-Halim Abu Shuqqa, *Taḥrīr al-mar'a fī 'aṣr al-risāla* [The liberation of women in the time of Revelation], 6 vols., edition Dar al-Qalam, Kuwait, 1990. This study is of prime importance and its usefulness is incomparable as the two shaykhs Muḥammad al-Ghazālī and Yusuf al-Qaradawi, remind us in their respective Prefaces.
29. See on this subject our translation of the Arabic text produced by the Muslim Brotherhood of Egypt which deals with the social role of women (whereby the right of women to elect and be elected is clearly indicated, and by extension, their participation in the running of the city). The second part deals with multipartism. *La femme dans la société Islamique* [Woman in Islamic Society], Lyon: Tawhid, 1995.
30. There are a great number of educated, graduates of universities and socially committed women who wear the veil of their own free-will, and who claim at the same time that the fact of wearing and respecting it is one of their rights. We hear today talk of the kind that "the veil is the yellow star of the Muslim woman" which conveys – by their elaboration – an extremism which is as dangerous as that which their defenders pretend to fight. It is sad to see that the Western media give so much opportunity to these spokesmen of openness and modernity, while spluttering the beliefs of thousands of women who are neither extremists nor alienated.
31. See the last part of this book.
32. Narrated by Bukhārī and Muslim.
33. At the very time that we are re-reading these lines, the Pope has adopted a position which goes along these lines: violence is allowed, he says, if it is a question of defending oneself against an indignant aggressor such as the case in Bosnia. The same ringing of bells from Abbot Pierre can also be heard, who, from Sarajevo and basing himself on the teachings of Jesus, called for armed intervention from the West. In this sense, one finds new exegeses concerning the rapport of the political to Christian action. Cf., for example, the exegesis of François Vaillant: "Rendez à César", *Le Courrier de Genève*, 19–20 August 1995.
34. From the verbal form *Jāhada*, the same root as the *maṣdar* (verbal noun) *jihād*.
35. The pronoun "*hi*" of "*bihi*" refers here, according to the majority of commentators, to the Qur'ān (cf., *inter alia*, Ṭabarī, Qurṭubī and Ibn Kathīr).

36. There exists a great number of traditions which point to the broader sense of this term.

37. *Mushkilat al-Faqr wa kayfa ʿālajahā al-Islām* (The problem of poverty and how Islam remedied it) [in Arabic], Cairo, 1986. The author points out that Islam has never encouraged poverty neither for the religious nor for the Sufis, and as such this appears as a distortion of the order of things which must be rectified. Then, he mentions six domains upon which Islam has insisted and which should lead to a solution: (1) personal work, (2) supporting relatives, (3) *zakāt*, (4) maintaining a state budget, (5) the necessity of other rights other than that of *zakāt*, (6) all types of voluntary charity and supportive engagement.

38. See our contribution to the colloquium *L'Encyclique sociale du Pape Jean Paul II Centesimus Annus,* "Travail, Culture et Religions" presented by Louis Christiaens, s.j., Institut international d'études Sociales, Geneva, 1992.

II. Political Orientations

Things are very clear: either the political has a link with the religious, and in this case, we are dealing with a theocratic organisation, the dogmatic drifts of which have already been shown by history. Or, the political is separated from the divine point of reference and, hence, there opens the horizon of the state of law, which is founded on rationality, the perfection of which can be found in the democratic model. The terms of the alternative are plain, and it would be premature to maintain that Islamists' claims are a retreat, and a dangerous, fanatic obscurantism. Analyses sometimes go very far and are not congested by embellishments. It is the whole Islam, which seems irreducible to "democratic reason". Additionally, in order to prove the soundness of this anathema, the declarations of such and such an "Islamic leader" are relied on, a practice much in vogue nowadays. It is suggested that one must choose either *Islam or democracy*. In other words, either a theocratic organisation or a state of law? All seems to have been said. So much so that certain governments and intellectuals attribute to themselves "a democratic quality" not through a concrete exercise of democratic principles, but rather simply because of their nominal opposition to Islamists. If the latter are "obscure theocrats", their opposites are surely "democrats". This regardless of whether there is torture, suppression or death accompanying the political process. The powers in place have cleverly played on this hypersensitivity.

Yet, one must go back to fundamental principles which are as much orientations of political activity in Islam. First, as we have already indicated in Part One, the articulation between the religious fact and the rational fact, in Islam, does not correspond to what it is, nor to what it used to be historically, in the strictly Judaeo-Christian culture. There is a methodological exactness that we cannot be distracted from when we approach the points of reference of these two civilisations. This consists, first, of looking for a general concept behind the terms used, a concept that gives these terms meaning. Then, extracting a conceptual range out of the logic from which these terms emanate. This, unless one insists on engaging in a political analysis of Islam, newly named "political Islam", starting from the principle that all actions related to government are of the same nature in all religions, cultures and civilisations, and that it is sufficient to judge *all* by the established norm in the West. This formulation smells of excess, and yet it is this perfume that nowadays emanates from the declarations of some researchers. Furthermore, absolute rejection of the questioning suggested by Western intellectuals is also thoughtless. In everything, and *a fortiori* in politics, one must take things into consideration.

One often stumbles on words and notions without taking into account the real content of the respective points of reference. Thus, some Muslims reject the word "democracy" because it is part of Western history as also because "it is not found in the Qur'ān". Similarly, some Western intellectuals have only a very vague notion of the Islamic concept of "*shūrā*". For, they often ignore the latter or suspect it "hides" the famous model of theocratic organisation already referred to. It is, therefore, appropriate to clarify these elements.

1.   The Religious and the Political

We have noted, in Part One, the status of the Qur'ān and that of the *Sunna* within Islamic thought. They are the points of reference that, in offering a concept of the universe and man, orientate thought by means of providing it with general principles. The latter are absolute, as they are for the believer the essence of what he believes in. Concrete realisation of these, according to time and place, is not given in the sources. Moreover, specific situations do not find a single and definitive solution. It is the *ijtihād* of the jurists which connects the general principle to its practical application. *Ijtihād* requires a rational process which imposes upon savants (*'ulamā'*) the development of a specific and understood reflection by means of an internal logic, and this via a search of consensus (*ijmā'*) to deduction by analogy (*qiyās*), and from taking account of the historical or geographical context to consideration of customs (*'urf*).

Islamic law swiftly accepted, in its formulation, the idea of plurality in interpretation and this even in rules of worship and from as early as the time of the Prophet himself (peace be upon him). 'Ā'isha in this respect reports the following tradition:"One day in Ramaḍān, I travelled with the Prophet (peace be upon him) to perform the lesser pilgrimage (*'Umra*). On the way, he broke his fast while I kept mine; he shortened his prayer whereas I performed the full version of it. Then, I said to him: 'May my father and mother be ransom to thee! You eat while I fast, you shorten your prayer whereas I perform them fully', and the Prophet answered: 'You have done well.'"[1]

Without a shadow of doubt, there are rules of interpretation. However, there exists, in a less certain fashion, a latitude in the reading and application of principles. The latter varies in function of the intelligence and experience of the reader and jurist. This plurality was lived, as it is nowadays, by the diversity of juridical schools, the most well known of which among the *Sunnis* are four. The *'ulamā'* (savants) are in agreement with regard to the pillars and fundamental principles of Islam. However, their differences are numerous with regard to the domain of worship, just as they are substantial in that which concerns social affairs (in their ramifications, *furū'*). Each scholar thus developed his own method with its rules of reading and modalities of verification. Some by virtually thinking the most particular and potential (Abū Ḥanīfa), and others abstaining from doing so (al-Shāfi'ī and Mālik). But all were influenced by the milieu in which they lived.[2] We know the story of the meeting between al-Shāfi'ī and Ibn Ḥanbal who were in disagreement about the qualification of one who does not observe prayer, that is whether he is a Muslim or not. This is an important question of theology, one which gave place to an exchange of views revolving around reasoning and logic. In this respect, al-Subkī reported the following story: "Al-Shāfiʿī and Aḥmad disagreed one day on the subject of the person who fails to observe prayer. Al-Shāfiʿī said: 'O Aḥmad! Do you say that the person who does not observe prayer is an infidel?' Aḥmad responded: 'Certainly he is.' Al-Shāfiʿī continued: 'And if he wants to become Muslim what should he do?' Aḥmad answered: 'He should declare that there is no deity but God and Muḥammad is His Messenger.' 'But our man has already pronounced the formula and has never denied it', retorted al-Shāfiʿī. Aḥmad said: 'He becomes Muslim by performing prayer.' But al-Shāfiʿī concluded: 'The prayer of the infidel is not allowed and it is not it that makes a person a Muslim.' *Imām* Aḥmad at this point remained quiet."

This, however, is but a difference of opinion on a point which is certainly fundamental and one can multiply such examples. Nonetheless, this has not prevented any Muslim from thinking that all juridical responses (*fatāwā*, sing. *fatwā*) are Islamic as long as they do not contradict the two sources which are accepted by all, and as long as they are given by acknowledged, competent persons. We can, therefore, retain at least four interdependent, fundamental principles regarding the relation of the religious with the political. The fundamentals which follow are part of the universe of Islamic rationality:

1. The Qurʾān and the *Sunna* are the two basic sources of reference. By means of these, a holistic concept of man and life is conveyed. However, these two sources do not respond concretely to the needs and relativity of historical and geographical situations.
2. Reflections based on these two sources, *ijtihād*, can be numerous so long as they do not contradict the former.
3. Each epoch and each community is responsible for the sane management of this diversity of situations and plurality of views.

4. The field of rational experimentation is huge and offers to reason a consequent autonomy to the point whereby very different applications are considered as "Islamic" if they respect the second enunciated principle. Thus, reason, backed by logic and the most modern scientific means, produce answers which are religious, in the sense of being Islamically qualified and justified.

We can see that the comprehension of "the religious" here does not cover what is meant by the same in the Judaeo-Christian tradition. The spheres of the religious and the rational, the sacred and the profane are defined differently. They do not have the same limits, and they are articulated very specifically from one tradition to another. It is undoubtedly in the domain of the management of the political that these specificities are meaningful today. The debates on secularisation, laicity and democracy are there to prove the point. We realise, moreover, that it is very difficult for Western intellectuals to think the political with categories other than those which are the product of their history. Any formulation which departs slightly from that which is known is suspect. As for that which is only reducible to social categories with difficulty, it is appropriate for them to invent expressions which makes that which is unknown accessible. It is this that Louis Gardet undertook in the middle of this century when he described Islamic, political organisation as "a laic, egalitarian theocracy".[3] A truly strange expression which tends to confuse anyone who tries to see clearly.

a.   *The domain of the political: the Islamic framework*

What has just been said is of prime importance to the question which concerns us here. In effect, it is fundamental to attempt to arrange and distinguish that which belongs properly to the domain of Islamic sources revealed by God and/or stipulated by the Prophet (peace be upon him) from that which pertains to human contribution, which allows the applicability of the project according to time and place.

In the political domain, as also in social and economic spheres, there exists a framework of the Islamic point of reference defined by the Qur'ān and the *Sunna* which corresponds, more or less, to the status of a fundamental law – the constitution (in that it allows its formation) – *vis-à-vis* national legislations.[4] One finds therein the general orientation, and the fundamental principles and laws which should respect the legislative instances of diverse communities. This respect does not, however, mean that national legislations will be identical everywhere. Instead, we shall see that the principles are general enough to allow the formulation of very diversified laws. For Muslims, this frame is of Divine origin and the directives which are related to it are intangible. This is what is understood – here in public affairs – by the term *al-rabbāniyya*, which consists of placing action in a permanent link with the remembrance of the Divine ordinances.

On an ethnological level, we can say that the sources imply a concept of the universe, of man and his organisation of the city as a system of values and as a culture which engenders a mode of structuration which is proper to it. Incidentally, nothing is more legitimate than to assert that Islam, in Muslim majority countries, is a fact which should be taken into account. To think that only French or English legislations are good, no matter to which populations they are addressed, smacks of colonialism. What a great number of Muslim intellectuals say today is that Islam is their point of reference; it is part of their history and identity. To deny this is to want to amputate a part of their being by imposing the idea that Western norms are the only universals (we note, in passing, that this view reveals the nonsense of its own conclusion). That this point of reference be religious is not sufficient to disqualify it, under the pretext that it will take us back to the most obscure periods of human history. Moreover Islam, and this is indeed proof for them, has a law which codifies barbarity and the most inhuman of punishments. It is, therefore, concluded that one cannot, under the pretext of respecting religions and cultures, admit the inadmissible.[5] It is appropriate here to recall that references to religious tradition are present in a great many Western countries' constitutions. These clearly mention religion (at least the ones they recognise) and even go so far as to limit access to the crown or presidency on the basis of religion, for example to Catholic or Protestant.[6]

As for the second objection, we limit ourselves here to pointing out that the general principles of Islam are both exigent and open. Moreover, they orientate human beings towards respect for justice and the dignity of everyone. Louis Gardet, reminding of the central place of the Qur'ān, rightly clarifies this as follows: "But in fact the Qur'ān is the seal of prophecy. It operates for men, and until the Judgement of the end of the world, the 'separation of good and evil'. Now, that which God has thus decreed 'good' in the Qur'ān finds itself taking a number of principles, which are objectively of morals and natural laws. These include observing justice, keeping one's word, respecting 'the rights of God and men', etc. It has prescribed obedience to those who hold power. But it has also ordained the faithful to 'consult one another'. On voluntary and uniquely positive bases we find ourselves joining, in fact, a certain number of facts that are susceptible of founding a democratic notion of authority."[7] This reflection is interesting because it looks beyond the simple fact of referring to the Qur'ān, and that it is the holder of a prescribed message. Louis Gardet points out that similarities exist between certain fundamental principles decreed by the Islamic sources and the foundations of natural law, even if their formulations are different. This author mentions further the Islamic notion of *shūrā* which is at the heart of the thought of the *'ulamā'* (savants) and intellectuals in the political domain. *Shūrā*, then, is the first major principle that we must study.

b. *The notion of shūrā*

Shūrā is the space which allows Islam the management of pluralism. The Arabic word signifies "consultation", "concertation" or "deliberation". It appears in several instances in the Qur'ān. However, two verses are generally cited, since it is from these that the principle of general orientation is conveyed. In *Sūra* 42 which has the same name (*al-Shūrā*) we read:

> *... but what is with God is better and more enduring for those who believe and put their trust in their Lord. And those who avoid the heinous sins and indecencies and when they are angry forgive, and those who answer their Lord, and perform the prayer, their affair being counsel between them, and they expend of that We have provided them...* (Qur'ān, 42:36–8)

Gradation, here, owes nothing to chance and we should notice, after qualifying the believer on the moral plane, an expression of the classification of attitudes. Response to God (meaning here the following of His ordinances), the performance of prayer (the second pillar of Islam after the testimony of faith), then, on the collective plane, the practice of deliberation and supportive social engagement. Thus, the formulation is clear, the very fact of submitting to God on the personal level does not mean that there exists ready-made solutions to settle collective affairs. We have said, above, a word about the concertation (the same verbal root) which must exist between the wife and the husband on the question of weaning the child. In the same way, the faithful are characterised here by the fact that they deliberate among themselves on the subject of their affairs. We know that the Prophet (peace be upon him) continually practised concertation with his Companions, and the traditions which report this are numerous. Whenever a situation, about which no revelation had intervened, presented itself the Prophet (peace be upon him) used to listen to those around him and consequently take decisions. Upon the first confrontation with the people of Makka at Badr, Muḥammad called his Companions: "O people! Share with me your views." Ibn al-Mundhir asked him whether the placement chosen for confrontation was the object of a revelation or whether it was a personal decision. The Prophet responded that it was his own choice. Ibn al-Mundhir suggested a different strategy which meant the Muslims taking up a different position. Muḥammad (peace be upon him) yielded to this argument and moved his entire army. In running affairs, the Prophet (peace be upon him) himself took into consideration and distinguished the absolute origin of the principles and the relativity of his own personal opinion. This, as it is in this instance, even in a situation which might determine the life or death of the whole community.

This fact is even more explicit in the context of the revelation (*sabab al-nuzūl*) of the second verse which acts as a point of reference. Before the Battle of Uḥud, there were different views about whether to advance to encounter their Makkan adversaries or whether to wait for them. The Prophet was of the opinion that they should wait. However, upon deliberation, it was the other view, following the opinions of the majority, which prevailed. The Muslims advanced, thus, and after the actions taken in the fight whereby a group did not follow their orders, the Muslims lost the battle. It was in these conditions of defeat that the verse in question was revealed:

> *It was by some mercy of God that thou wast gentle to them; hadst thou been harsh and hard of heart, they would have scattered from about thee. So pardon them, and pray forgiveness for them, and take counsel with them in the affair; and when thou art resolved, put thy trust in God; surely God loves those who put their trust in Him.* (Qur'ān, 3:159)

After this defeat, the Prophet (peace be upon him) forgave the Companions who had let themselves be carried away by their desires thus causing the first Muslim setback. Despite this, however, the Revelation confirms the principle "consult them on all things". Whatever the result, deliberation imposes itself and the opinion of the majority is decisive. The example of the Prophet (peace be upon him) was followed well by his successors. Abū Bakr used to gather together the most competent and reliable Companions and consult them about juridical, social or political decisions. Upon his accession to the Caliphate, he addressed the community: "If you see me in the right, help me; if you see me in error, correct me." These were, more or less, the same words which were uttered by his successor ʿUmar when he said: "If any of you sees distortion in my actions, let him rectify them." Such behaviour is born out of respect for the principle prescribed in the above two verses. However, reading history, one realises that each among the successors thought out a specific mode of consultation. For the principle of deliberation enunciated by the Qur'ān does not say anything about the actualisation of its form.

Supported by these considerations, while equally taking into account the diversity of practices of consultation in the history of Islamic civilisation and the reflections produced by the 'ulamā',[8] we can extract seven principles which are inherent in the notion of shūrā:

1. The political must offer to the community the means of deliberation and, hence, of participation in running its affairs. This is either by direct elections, or under the model of representation. The form may depend on historical situations,[9] habits or existing social structures.

2. The creation of a "Council of Shūrā (deliberation)" – majlis al-shūrā – imposes itself and necessitates structuring the modes of people's consultation which allows for the election of members to this Council. Whether it is direct elections, the formation of regional councils or something else, all these forms are acceptable so long as they allow participation and consultation of the grass roots according to the Qur'ānic expression.

3. Members of this Council are chosen with regard to their competence[10] according to the specific role devolved upon the Council. It seems evident that there must exist two types of competence in this Council. On the one hand, those related to the knowledge of the acknowledged principles of Islamic orientation, to which must be added mastery of economic, political and social affairs according to the domains whereby reflection is engaged.[11] Suitably appointed commissions, as nowadays found in all parliaments, can legitimately do this job. It is inside this authority or another, which is appointed to it, that the practice of ijtihād must be elaborated, and which links the sources with concrete realities. This is the role of those

who are known in Islamic jurisprudence as "the people
who tie and untie" (*ahl al-ḥal wa'l-ʿaqd*). It is impossible
nowadays to leave this function to theologians alone.
Social, political, economic and even medical and
experimental sciences have reached such a level of
complexity that it is not possible to deal with related
juridical and ethical questions without consultation with
experts in these various domains.

4. Selection of the person responsible for the nation (the
    President or *Imām* – the one who is placed ahead) can be
    delegated to the *Shūrā* Council (or to regional councils, if
    they exist), but it can also be the choice of the people.
    Once again, the principle of choosing people is
    inalienable in Islam. The form which its realisation takes
    depends on a great number of historical, geographical
    and even cultural factors. The idea of a mandate of a
    determined period does not contravene Islamic teachings.

5. The President of the nation is, thus, chosen by the
    community (both men and women must have the right
    to participate in this choice). As any other President
    bound by the constitution of his country, he must respect
    the principles of the Islamic reference. He must also be
    its guarantor before the *Shūrā* Council (as also before the
    people) to whom he must give an account of his general
    politics as also that of his ministers.[12] This is exactly what
    Abū Bakr and ʿUmar did, and it is in this sense that, in
    modern societies, the executive and legislative powers are
    articulated.

6. The separation of power is one of the fundamental
    principles of the organisation of the city, and this was
    respected from the moment Abū Bakr succeeded to the
    Caliphate. The judges (*quḍāt,* sing. *qāḍī*) had to exercise
    their function in an autonomous fashion and according
    to the principle of equality of all before the law.[13] In this
    sense, ʿUmar addressed very firm recommendations to a
    judge of one of his provinces which are still well known
    today.

7. The people, as long as the principles of election have
    been respected, make an act of allegiance (*bay'a*)[14] to the
    one whom the majority has chosen. This allegiance
    presupposes conditions and cannot be one of blind
    submission. It requires a critical conscience from the
    people towards the one who has the responsibility of
    running their affairs. This critical participation, for Islam,
    is one of the fundamental duties of the citizen. One
    tradition reports: "The Muslim must hear and obey that
    which he likes and that which he dislikes, unless it is a
    question of disobedience (of the principles of the Creator).
    If the latter is the case, then, they ought to neither listen
    nor obey."[15] A president or king who spreads injustice,
    corruption and denies citizens their rights cannot receive
    allegiance. This because he betrays the message which he
    claims to defend. The population, then, must make use
    of all legal means to remove him from office.

2. *Shūrā* or Democracy?

"There is no democracy in Islam"; "Islam is opposed to
democratic principles." Such statements have been made by
Muslims and some researchers have registered them. Hence, a
thought which comes to disturb the clarity of such a formulation
may appear dubious. If, incidentally, one dares to assert that
things are a little bit more complex than this, one may be accused
of casting a shadow where there is so much light. Therefore, an
explanation imposes itself.

Many Western researchers and intellectuals, regardless of how
good their intention is, make the mistake of apprehending the
domains of the religious and the political, at the same time as
their articulation and interaction, according to points of reference
which are theirs and in the light of their own history. In the
same way, the terms used take the meaning of their historical
evolution from which they cannot be subtracted. It is impossible
to stop at the "actual" meaning of terms for one risks committing
serious methodological errors. This happens by starting, for

example, to compare that which is incomparable within two points of reference and two different cultures. To recall this is not tantamount to sidestepping the custom. It is rather purifying turbid water by refusing to have a dispute about expressions when it is a question of evaluating the respective principles of structuration in the political field.

Numerous Muslim intellectuals have not been immune from such clumsiness. They express, without any great anxiety for being well understood, Islamic specificities with a terminological arsenal which is liable to produce damaging shifts of meaning. Out of reaction against the universal, universalist pretension of the West, they combat notions for what they represent in the rapport between the West and Islam and not in what they are in themselves. This to the extent that this criticism, whose source we can well understand, ends up by clouding over the Islamic points of view themselves. As for concepts of "democracy", "human rights" and "freedom of expression," it is appropriate, all the same in this discussion, to distinguish between normative definitions and ideological and political tools.[16]

In Part One of this book, we revealed some bases of the Islamic concept of the universe and man: this allowed us to arrange, with more clarity, the domains of Revelation, tradition and rational research in order to show how their interactions were elaborated. When establishing a strict comparison with points of reference proper to the Judaeo-Christian tradition, one realises that there are some significant differences between the two concepts,[17] and this despite the apparent similarities. The history of Islamic civilisation confirms that there exists a primal difference between the elements which have given meaning to its internal dynamic and that which, in the West, has produced the phenomenon of secularisation, at least since the Renaissance. This is not only a simple historical acknowledged fact, rather there exists a difference of concept in the rapport with the Creator, and in the perception of the universe and man. The latter's social thought is inevitably oriented by the holistic vision which is implied in it. The contrary of this would be strange indeed.[18] To speak of political organisation around the idea of *shūrā* and looking for points of anchorage with democracy requires first that we speak, even if succinctly, about the philosophies and systems of values which found these projects.

In order to do so, let us go back to those categories we have already talked about and which render our reflection more explicit. It can be a question of a parable, that which engages *the proprietor* and *the gerent*.[19] What can straightaway mislead us is that both in the Judaeo-Christian tradition as in the Islamic concept this parable is eloquent.[20] God, the Proprietor, has rights over both the universe and man, who is the gerent. Certainly, but the comparison, barely started, must stop and loses all pertinence if it goes beyond this threshold of this consideration of role. In fact, in analysing the roles attributed to the actions of this parable, all is disclosed differently.

Western history is marked by the way in which it represents the rapport with God through the institutionalisation of its terrestrial Church. The sphere of the religious was, thus, founded on authority and dogma. The Church, strong with the powers it had, acted as if it retained not only gerency but also property of the world and reality. For a long time it opposed science, rationality, and free thought. The process of secularisation is very clearly the process by which the gerent claimed his rights after being long suppressed by the authority of the Church. He wanted, as he was later to liberate one by one, the domains of thought and management of the world from dogmatic tutelage. Here, the gerent is opposed to the Proprietor, or to the one who represents Him, and will go as far as willingly getting rid of Him.[21] From now on, the gerent runs things without the Proprietor. He fixes norms, establishes values and develops all the means he is in need of. If God remains "useful" for "private" questions concerning the meaning of life, marriage or death, He, nevertheless, never enters into consideration as regards the running of the city. Here, nothing is imposed and everything is discussed and discussible. Moral law may well be in us, but the sky full of stars above our heads remains silent.[22] The gerent is from now on responsible for the whole management. The

democratic principle is, in the domain of social organisation,
the result of this same process. It is founded on the idea that
nothing should be imposed upon men except that which men
decide amongst themselves, by majority, only in the mirror of
rationality which is from now on normative. This concept of
liberty was formed against authority and cannot seem real unless
it is total. God and the sacred are outside the world, and the
disenchantment of the latter seems to be, from the beginning,
programmed.[23] The gerent is absolutely free; that is to say, the
gerent is the proprietor.

When Muslim theologians or intellectuals are opposed to
the idea of "democracy", it is an opposition to the philosophy
which it implies that they are expressing. Everything in the basic
concept of life, man and his destiny; everything in the history of
this civilisation is constructed around the presence of the
Proprietor who invests the three spheres of the human. He gives
meaning to the fact of being, He exposes the means to be with
the Being. Finally, He prescribes the orientations to which man
must remain faithful in history. The Proprietor is present by
means of a Book and a human example – the Prophet (peace
be upon him) – and not by means of an institution or an
incarnation. Man finds therein a very encompassing concept of
the religious, a relationship with the sacred which is both intimate
and vast, and also a permanent, rational exigency. God, the
Proprietor of the heavens and earth, indicates the moral norms
of action and the general orientation of their achievement. He
has entrusted gerents of all men at all times with calling upon
all the qualities of their humanity, intelligence and reason. This
in order to give shape to this teaching. Here, authority does not
suppress, it awakens and stimulates. Nonetheless, one cannot
do without this authority. The specificity of the Islamic concept
is here entirely accessible. God does not require anything from
man which is against his humanity. The latter must think, act,
undertake and manage according to his nature but always in
acknowledgement of the rights of the Proprietor. This
acknowledgement may take diverse forms according to time
and place. However, it always remains nourished by the

interpretation of the sources of which no one can claim the monopoly of comprehension. The process which liberated the gerent of all tutelage in Western history does not have its counterpart in the history of Islamic civilisation. In the latter, research and experimental and human sciences were developed in the name of religion and faith, not against them. On the contrary, the Proprietor required from the gerent that he should seek understanding and always act more. His liberty was not supposed to be the expression of opposition but rather the testimony of a responsibility that he carries and acknowledges before the Creator. Such a concept of liberty differs from that which we have spoken about above. There cannot be total liberty which would deny his own reality, as well as the bases of the relationship between the Creator and men. There cannot be a dogmatic authority which would likewise deny the responsibility of man before God.

The way lies between these two extremes and the principle of the organisation of *shūrā* is born from this concept of man. It is a Revelation as it is a Messenger. It is these two sources which convey to man the exigencies of the Proprietor who, in matter of political organisation as in all other domains, does not stop only at the details. Management is incumbent upon the men who must read, interpret, discuss, consult with one another, oppose one another and, finally, elaborate a project about which we can say it is a test of their liberty. This test, when it is lived in constant remembrance of divine exigencies, gratitude, respect and justice, is the translation of the meaning of *rabbāniyya* which we have already discussed. It is wanting to be a human being without obliviousness of God. It is knowing oneself to be a gerent, albeit free, but still only a gerent.

The two concepts are, without a doubt, basically different, and it is necessary to know the nature of these divergences. Yet, it remains that one must avoid enunciating conclusions hastily, two of which appear to us to be erroneous. The first consists in thinking that these differences are, in short, due to different rhythms of evolution in history. Thus, it is asserted, without turning a hair, that the "progresses" which allowed real autonomy of thought in the West are the expression of a greater "development". Hence, the Islamic concept with this authority, which is always paraded by God, the Proprietor, is the expression of backwardness in a culture which has not developed sufficiently, one which could not accede to modernity. "Soon, *with our help*, Muslims will evolve in the right direction and their idea of religion will resemble ours. They will be free by means of the same freedom as ours." Such is the reasoning, and how dangerous it is, which we increasingly hear in certain interreligious dialogues or in political and cultural discussions.

With a pronounced condescendence, we recognise, in the formulations of Muslims, certain accents of medieval thought which we have fortunately passed, and of which, it is hoped that, for the future of the world, the world of Islam will be able to liberate itself. As the West did in history, concepts, values and progress appear insidiously as the norm of the good. Those who think differently are way behind; or else they think badly, it all depends. For asserting one's identity one has a choice between walking quicker or "refraining" oneself. Cultural pluralism, in many respects, seems to have limits. The second shortcoming consists of maintaining that if the differences are such, it is, therefore, because we find ourselves in the face of a conflict whose aspects are irreducible. On account of the nature of the prevailing concept and respective histories, we can but notice what seems to be conveyed by no other term except conflict.[24] As for that which concerns the organisation of the political, it is asserted that nothing which is Islamic is democratic, because at the end the democratic ideal does not find an echo in the foundation of the Muslim's points of reference. One again asks, does one have to choose either Islam or democracy? We shall make the reprehensible economy of analysing things in their respective context in order to disengage, behind terms and points of reference, the principles which orientate the organisation of the city. Once the differences of concept which orientate the running of the political are understood well, we shall find that the principles of *shūrā* echo many elements of economic rationality, at least in four respects:

a.   *The principle of managing pluralism*

On the question of managing the political, Islam seems to be like a culture which produces a specific concept of the world. This we have already said and repeated. There are orientations, limits, obligations which we cannot question, and, furthermore, we do not see in the name of what they can be. Just as one finds, in values produced by Western rationality, a certain number of postulates which are referred to as principles of truth. Thus, there exist principles which are, for Muslims, inalienable foundations of their faith which one should respect. No human being can give himself the right to make a definitive ruling whether in one sense or in another. "Freedom of conscience" here echoes the Qur'ānic "there is no compulsion in religion".

It remains, therefore, to consider how, within its field of reference, Islam conceives of the management of pluralism. It is this question which interests us mainly, and which alone can make us avoid "disputes over words". The important thing is to know the fate that Islam reserves for opinions and their plurality. Is the ideal organisation of the theocratic type or not? Does reference to God, Revelation or the Prophet (peace be upon him) prevent men from being responsible and free citizens? It seems to us that we have shown, in the discussion which led us to disengage the seven most general principles extracted from the notion of *shūrā*, that Islamic political organisation is in complete opposition to the idea of theocracy as it was lived in Europe! The *rabbāniyya* – the relationship with God – cannot be made, in the political domain without rational development or pluralist discussion or looking out for appropriate historical and geographical solutions. This *rabbāniyya* enhances, around *tawḥīd* (the principle of Divine unicity), the unicity of God's remembrance and the multiplicity of views on the affairs of the world. There is only one God, one Prophet and one Text. But there are different interpretations, opinions and deliberations. From this running of pluralism, we can disengage elements which find their counterparts in the democratic project, and which are even among its most basic foundations. Without having fixed a finished model of political organisation (republican, monarchy, parliamentary regime or others), we find very strict conditions, the respect of which alone testifies to the Islamic nature of the project.

* *The choice of the people.* The choice of the one placed ahead is delegated in Islam to those who place themselves behind. One can be chosen by means of elections, a representative system or any other original idea. The important thing is that the people choose their representative. This means, *a fortiori*, that one must be granted all the conditions that allow one the opportunity to choose with full knowledge of the facts. Any pressure or attempt to influence public opinion must be the subject of strict regulations, for this means that there is a deficit in the real participation of the people. Just as is the case, moreover, with ignorance, illiteracy and misery which are, as many social phenomena, obstructing the real participation of the grass roots.

* *Freedom of opinion.* The first element cannot be without this second. One cannot have the right to choose one's representative and, at the same time, be prohibited from formulating one's own opinion. Thus, freedom of opinion and expression is granted in the political debate within a legitimate respect of the constitution. We can imagine an organisation based on parties or of any other form of pluralism in this domain. The expressions of the political in Islam cannot be confined to a debate on the politicking political whose only aim is access to power.[25] Political programmes must contribute in proposing solutions to the problems of society. In this, and taking into account the experience of multipartism in the West (or parties with programmes often similar, disputing only power), it is legitimate to turn towards new forms of pluralistic participation. The party system, with increasing absenteeism apparent in the North, seems to reveal its limits. To respect freedom of expression and opinion nowadays requires some reforms.

* *Alternation.* To govern is tantamount to being responsible before the people who choose us and before the institutional

organs which play this role in the society in question (*shūrā*, high legislative court, parliament, etc.). It cannot, therefore, be a man, a family or a clan, who take hold of power in a definitive fashion simply because their name or actions enhanced their reputation in a given moment of history. Competence in matters of governing, as indeed moral responsibility, are not hereditary.[26] In the *Sunnī* tradition, things are clear. Competence prevails over blood, and each person carries the testimony of his own honourability in matters of running political affairs. The name of the father never justifies the credibility of the son. Having said this, and in conformity with respect to the choice of the people and freedom of opinion, it is evident that alternation is a founding element of the Islamic project. Each society is in charge of determining the period devolved upon the magistrate for the exercise of power and the modalities, which regulate its respect. Allowing alternation is tantamount to offering the possibility of establishing a critique of the politics devised by the government under the form of an intermediary or definitive assessment. It is exactly what Abū Bakr and ʿUmar requested, for example, from those who had chosen them: "Remain vigilant, take account of our actions and rectify what ought to be rectified."[27]

• *The state of Law.* Whoever reads the First Constitution of Madina will be convinced that from the very beginning Islam thought its social and political organisation around the question of law.[28] The priority of the law is indeed apparent in all domains of Islamic sciences. The domain of social affairs is no exception. Social organisation is based on the foundation of the constitution which, in conformity with the orientations of Islamic teachings, stipulates equality of all before the law, whether they be Muslims or not. It also stipulates respect for the dignity of each person. Every man and woman should have the means to see their rights respected, as much on the political plane as on the juridical. A society which does not respond to these requirements and which, by its own legal system, sanctions inequalities, unjust treatment, or denominational preferences, would be violating the elementary principles of legislation. In this sense, the Islamic reflection joins that of democratic societies which always attempts an evolution towards a greater respect for individuals and groups. The delicate discussion on the rights of minorities (a very sensible debate in the United Nations of Europe) is far from being exhausted. In the same sense, there exists a debate in the Muslim world on the kind of organisation which will be in a position to respect the rights of non-Muslims.[29]

It is appropriate to recall that there does not exist a unique model of Islamic organisation which is thought out for eternity. Rather, on the contrary, it is the principle of adaptability which prevails. This is the basic function of *ijtihād*. In reality, to consider things closely, one notices, if we discard phraseology, that Islamic rationality is echoed, on a number of capital points, in democratic rationality. The fundamental points of reference are different, histories are divergent, and terms are not the same. However, one finds oneself obligated to point out similarities in the principles of articulation and the objectives granted to the respect of pluralism and differences of expression with regard to the political. Without failing to notice that, in the two spheres, there exists a dynamic which advances research and which modulates achievements by taking account of new realities. With this difference – which is fundamental insofar as it identifies the two different concepts of the world – one may add that the pragmatism of democratic rationality draws its vigour from the consideration of situations and events which require forward readjusting. This in the thought of a history that man had to edify in an absolutely autonomous fashion. The Islamic concept finds its strength in a vision of history which, at each stage, refers man to his points of reference and to their interpretation in order to find a forward solution, but one which legitimates its link with the original orientation. This type of rationality, which is the basis of *ijtihād* (one which Iqbal, while giving account of the same idea, called "the principle of movement in the structure of Islam") revolves around a dynamic of memory. Inversely, the democratic experience exposes the dynamic of projection.[30]

There does exist in Islam a framework to run pluralism. Moreover, we can say that a number of principles pertaining to democratic societies have a place therein. The expression of an absolute opposition between Islam and democracy cannot hold from the moment we bring to the fore the bases which distinguish them apart and the principles which unite them together.[31] Each religion, civilisation and culture has the right to have its values considered in the light of the general frame which gives these meaning. This remark applies as much in the sense of a critique against Western sufficiency, as it is a questioning of the rejection, sometimes simplistic, that certain Muslims manifest towards European and American points of reference. This because if there exists a pluralism to manage within societies, there is another pluralism, no less enriching, which comes as a result of the diversity of religions and cultures. It is appropriate to point out the riches of each one among them and to measure that which they bring to the conscience of their faithful or adherents in terms of obligations, rights, responsibilities and values. Undoubtedly, this is the only means to reach a coexistence which is respectful of specificities. For the case which interests us here, it must be admitted that the West has reached a level of scientific mastery and outstanding specialisation. In its points of reference, this evolution commands admiration and all civilisations have to benefit from the dynamic of this rationality, as they can derive lessons from the progress achieved. "Benefiting", "deriving lessons" do not, nevertheless, mean submission. In the same way, it must be acknowledged that other civilisations and cultures propose a rich vision of the world, and that some of these have managed to preserve the basic values of life, and glimpses of their fundamental shape are beginning to be seen in the West.[32] It is not a question of suggesting a new wave of "love for exotisms and folklore". On the contrary, it is a question of engaging in an exigent reflection about cultural specificities and possible enrichment starting from within cultures and not at their peripheries.

Islam, as other civilisations and in the same entitlement as any other culture, has nowadays to bring forth its contribution in the different domains of human thought and action. That this "religion" arouses the fears of the West is not something new.

The conflict is several centuries old. What is new in our epoch is the differential treatment to which some Westerners subject other cultures. In evaluating the profound crisis of values in the West, the wisdom of Buddhist or Sioux thought are in this context legitimately singled out. Basically, it is "allowed" for these cultures to have differences on fundamental concepts because they are not dangerous to the West. As for Islam, the case is different. There are more than a billion faithful today, and a quarter of the planet tomorrow. For the West, the enriching specificity and constructive particularity of Islam are not sought. It is rather repulsive difference that is fixed in mind. The danger appears to be such, and the aggression against the model so evident, that only when the world of Islam speaks "our" language and borrows "our" tools are we going to acknowledge its positive presence. Thus, we could see the same intellectuals accuse, on the one hand, the Declaration of Human Rights for being too ethnocentrist in its formulation (when they defend the rights of South American cultures for example) and, on the other hand, set against Islam because it does not respect the text of 1948. This without being afraid of claiming one thing and applying its contrary.

The debate about the democratic frame, as we can see, opens very vast perspectives. Let us retain for the time being those questions which are directly linked to it (we shall come back to cultural questions in the last part of this book) and which today make great noise; human rights, freedom of expression and opinion and the question of non-Muslims in Islamic societies.

b. *Human rights*

The question of human rights, their formulation and, in a more general fashion, their universality have been much discussed. However, quickly, and from one side and the other, blunders were committed due to an over-simplification of things. For the defenders of human rights, the founding text must be taken as it is. Any remark or criticism reflects an unclean positioning "which hides something". In their view, to discuss the formulation of these rights or their universality is a dissimulated way of not wanting to respect them. One finds in the argumentation of their Muslim contradictors the same hastiness. According to the latter, these rights are based on reason alone and do not refer to the link which unites man with his Creator. As such, this Declaration is in opposition to the teachings of the Qur'ān and the traditions. Here we have reached, from one side as from the other, a conclusion slightly similar to the one we encountered regarding the question of democracy. Islam and human rights, then, cannot go hand in hand.

It is, nonetheless, important to stop for a moment and consider that we cannot make such an economy in this debate. To read a text without taking account of the circumstances and context which brought it forth can lead to serious inconsequences. To forget the historical origin of the Declaration of Human Rights and the compost of human philosophy, which gave it shape, is strictly speaking a nonsense that is justified only by this fierce will to make it a universal tool. This along the disconcerting paradox of a rationality which has its source and meaning in the rejection of absolute principles and which will end up producing one itself. It is a strange approach indeed!

Without entering too much into the detail of historical elaboration, it should be pointed out that diverse English, French and American Declarations, since the seventeenth century, have been, first, the effect of a mobilisation of religious and humanist minorities desiring to defend their rights. It is this viewpoint which, after the Renaissance, was conveyed in the course of its struggle and which opposed both the humanists and the precursors of rationalist thought to religious authority. Born and nurtured in the West by intellectuals who were battling against oppressive forces – themselves justified in the name of the absolute – the philosophy of human rights is marked, in its essence, by such an origin. Before being a universal tool, it indicates a moment of the history of the liberation of reason *vis-à-vis* dogma, and of the assertion of the individual and his autonomy against the oppression of a power and a religion which denied him. Thus, historically speaking, the process is of the order of a reaction. It was an attempt to assert oneself and liberate oneself from imposed duties that rights based solely on rationality were codified and declared. Whatever our desire to defend the rights of human beings, we find ourselves with the obligation to acknowledge that the dynamic which gave rise to these texts contains three basic characteristics. By its own history, it determines the primacy of rational norm. It bases itself on a defence of human autonomy. Lastly, it is the realisation of the rejection of any absolute.

The philosophy which is implied by human rights is culturally marked and belongs to a vast elaboration of analytic thought where all the postulates are significant in the Western history of mentalities. It carries in itself stigmas of the tensions which marked its history. Moreover, this same characteristic is found in the notion of "tolerance". It is indeed a question of a human interpretation of the relations between men. But the point of view is here reversed. By the idea of tolerance is meant a peculiar attitude ensuing from a position of strength at the level of the rapport between human beings. Human rights convey a reaction in order to assert the right of each human being. Tolerance consists of measuring its action in order not to prevent the other from being who he is. The viewpoints expressed are not identical, but the source is the same. The formulation of the principle of tolerance is linked to the formation of rationalist thought. Other cultures, and Islam in particular, do not formulate the universe of coexistence placed at the level of rational norm only.[33]

Does this mean that the origin and philosophy of human rights justifies their pure and simple rejection and takes away any weight *vis-à-vis* their respect? A conclusion of such nature would be baseless. Reinserted in the context of the rationalist dynamic, human rights are one of the most positive achievements and one must point out the well-known improvement that the juridical instrument – which accompanied the declarations – helped to bring about. The Declaration of 1948 is a point of reference from which we can derive today basic, general principles which go along the lines of respect for human dignity.

The same can be said about all philosophical developments since Locke which have allowed Western societies to be more tolerant. The facts are there, it is not possible to deny them. These societies, nurtured by their reference to human rights, have concern for the respect of human beings, their equality and liberty. The lacunae are important, everyone knows it, but the progress is undeniable.

We should not have any pain in acknowledging these realities, for intellectual probity invites us to do so. One has, nevertheless, to go further in the analysis. Once the philosophical nature of "human rights" and, at the same time their positive contribution in the context of their elaboration, are acknowledged, we have to summarily explain how the question of man and his rights are elaborated in Islam. Not with the idea of opposing one concept with another, but rather with a concern for showing that if, on strictly philosophical substance, there are differences, one also finds points of convergence which should allow us to go beyond debates of reciprocal rejection.

The fact that there exists in Islam two points of reference, where human thought derives its orientation, shatters the perspective which we talked about. Moreover, we cannot, in all logic, be satisfied with the formulation which is relative to it.[34] There exists, as we have said, a vast domain of Islamic rationality, but the latter does not fix its marks in an autonomous fashion, or solely in function of the tension which it perceives among men. Before that, there exists a holistic concept which radiates the entire domain of action. That is in the relation between God and men, men between themselves and finally between men and nature. The relationship with God comes first and this in each one of these domains. The notion of responsibility and duty come first. Beyond the peripheries of history, conflicts, claims and reactions, the Islamic teaching imprints its mark first on the action of each individual. The latter has obligations towards God, himself, other human beings as also towards nature before possessing rights. Moreover, the rights of each one will be better respected in the exact proportion whereby each individual respects his own duties. As we have said earlier, human rights are the outcome of a historical process of liberation. The Islamic concept is differently based on an exigency of balance. It does not formulate rights in function of a threat of oppression, but rather with the idea that man is from the outset a responsible being[35] who must be accountable for his choice. Human rights exist in Islam, but they are, nevertheless, part of a holistic vision which orientates their scope.[36] The differences are substantial but they must not lead us to conclude the impossibility of dialogue between the two civilisations. On the contrary, if the source is different, it is nonetheless possible to find in Islam, (as indeed in the texts of Jewish and Christian traditions), orientations and fundamental principles of rights stemming from obligations which agree with those emanating from the text of 1948.

It is this, when all is said and done, that one must look for. It is putting as evidence, within the framework of the Islamic point of reference, as indeed at the heart of each diverse culture, the elements that allow the disengagement of a concept of man (of his rights) thanks to which the discovery of common points will be possible. By referring to the Qur'ān and the *Sunna*, by considering the work of *ijtihād* of the *'ulamā'* and by developing and pursuing reflection in this sense, one realises that one can subtract from the centre of Islamic legislation, from the *Sharī'a*, elements relating to rights. Respect of the latter is primal in comparison to any application of punishments (*'uqūbāt*). These include the right to life, freedom, equality, non-discrimination, justice, asylum, and the right to liberty of conscience, etc.[37]

In fact, if the universality of human rights – as stated in the version of the 1948 Declaration – causes a problem for Muslims, this does not mean that Islam rejects or refutes any thought relating to human rights if understood as the protection of human dignity. On the contrary, all the juridical thought of Islam revolves, so much in the objective of its obligations as in that of its rights, around the respect and inviolability of the person, whether man, woman or child. Now that the points of reference are identified, the differences arranged and the similarities recognised, what is appropriate now is to look beyond a dispute over words to the means to achieve a concrete and better respect of human rights. To use the latter as an ideological tool which confirms Western superiority over other civilisations would be unfortunate. The important thing, and this is so in each culture, is to set in motion the movement that allows approach of the respective models which enable the application of fundamental rights.

If there really exists a pluralism, and if there is a sincere will to engage in the coexistence of civilisations and cultures, then this must proceed from here. Imposing one's norms on others will inevitably mean conflicts. But to call upon each religion and culture to develop from within spaces of protection for the dignity of woman, man and child is, in our view, the choice of the future. Moreover, there must also exist the resolve to want to make one's rights respected everywhere, at all times with the greatest of equities. It is in a concrete, permanent engagement in the field that the living forces of civilisations can encounter one another, have dialogue and a common cause against the suicidal by-products of our time. This for the sake of God, men, our children and before our own consciences.

During the last decade, the world witnessed a live massacre. The ethnic cleansing led by the Serbs was being carried out before the hearing and sight of all the inhabitants of our planet. Mass executions, rapes and deportations were perpetrated, while the cynicism of Serb officials was met with the biased calculations of the great powers. Bosnia was on fire, covered with blood while the waffle went on. While human rights are suppressed, trampled on, and denied, people gather and keep gathering. In 1992, we were presented with a formidable mobilisation against Iraq, who invaded Kuwait, as the concerted action of the great powers for the safeguarding of freedom, human rights and democracy. Everything was good in order to justify for us the good "Desert Storm". We have been told lies, so many lies, and the lies continue. Humanitarian arguments are weighed with the interests which they defend and the dead are valued according to the interest which justifies them. The worst enemy of human rights and the worst insult to the 1948 Declaration is not caused by Islamic, Indian or other differences, rather the worst enemy is indeed this variable utilisation of the most beautiful texts for the most sombre of interests. The worst insult lies indeed in this unconditional support for the most bloody and repressive dictatorial regimes ever to exist. This unconditional support coupled with "non-violent" inclination in discourse and which denounces the violence of those who are forced to take arms because of the suppression they live under. Political violence must be denounced, but how is it not possible to understand, from the depth of what gives meaning to the life of a human being, that after years of terrible repression, men mobilise themselves and decide to put a stop to such situations. For, if one must die being denied in one's being, then one would rather die in dignity. This attitude is understood, but it certainly cannot be justified. However, with the same force one must say, and repeat, say and denounce, say and say again, that nothing justifies the sinister calculations of rich countries nor the passivity of their public opinion. Before God and before our consciences, nothing justifies them nor does anything enable the understanding of such a degree of acceptance and lassitude bordering on complicity.

How can it be imagined that the inhabitants of the South, whether Muslim or not, still believe in the grandeur of human rights? How is it still to be hoped that they trust those who do not hesitate to ward off the most valued of their interests by means of the most beautiful discourse of humanist intentions. It would be just as insane to ask the homeless, unemployed and those excluded from society to believe the sincere respect that their politicians have towards them. The problem of human rights today, like the problem of the rights acknowledged by Islam but which are violated every day, is that it still belongs to the domain of theory and intention while everything is allowed in practice. Whether it be from the side of Western powers or from the majority of Muslim governments, of which we can today measure the strength of hypocrisy, the points of reference are suppressed. The same people who cite articles of diverse humanist declarations, and the same people who recite from memory a Qur'ānic verse or a Prophetic tradition, have blood on their hands and prisons consecrated to the denial of rights and to torture. The most beautiful poem which is stained with blood has a bitter tone. Undoubtedly, silence is better than this betrayal. Our common engagement starts exactly here. With determination, rigour and conviction one must give witness to our faithfulness in the face of all betrayals. We should do this firmly, conversely and practically, for it is a duty of conscience for those who defend the dignity of rights.

c.   *"Non-Muslims" in Islamic society*

Concerning the status of non-Muslims in Islamic societies we have heard everything, from the worst to the idealistic. Muslim thinkers sought in the Qur'ān, the *Sunna* as well as in the action of such and such a ruler the proofs that Islam gave to *ahl al-dhimma*, the greatest respect and the best of recognition. As for Orientalists and intellectuals, they have made no less an exhaustive compilation of Qur'ānic verses, traditions and historical events which confirm, once and for all, that Islam reserves the worst treatment for those men and women who do not share the Muslim conviction. A discussion appears impossible as much because these points of view, armed respectively with argumentative stuff, are irreducible and irreconcilable. Only, is it possible to find a field of understanding?

One must take things into account and delimit the subject of discussion. Once again, it is appropriate to present the Islamic bases of coexistence and, at the same time, bring to the fore the principle which should orientate social organisation in this domain. It cannot be a question, subsequently, of idealising the history of Islamic civilisation. There were yesterday, as there is today, discrimination, injustice and exploitation. To deny this would be a folly. In the same fashion, to retain nothing but deviations would be unjust. Valery has rightly pointed out that history can prove everything. In other words, if we want to have a useful discussion, it becomes imperative, after having been reminded of the Islamic principles on the question, to analyse concretely, the situation in the field by trying to plan the stages of reforms which are necessary to guarantee the fundamental rights of those who do not have a Muslim confession.

The Foundations

Starting from the Qur'ān and the *Sunna*, and taking support from the practice of the first Companion of the Prophet (peace be upon him), we can disengage the basic foundations of coexistence between Muslims and non-Muslims. We shall confine ourselves to bringing to the fore six principles which present the general orientation that Islam offers, even if their analysis cannot here be exhaustive:

1. The principle of coexistence between the faithful of diverse confessions is one of the bases of the social and political organisation of Islam. The Prophet (peace be upon him), upon drawing up the Constitution of the State of Madina, considered the Jews (the tribe of Banū ʿAwf) as a permanent part of the new society, linked by contract. In the text of the said Constitution we find two very meaningful expressions. "The Jews of Banū ʿAwf form one community with the believers (Muslims)." This explicitly means that the constitutional community covers both Muslims and non-Muslims. And again: "All the Jews who choose to be joined to us shall benefit from all the protection that the Muslims have a right to. They will not be oppressed and there shall be no collective agitation against them. To the Jews their religion and to Muslims theirs."[38] Thus, coexistence is based on the free-will of the partners, equality of treatment and the respect of consciences.[39]

2. The citizens who are not of a Muslim confession participate fully in the social and political life of the society of which they are members. But for the function of the Head of State (devolved, in a society of a Muslim majority, to a Muslim),[40] they can be elected to any government

post in accordance with their competence and without any discrimination. It is indeed this that 'Umar did by naming a Christian as chief accountant in Madina. The same was done by a great number of his successors. Al-Māwardī presents the nomination of non-Muslim ministers as a choice left to the head of the executive. Thus, the possibility of eligibility supposes and renders necessary the fact of electing. It is a fact that this right must be inalienable.

3. Citizens who are not of Muslim confession are referred to as *ahl al-dhimma* or *al-mu'āhidūn* – "those who have agreed a contract". This contract is clearly a contract of protection of these persons and their fundamental rights. The State commits itself to offering them all the conditions which allow them to live in serenity. They are not subjected to the purifying social tax (*zakāt*), the third pillar of Islam, nor to military service.[41] They are obliged to pay a tax, *jizya*, which is the equivalent of a military tax,[42] although women, children, old men, the poor and the clergy are exempted as are all men who prefer to serve their country militarily rather than pay *jizya*.[43] It is in this sense that the contract signed by the Prophet (peace be upon him) with the Christians of Najrān was inscribed.

4. *Ahl al-dhimma* are held, in the same title as Muslims and on the same footing of equality, by the Constitution of the country and its legislation. However, they must entertain a total autonomy with regard to their private affairs (on the judiciary plane also) and anything relating to their religion and spirituality too, whether closely or remotely. Their language, culture and traditions must be defended and protected. For example, there was, in Madina, a Jewish Centre of Education (*Bayt al-Midrās*) which the Prophet (peace be upon him) visited and about which he inquired after its state of affairs. In the same vein, and as the pact with the Christians of Najrān mentions, non-Muslims' places of worship are sacred and inviolable; religious practices must be absolutely protected. Again, the Prophet

(peace be upon him) allowed the delegation of Najrān to pray in the Mosque of Madina.

5. We have said above a word about freedom of opinion and expression in relation to political management in Islam. Here, plus freedom of conscience, non-Muslim citizens, like all other citizens, must enjoy the same fundamental liberties. Conveying an opinion, expressing a critical view, and engaging in a political reflection are all actions which must be granted to them. They must also be granted, as Muhammad Hamidullah reminds us, the possibility of getting involved in deliberations, as much on the executive as on legislative levels.[44] The sole restriction relates to respect of the constitutional framework, as is the case nowadays in any state of law.

6. The responsibility of the state is important in the protection of the rights of non-Muslims. It is, besides, this idea which is derived from the term "dhimmīs". The latter are those whose obligations are the responsibility of the state and nation. It is this that 'Umar understood when he asserted, on his death-bed, that the contract with non-Muslims must be respected, that their life and properties must be defended, that they should not be charged with that which is beyond their means and, lastly, that if necessary they are to go to war in order to defend their rights. As full citizens, their persons, traditions and wealth are sacred. They must be treated with the greatest equity in a social space which, in order to welcome plurality, admits adversity of legislation for that which relates to private affairs. The Prophet (peace be upon him) maintained with force: "Whosoever is cruel and harsh towards a mu'āhid (one who is under a contract), restrains his rights, burdens him with that which he cannot endure or takes anything of his property against his will, I shall be myself his adversary on the Day of Judgement."[45] This saying is clear, as is the saying which he uttered before his death, as reported by Māwardī: "Treat non-Muslim subjects well."

The above six foundations bring to the fore that Islam, in its basic teachings, acknowledges religious and cultural pluralism and that the principles of coexistence are based on respect, liberty, justice and participation. This depiction seems ideal and, in effect, it is so. The Qur'ānic text, the practice of the Prophet (peace be upon him) and that of his Companions, though they offer the best examples, were not always respected as they should have been. Moreover, mention of these elements is not sufficient to resolve the important problems which Muslim societies are facing in their management of "minorities". These principles should orientate us and not, in their ideal dimension, blind us about history and about the real status quo today.

History

We have just put forward the general orientation which emanates from Islamic sources as from the first Companions. In early times, one must acknowledge, coexistence was relatively possible despite important conflicts resulting from the permanent situation of war between the Muslims and the Quraysh of Makka (who made alliances with other Arab and Jewish tribes in order to destabilise and then defeat the new Madinan society). Within a span of 12 years – from 633 to 645 – Islam spread, however, and was established in Palestine, Syria, Mesopotamia and Egypt. This expansion continued for almost another century.

The history of this epoch, and those which followed it, has been written and rewritten. The fiercest opponents of Islam, and of the message this religion conveys, have presented it as the most sombre period, full of bodies, torture, forced conversions and organised slavery. Carried by the obligation of *jihād* (translated as holy war), the Muslim thirst for conquest saw weakened empires, one after the other (Roman Empire of the East, Sassanid Empire of Persia, the Visigoth Empire of Spain) subject themselves. Furthermore, the Muslims imposed their law by humiliating the defeated by means of exorbitant taxes (the famous *jizya*), specific styles of dress, or simply putting their enemies to death.[46] Other historians, not only Muslims, however have emphasised the peaceful character of this expansion. Undoubtedly there were wars, but on the whole the Muslims often numbered less than their adversaries and did not have to engage in fierce fighting. The simplicity of their message, their will for social justice and their respect for the cultures and traditions of the indigenous people meant that they were sometimes welcomed as liberators considering the way in which the despots of the time treated their own subjects in their new territories, Muslims allowed the inhabitants to retain their religion, practise it freely and respected alternative places of worship. Arabic was not imposed and people continued to express themselves in their mother tongue. Moreover, local notables were called upon to take care of the administration of affairs (especially during the ʿAbbāsid period) and often occupied important posts.

The story reported about Michael the Syrian, who was happy to be liberated by Muslims from the tyranny and "cruelty of the Romans", the rallying of "Unitarian" Christian sects (Monophysite, Arian and Nestorian) upon the victory of Spain, and at the same time, the studies carried out by diverse historians (Ibn Khaldūn, Dozy, Ibanez, Olague, Hundke, Velasquez) seem to back, at least partly, this second interpretation. The fact remains, nonetheless, that there were equally during this long period of history, patent injustices committed against non-Muslims. Under the Umayyads, important exactions were made, populations displaced, and humiliation and distinctively-marked clothing imposed. These are many recognised events which give nuance to the picture of a Muslim presence depicted as always tolerant and well-intentioned. Such was not the case, for the betrayals of the orientations formulated by the Qur'ānic and traditional references were numerous. One may delight in the general vigour of Muslims wherever it was the case, but it is appropriate to acknowledge the deviation and propose a firm criticism, without complacency, of all injustices and exploitation which have been committed by Muslims in the name of Islam. It is hoped that this critical attitude towards their history will encourage in Muslims the habit of a similar posture today. This not in order to self-scourge themselves, but in order to constructively engage themselves in a project for the future.

Moderation, from both sides, and acknowledgement of the positive contribution of the Islamic civilisation, without concealing its most sombre period, seems to be the wisest attitude. This equally means that one must admit that Islam is not reducible to some notions of which one offers a definition only in the light of the saddest events of its history, as was done concerning *jihād*, the *dhimmīs* or again the text of *jizya*. This clearly means that one must go beyond the frame of conflicting analysis alone whose only objective is to show that Islam, in itself, is a danger which threatens the progress of Western norms of coexistence. In other words, finally, one must acknowledge that along the centuries, civilisation has proposed and achieved models of coexistence between different communities based on respect and freedom of conscience and worship. For, there were indeed in the history of this civilisation, so much discredited today, spaces of pluralism, exchanges and relations. From the eighth to the eleventh century, at least, one must point out that coexistence, even when it was not always perfect, was real, institutionalised and administered. We have examples of this under the 'Abbāsids, we also know the history of Andalusia and its intellectual flourishing. This alone enables as to prove that Islam is not inherently opposed to pluralism carried out with justice and respect for other religions. To remember this is imperative today, as one must be aware that Muslims have been, in many times, worthy of the message they carried.

Contemporary Problems

Coexistence, in Muslim-majority countries, between Jews, Christians and Muslims is a few centuries old. The different communities have survived and pluralism has sometimes been real and positive in the Ottoman Empire, Egypt, Lebanon, Morocco, Algeria, Iraq, and Iran, etc. There exists, however, problems, important sources of tension which put in peril the serenity of inter-community life. Identifying and finding solutions is urgent. In order to do so, it is sufficient to remind ourselves of the great principles of Islam which we have mentioned before, convincing ourselves of their immediate applicability. This would be a dangerous over-simplification of things and would mean, at the same time, avoiding the most important question of all. Namely, how to set in motion the reforms which would enable us today, while taking into account the state of different countries, to draw nearer to a model of coexistence based on pluralism, while respecting religious, linguistic, and broadly-speaking, identity-based differences? The primary Islamic sources require from each society and epoch that it finds the means of this actualisation. The same applies to our responsibility and we must activate this debate on the internal level without failing to take into account all the juridical studies carried out on these questions at the international level (UNO, CSCE, and the European Council).[47]

Two important remarks have to be made here in that they have consequences for the debate which interests us. In the first place, it is appropriate to note that the legislation "imported" into Muslim countries during the colonial period and "plastered" (or applied with a very relative degree of adaptability) on a very different social reality, have not solved at all the question of coexistence between different communities. The tensions are vivid, and under the varnish of a "unitary" legislation which does not distinguish between state and nation, citizenship and nationality, are expressed in particular adherence and identity-based networks which imprint their mark on social life. The assurance that the powers apply the best of models – since it comes from the "so advanced"[48] West – may not hold under a rigorous analysis of the situation. A constitutional model guaranteeing justice in a given place may produce, when exported, significant injustices as a result of the gap which exists between the philosophy which thought it out and the reality on which it is supposed to be applied. We have many examples of this in developing countries, whether they have a Muslim majority or not (as also in Eastern Europe as we shall see).

One must remember that neither the United States nor Europe have provided today a satisfactory answer to the question of the pluralism of collectivities based on religion, language or ethnicity. The disintegration process of the great empires in Eastern Europe, wherein many "nationalities" coexist, has given rise to states whose territorialities do not correspond to different identity belongings.

As early as 1878, at the Berlin Conference, the question of the protection of minorities was tackled. It was then a problem and it will always continue to be so. The 1919 "Treaty of Minorities" thought out after the Balkan Wars of 1912–13 which changed "national" structures, show a difference between the Polish citizen and his identity. Stated in this Treaty: "Polish nationals belonging to minorities of race, religion or language benefit of the same treatment and guarantees, by right and fact, as other Polish nationals."[49] A strange formulation indeed! The allied powers of the West exported their model of nation state and, due to the particularity of the population of Eastern Europe, found themselves in an impasse. Namely, it is a question of how to create a state possessing a unitary structure by trying to make live collectivities that all require the legitimate respect of their specificities. The principle of nation state found it difficult to apprehend this other reality. The end of the nineteenth century saw the rise of new minorities, but the Treaty brings forth an original juridical expression – "national minority" – which used much ink, and is still at the centre of the debate that we have not come out of even today.[50]

Endless discussions have revolved around the question of minorities, upon the elaboration of the Declaration of Human Rights, at the level of states, in the commissions, etc. Was it necessary to mention in a specific article the question of the protection of minorities? A number of European countries, and the United States, were opposed to this. For, according to them, human rights contained and encompassed the right of minorities in what they have accepted to recognise in Eastern Europe. But they refused to consider it in their own countries. The great powers took part in the elaboration of an international juridical instrument which did not oblige them to investigate their own national law. This was more so during the elaboration of the European Convention of Human Rights (1950), the Additional Pacts (1966) and the Declaration.[51]

During years of colloquia, suspensions of meetings, of formed and discharged commissions, for over what is now eight decades, at least, it has not been possible to agree on an official definition which covers the notion of "minority". Yet, we know well what this comes to, but these states are opposed to any formulation which may bring to the fold shortcomings on an internal level which may impose constitutional reforms upon them. The nation-state, more clearly the nationalist state, has some difficulty in giving a juridical form to pluralism. Often things were confined to calling upon human rights and the democratic ideal in order to guarantee the respect of identities, without, that is, being subjected to any constraint. Yet, the problem is far from being solved. For the ideal and legal effacement of the specificities pertaining to identity does not mean that they do not exist any longer. Almost all Western countries are facing surges of reaffirmation of particulariness and there is difficulty in resolving this problem. That is unless one treats its supporters as reactionary elements, who march against the course of history which "the great Europe" constructed against "small identities". Contempt vies with mockery and rejection when we come to consider such claims in Eastern Europe: "Such things, they can happen in Africa, perhaps, ... but in Europe, its unthinkable!"[52]

Fabienne Rousso-Lenoir circumscribes the problem: "Apprehended in the sole vision of the nation-state by the law of human rights, the man belonging to a minority acquires the same rights as the others but loses this part of himself which is different and which cannot be expressed except in, and by, the group to which he belongs."[53]

There exists, therefore, gaps which we cannot afford not to consider, and this, especially, if we think to export the democratic model to the countries of Eastern Europe.

"The political men of the old Western democratic nation-states, where nation and state have developed together, still have difficulties perceiving how much centralising (and, in the best of cases, integrationist) nationalism, may undermine any tentative attempt to establish in the East real and effective democracies, by locking up nation-state and national minorities in an infernal game of mirrors."[54]

It is imperative to weigh the specific realities in order to work out structures which would allow each one to entertain his fundamental rights. The model of Western Europe alone cannot be applied to the whole continent, otherwise it will provoke tension and war whose sad spectacle is offered to us every day. The question of minorities, therefore, requires an inventive spirit. Rousso-Lenoir mentions the research of two Austrians, Karl Renner and Otto Bauer, who have elaborated that a "political and juridical system or a state, nation and even territory do not necessarily correspond". According to these two researchers: "The choice of nationality is like that of a religion, it is a private matter... The quality of national does not ensue from belonging to a state but rather from belonging to a nation ... The state, made up of nations that compose it, conserves the sphere of general interest and the national undertakes with him relations of a citizen. The proportional system guarantees the representation of nations in the Parliament of the State."[55]

A political project which aims at promoting a real participation of the people in respect of diversities and identities must propose a flexible structure which respects values and protects rights. It is this that is conveyed in the conclusion of the book: "Political unity and national unity are not necessarily superimposed, in the same way as national life and political system, nationality and citizenship or civic loyalty and ethnic or cultural attachments are not" (p.91).

One is obliged to note that the difficulties felt in Eastern Europe find an echo in the Muslim world. The exported nation-state model has not been appropriate. Being the outcome of several centuries of gestation mixed up with the process of secularisation, this model is linked to the circumstances of its elaboration and is conditioned by a certain number of elements, the least of which is not the formation of the individual citizen.

All the attempts which, after independence, have based their legitimacy on "modernity" and "the progressist scope" of their management have demonstrated their limits. From Nasser to Bourguiba and from Ben Bella to Asad, the failure is total and the principle of citizenship is everywhere absent. One realises, on the other hand, that the religious referent is today irreversible. Kings as the most secular heads of states derive their popular legitimacy from a constant reminder of their faithfulness to Islam.[56] The histories are not the same and the secularisation which was operated in the West is not achieved in the Muslim world, first and foremost, because the links between the religious, the political and the cultural are not the same. We would be wrong not to draw a lesson from this state of affairs, as it is appropriate, furthermore, to take stock of the traditional links which permeate through the populations at the familial, tribal and ethnic levels.

A political structure which allows pluralism presupposes that we take account of these specificities, and before that, as we have already noted, of the omnipresent religious reference. The political structure must without any doubt be original, new and in tune with the field on which it should be applied. But it is certain that Islam, according to reading of the bases that we have discussed, holds, as a point of reference, a wide range of possibilities in political achievements.[57] Unlike the West which is more or less relatively liberated of the religious in order to create an individual citizen, our epoch reminds us that it is within Islam that a dynamic must develop that enables a citizenship which is respectful of the values of each one. We cannot continue thinking, unless we want to be blinded indefinitely, that we can reach a result by denying the religious and cultural substratum of identity. Difficulties still persist to prove this fact. So how to manage religious pluralism, in Muslim countries, at the end of the twentieth century? Is it by introducing the troublesome concept of "minority"? Or is it by distinguishing citizenship from nationality? What exactly is this model which is bound to principles and, in line with contemporary social realities? Muslims today, if they consider the principles of coexistence which are extracted from the two sources of reference, find themselves facing a problem similar to that faced by the new democracies of the West with, it goes without saying, the religious and cultural specificities which are theirs. They have to envisage a new structure which offers citizenship to all as well as respect for their beliefs. On the purely juridical level, Muslim thinkers have never formulated the question of coexistence in terms of the binary "majority-minority". This is undoubtedly because they have straightaway understood, with the example of Madina, that there existed two distinct belongings. The first is that of the state which makes of each person a full-bodied citizen whereby there is no majority other than that resulting from the vote. The second is that of the religious community[58] for which there exists an autonomy of worship, language and legislation (for personal affairs).

Without insisting on the terminology, we can see that the reflections produced by Renner and Bauer go exactly along the lines of contemporary Islamic preoccupations. Shaping a society that realises the Islamic bases of respect, autonomy and the participation of diverse communities will never be an easy task. Investigations should be numerous and we should fix the stages which allow us to transfer from the known regimes, most of which are dictatorial, to structures of participation at the grass roots level which offer non-Muslims a real space of internal autonomy, and at the same time a true political role.

Coexistence between Muslims and *ahl al-dhimma*, if we do not want to stick to theoretical elaboration, is not easy and further necessitates an in-depth reflection, far from any simplification. The social justice which Islam imposes is achieved at this price. We can afford not to imitate the Western model of nation–state and still have the possibility of establishing other things. Some Western researches, as we have seen, have done it and many others today are coming to the same conclusion, persuaded that this model has fallen apart. We can and must go along this path. But it cannot be a question of producing simplistic caricatures, nor of responding to the humiliation sustained under terror by another humiliation which we would impose on those non-Muslims who "made the wrong choice". This kind of reaction exists among Muslims, and everyone can hear these reflections which mix the beauty of hope with a terrible simplification of reality. That is when this does not carry the germs of a dangerous intransigence. Nothing in the message of Islam can allow such short cuts. On the contrary, to assert that the revealed principles are suitable – as principles and not as concrete solutions – to all times and places, requires that we try to understand our time with its complexities and respond, to the best of our abilities, to the requirements of equity embodied in the Muslim faith. This should be carried out stage by stage with humility, while being conscious of the extent of this burden. The sources should not only brighten our hopes, they should also awaken our intelligence. For if this does not happen, they may produce that which is worse than what they claim to want to reform.

It is imperative to assess the state of each society and to consider the daily and regional tensions. Pluralism must be given shape, within the respect of the Islamic bases, while taking into account contemporary situations, social stratification, that which is at stake, as also the necessary time to achieve such reforms in depth. After all, it is a question of providing a real political culture to those people who were denied any other choices for a long time. The establishment of a large process of representativity and the principle of deliberation (shūrā), which should give to each citizen his rights, whether he be Muslim or not, must be drafted at the same time as the researches on the legislative plans (project of constitution, specific laws, etc.) be carried out. This double mobilisation is nowadays perceptible in the Muslim world. From the North, one has the impression that everything is played out between the established powers and their most radical opposition. That outside this perceptible conflict, nothing that may have political weight happens. This error of analysis has no possible comparison. There is in the whole Muslim world grass roots movements that by means of literacy and social work develop the germs of a more consequent political participation. It is this work first that, in the long term, will enable us to tackle and go beyond communal tension. Taking the latter into account presupposes real work in the field and continuous collaboration efforts. On the more theoretical level, theologians, researchers, and Muslim intellectuals have increasingly, over a number of decades, produced books and documents aiming at promoting this reflection. Islamic references have been commented upon and explained; constitutional projects have been drafted; specialised colloquia have been organised in order to better classify the problematic. Intellectual and social activity is abundant, even if it is not always organised and constructive. There exists today juridical tools of reference which should serve to elaborate a strategy of a wider political openness. This alone can allow us to reconcile participating citizenship with pluralism in the Muslim world. But this requires that the powers in place must have a real political will for change; and the great powers must have other things than speeches of good intention. One must finally remember that if we have sometimes deplored the treatment of Jews, Christians and others in Muslim countries, it is appropriate not to forget that Muslims themselves are subjected to worse humiliation in their own countries. Hoping for an improvement in the fate of non-Muslims goes, naturally, by means of a requirement of respect and dignity given equally to Muslims.

3.   The Pitfalls

We have attempted to show the fundamental principles of political orientation by tackling the theoretical level, certainly, but without concealing here and there, the difficulties on the practical level. In order to complete the analysis in this sense, it is important to enumerate the concrete problems which undermine the Islamic world in the specifically political domain, which interest us in this chapter.[59] The latter are numerous and complex. For this reason we shall confine ourselves to four which appear to us to be decisive.

a.   *The compartmentalisation of competences*

To refer to the sources requires an in-depth knowledge of the Islamic sciences relative to the domain in question. The Muslim world abounds with trained personalities who have authority. Unfortunately, often these *'ulamā'* (savants) and *fuqahā'* (jurists), who have the ability to practise *ijtihād* and give legal edicts relating to social affairs, are locked up in theory or, at best, deal with a precise question in a specific context. Far from realities and social dynamics, it is impossible for them to apprehend the problems from within which, in order to be solved, require another kind of specialisation. The latter allows a different and in-depth comprehension which is based on other parameters and which takes account of other criteria. However, this approach is decisive and imperative, in order not to disfigure the principle of *ijtihād* which is not an exercise of application of *fatāwā* (pl. of *fatwā*) on an *ad hoc* basis, but rather the elaboration of a reasoning which comes within the scope of a strategy of reform and planned evolution. Few theologians of Islam take part in the formation of a long-term project by thinking, one by one, the stages which need to be crossed. How could they? Nothing in their training allows them to do so and their role is often confined to formulating views, in an absolute or within the space of a limited practice, on the licit or illicit character of such and such action or process.

This cannot be sufficient today. Wanting reform from the roots requires that we develop our competences and bring together our specialisations. It is imperative that we increase contact between the intellectuals who are skilled in contemporary political sciences, sociology, law, economy, field specialists (urbanists, architects, members of NGOs) as also with theologians whom we have talked about. It is the common, associated reflection which will enable us to think a real strategy. A strategy which, by taking into consideration the complexity of situations, will allow us to put on course a profound programme of reform. It is impossible to be content with a political tinkering by trusting only in the salvific value of Islam, since we rely on God. We have already cited the verse:

> *God changes not what is in a people, until they change what is in*
> *themselves.* (Qur'ān, 13:11)

To change what is in ourselves is not a simple task. Wanting
to give to Muslim populations the sense of responsibility and
the desire of participation is a gigantic job if we consider the
actual situation. This means that it is impossible that the *'ulamā'*
think in a closed circle, that the intellectuals isolate themselves
and that the field specialists attend, day after day, to the most
urgent things first. Wherever possible, at the scale of
neighbourhoods, regions, countries and at the international level,
it is incumbent upon us to increase the occasions by synergy
and inscribe local action in global thought. If, *a fortiori*, we want
to give birth to an original Islamic project and avoid the imitation
of Western models, in order not to repeat both these mistakes
and also that which does not correspond to Muslim values, then
theological thought on its own, guided by the ritual '*yajūz, lā*
yajūz (allowed, forbidden)' cannot be enough and must be
oriented by in-depth and consequent analysis. At all levels and
in all domains, the contemporary practice of *ijtihād* requires
this kind of collaboration. Certainly, today this exists here and
there but in an insufficient manner.

b.   *The absence of a political culture*

To consider the recent history of Muslim countries before
and after colonisation, we have the right to ask whether there
really exists a political culture at the populations level. For
decades these peoples have very often been subjected to
dictatorships and their opinions have never been decisive for
the orientation of national politics. Independence has not
changed much the data of the problems. This we can see today,
and if moreover we take into consideration the frightening rates
of illiteracy in these societies, we have the right to ask how a
process of popular participation (we can say here a process of
democratisation) can be put in place. Everything has always been
decided somewhere else, and whatever is given is never

perceived as a right which belongs to us, but rather as a gift that the power grants.

We can minimise this problem. In truth, it is of prime importance. Willing to apply the principle of *shūrā* on a national plane presupposes that the people are ready for it. To put it plainly, this presupposes that we multiply the experiences of participation on the local level and at the level of neighbourhoods and countrysides in order to enable the people to take charge of themselves. In this sense, social work and literacy campaigns are of prime importance today, as they were yesterday; remember that after the Battle of Badr, the Prophet (peace be upon him) freed each prisoner who taught ten Muslims to read and write. Many experiences, though still insufficient, are achieved in Muslim countries and the ensuing results are remarkable. This to the great detriment of the powers in place which unfavourably watch their people educating themselves and taking charge of their affairs.

c.   *The absence of a political will*

Who really wants today, in the West and with the governments of developing countries, education of the people and the achievement of a real pluralism in the societies of the South? The question must be clearly put. Behind the beautiful speeches based on human rights and democracy, the great powers support regimes whose least concern is to be representative. Democracy, here, supports dictatorial terror there. And this without losing countenance. Dictators, conscious of their role as protectors of Western interests that they are made to play, do not behave either with regard to particular detail or with elegance. Thus, they do not hesitate to stop any enterprise, no matter how positive and humanitarian, which may put in peril the seats of their power. Should we really need reminding that an ignorant people, subjugated or silently suppressed, is the guarantee of the tranquillity of dictators, and when these latter are, themselves, the guarantors of the strategic security of countries of the North, then ignorance, subjugation and repression are, in one way or another, supported by the latter without any uncertainty. They will not hesitate to propagate the worst information on those who dare to contest this order of things. The latter used to be "communists", "theologians of liberation"; now they are "fanatics, fundamentalists, and reactionary", engaged Muslims, "Islamists". Focus is put on the most radical groups in order to discredit all the oppositions. All in all, better a dictator than a "madman of God" who promises us beards and will impose veils. Hotchpotches make good progress and they will deny that there are moderates. "Sophisms" and "fraud" as Interior Minister, Charles Pasqua, said, for, deep down they are the same.

On account of the interests in play, one is forced to notice that there does not exist the "political" will for changing things. The powers in place suppress any political expression, they halt any initiative, as they stifle any popular mobilisation. These governments do not represent the people, they represent interests, and it happens that the latter make them opposed to their own people. One has often thought that it is enough to overthrow power to be able to achieve a political project which is respectful of Islamic values. One knows now that things are more complicated than this and that the guarantee of success does not lie in a structure of state control that one runs, but rather in a dynamic that is brought about in the long term. The links uniting the governments of the North to those of the South are nourished by such a convergence of interests that it is naïve to think that it can be otherwise today. However, one must, against all odds, continue this work of training and participation for it is the only one to give back to women and men their dignity that the despots are stifling. This without use of violence, patient and determined in the face of governments who stole a power that history, God willing, will force them to give back.

d.   *Corruption*

Dictatorship and cronyism have caused havoc in Muslim societies. At all levels of structure under state control, one notices a degree of corruption such that one still wonders what exactly functions without privilege or under the table. The responsibility falls first upon the magistrates in place who are far from being models in matters of honesty and transparency. Moreover, it is difficult to blame small civil servants and ordinary men from whom, in the final analysis, recovered "bribery" is part of survival. What to say of the teachers who make money from their courses, of traffic wardens who get paid for their "blindness", of the administrator who sells time that needs to be gained. Definitive condemnation is delicate, the conditions of life being difficult. The only verified fact which stands out is that of a general corruption which has penetrated the most profound machinery of social organisation. How in such a state can one reinstall a more moral functioning, more respectful of the values of justice, equality and transparency?

Everything happens, in fact, as if we were facing a vicious circle. Dictatorships, which encourage the most dubious methods of survival, which themselves hinder real participation in the absence of which, in the course of the process, the inalienable authority of the sovereign is confirmed. We are so used to these gaps that they seem to be a normal part of social and political life. The situation of Muslim societies is, from this point of view, particularly serious and any project which does not take them into consideration will automatically be threatened. The re-establishment of a more sound functioning begins by individual responsibility at every level of the political structure, but equally also by the recognition and reinstatement of the fundamental rights that each one should enjoy. These four dangers are far from encompassing the whole problematic, but they allow appreciation of the work to be accomplished. The mobilisation of all intelligences – theologians, *'ulamā'*, intellectuals, field specialists – is a prime necessity. At the same time, it is necessary that we urgently create conditions which enable the population to engage itself and participate in political life by fighting against any form of corruption. It is also imperative that we remain aware of the interests at play and the absence of a political will on the part of the powers of the North and South. This also requires that the strategy in question determines the stages which, starting from the grass roots, allow us to cover the whole social and political field. Before such dangers, the only path is to concede nothing to those repressive powers that are disrespectful of fundamental rights. Determination nourished by reliance on God, will be stronger than any other weapon. It is itself a weapon, as we can see it today, where so many years of torture, oppression and execution have not overcome courageous mobilisations, determined claims and exigencies of justice. This before God, and in the name of the most fundamental rights, as taught by the Prophet (peace be upon him) to all Muslims of all generations. This is the echo that will recognise – in the duty of resistance – the supporters of human rights when reading the third preamble of the Declaration: "Considering that it is essential that human rights be protected by a regime of the law so that a person is not compelled, as a last resort, to revolt against tyranny and oppression."

The fight to achieve this "regime of the law", which is one of the political bases of Islam, starts with the duty of resisting "tyranny and oppression", as long as the strength and patience can endure it. And if the people and the powers of the North keep quiet or continue to support the untenable, "revolt" will be the price to pay for their folly and inconsequence. The injustice in their complicity, complacence or passivity, will then be responsible for the violence generated by those who are stifled, all the while blaming them for complaining and screaming. Perhaps, the following saying of the Prophet (peace be upon him) should be recalled: "Beware of the supplication of the one who is wronged, for there is no veil between this supplication and God."[60] Trusting in this supplication, nourished by the orientations of the sources and accompanied by analysis, researchers and the councils of competent men and women, the work at the grass roots level seems to be today the first stage of political engagement. It would be good, incidentally, that we return to this perversion which consists of thinking that taking power alone is political and, leading many movements towards short-term action. True, the support and engagement of the state, beginning from a certain limit of action, is necessary. But in the actual state of our societies, the road is still long and requires that the first step of political activity remains that of social action.

Notes

1. This *ḥadīth* is reported by Dāraquṭnī who declared it to be of a sound chain of transmission (*Nayl al-Awṭār*). On this subject consult the works of Taha Jabir al-ʿAlwani: *The Ethics of Disagreement in Islam*, IIIT, Herndon, Virginia, 1993. The situations of managing conflicts which are reported therein are the most interesting and ought to allow us to moderate our attitudes in situations of disagreement.

2. We know that geography, climate, habits, etc. have produced different juridical interpretations without this causing any shock to the different Schools.

3. Louis Gardet, *La Cité Musulmane, vie sociale et politique*, Vrin, 1954, 4th édition, 1981, p.48.

4. In his latest book, *L'Islamism en face*, La découverte, 1995, François Burgat rightly points out the groundlessness of the critique generally directed at the Islamic system. This critique reproaches to the latter its reference to divine, intangible principles, whereas Western legislations proceed solely from the rationality of the parliamentary majority: "The universal declaration [of human rights], the general principles of law and other 'natural laws' have indeed continued to impose upon the constituents superior, reputed principles on the will of whatever parliamentary majority" (p.202). See also the entire discussion (pp.200-3). If it is legitimate that the diverse declarations and principles of law are considered as basic fundamentals of legislation in the West (since they belong to its history), nevertheless, one cannot deny the Muslims their searching in their own points of reference the elements which would allow them to run their social, political and economic affairs.

5. This is the position of Alain Finkielkraut in his book *La défaite de la pensée* (Gallimard, 1987). This author, once again, displays a real lack of moderation. First he criticises Father Lelong and concludes with a good ironical flight of oratory: "Is there a culture where corporal punishments are inflicted on delinquents, where a sterile woman is repudiated and the adulterous woman sentenced to death, where the testimony of a man is equal to that of two women, where a sister gets only half of what her brother inherits, where excision is practised, where mixed marriages are prohibited and polygamy allowed? Love of neighbour expressly commands respect of these customs. This would be tantamount to mutilating his being and infringe upon his human dignity, in a word showing racism rather than deprive him. In our world which is deserted by transcendence, cultural identity sanctions barbaric traditions which God is no longer in a position to justify" (p.143). This declaration is serious, the counter-truths contained therein are multiple and

the intellectual probity of the author is dubious. Apart from the hotchpotch and reductionist formulation, we interestingly note that Islam – bearer of so many horrors – is not a culture for Finkielkraut, and that, by fact, nothing can be claimed in the name of Muslim cultural identity. The humanism of some intellectuals takes flight when they tackle certain subjects. This is the least that one can say.

6. See the British, Swedish, American, Swiss, Spanish and Irish constitutions, to cite but a few examples. We may add the cases of Burma or Thailand which make reference to Buddhism.

7. Op. cit., p.45.

8. The classic book of reference is that of Abū'l Ḥasan al-Māwardī (eleventh century) *al-Aḥkām al-Sulṭāniyya*. English translation under the title *The Ordinances of Government* (translated by Wafaa H. Wahba), Garnet Publishing Ltd., 1996. See also the excellent work of research and synthesis *Fiqh al-Shūrā* (The Comprehension of *Shūrā*) by Dr. Tawfiq al-Shawi, Dar al-Wafa, Cairo, 1992, 844pp. (in Arabic).

9. Taking account of these situations is decisive. We shall return later to the question of the people's participation in public affairs. When the latter has no political culture (either because a dictatorial power has bestowed this right upon it, or because the dynamic of participation drives to passivity) imposed upon it overnight, an organisation which takes account of the political opinion of each and every person is, strictly speaking, illusory, when it is not a question of deceitful manipulation. To forge an opinion for oneself would become known. The process of democratisation cannot jump this stage without itself becoming content with the form while betraying the essence of the project. When in certain African countries – in Benin for example – one moved from one single party to 80 in just a few months, one may doubt that the woman and man of the people will make sense of them. For years the people kept silent and listened to the only voice in power and had to digest the pluralist explosion completely disarmed. It was not a question of a real process of participation, but rather a show. The President of Benin understood it well in his electoral campaign, for he did not get rid of circumlocution. His message was simple: "I am, at least, known." In our discussion, one must keep this in mind. To impose stages upon participating life, is not, by means of undertaken precautions, rejecting the participation of the people. It is rather giving them hope of a real achievement, in profundity.

10. The question of competence is of capital importance. Straightaway, the Prophet (peace be upon him) warned against love of power and the relentless will to have access to it. To avoid this, he defined the responsibilities of both the elected and the elector. The following two traditions are clear. As regards the elected, Abū Mūsā al-Ash'arī reported: "I entered upon the Prophet (peace be upon him) and I was accompanied by two cousins. One of them asked the Prophet (peace be upon him): 'O Messenger of God! Grant me the rulership of one of the provinces that God bestowed upon you.' My other

cousin made the same request. The Prophet (peace be upon him) answered: 'By God, we do not entrust these functions to those who ask for it, nor to those who covet it.' (Narrated by Bukhārī and Muslim.) As for the elector: "Whosoever employs (mandate for a function) a man from a community while there exists a more competent person than him (who is better accepted by God) has betrayed God, His Prophet and all Muslims." (Narrated by Al-Ḥākim.) These two traditions render impossible, if we respect the principles of Islamic ethics, the type of electoral campaign, which we see in the USA and France, for example. Presentation of oneself and one's image, worked out by public relations agencies, in order to appear "the best", disparaging remarks about adversaries, permanent polls associated with the partisan spirit of the electors, are all to be registered as defects of the democratic ideal.

11. We limit ourselves here to giving the major principles. Numerous strategies of presentation have been thought out which modify reasonably well the nature of the "council of consultation", depending on whether one attributes to it the role of guardian of Islamic norms or on thinking about the creation of another authority – a kind of Supreme Court – which would be in charge of measuring the degree of the council's adaptability in decisions. In the latter case, the council would basically be composed of specialists in public affairs as well as experts.

12. The tradition to which we refer here is known: "Each one is a shepherd and each one is responsible for that which is under his responsibility, and thus the *Imām* is equally a shepherd and he is responsible (he must be accountable) for that which is under his guard (here the running of power)." (Narrated by Bukhārī.)

13. The Qur'ān stipulates: "And if you judge between people, judge according to justice." See Part Two of this book concerning social justice.

14. During the great constitutional manoeuvres which allowed Hosni Mubarak to obtain a third presidential mandate in Egypt (at a time when he was reaching a term of 12 years of legally authorised power), notices were placed over the whole Egyptian territory, calling the people to make allegiance to the dearly loved President. The choice of the word *bay'a* owed nothing to chance and made direct reference to the Islamic quality of the political act. We are not yet in front of a symbolic manipulation, but we note that in this trick, none of the conditions of *bay'a* were present. The power heard "the voice of allegiance", that the people have not even dreamt of.

15. Narrated by Bukhārī and Muslim.

16. Let us point out this example: that human rights are today the best achievement of humanist and rationalist philosophy, there is not a shadow of a doubt; that the argument for their respect be of variable geometrical use on the tongues of the great powers is also no less certain. See below.

17. Encounters and influences between the two civilisations were numerous. This is an evident fact. However, there remain basic specificities. One can retain here only that which concerns the understanding of the "religious".

See on this subject, the second part of *Les Musulmans dans la Laïcité: Islam et laïcité*, Tawhid, 1994.

18. Nevertheless, this basic principle of ethnology seems to have some difficulties explaining its pertinence when one speaks of Islamic points of reference. As if the elements of Islam, which are known in appearance, were blinding and misleading us on basic religious and cultural differences.

19. See Part One: At the Shores of Transcendence.

20. Proudhon, for example, in his book *What is Property?* develops all his thought around these two notions in order to conclude with a concept very close to that of Islam.

21. It is, absolutely, the sense of Michel Bakounine's reflection: "If God exists, we should get rid of Him." On a more fundamental philosophical plane, Nietzsche, who it is interesting to recall is acknowledged as "the last of the metaphysicians" by Martin Heidegger, founded his thought by pushing to extremes the process of liberation: "God is dead", he had to say to the madman in *Gay Knowledge*. The madman is, in fact, a prophet.

22. Kant's expression is reviewed here in its voluntarily disfigured sense.

23. Following the title of Marcel Gauchet's excellent book, *Le désenchantment du monde* [translated into English by Oscar Burge as *The Disenchantment of the World: A Political History of Religion*, Princeton University Press], whose theses are, in our view, of prime importance. They deserve, anyhow, a discussed development.

24. We shall say a few words below on the analysis developed by Samuel Huntington concerning the clash of civilisations.

25. Everything in the teachings derived from the traditions of the Prophet (peace be upon him) is in categorical opposition to this. The modern concept of multipartism posits a serious problem in this sense. We can imagine a similar system with very strict requirements which obliges that it is the parties' programmes – by means of their concrete propositions – which decide their access to the political debate, rather than the sole will to achieve power. It remains for us to think the creation of a neutral and independent authority which would have the mandate to arbitrate.

26. Even during the Umayyad period which saw the birth of the dynastic principle, governments were conscious that it was impossible for them to justify, Islamically, access to power by means of heredity right alone. They therefore based recognition of power on the allegiance (*bay'a*) of the people to the new sovereign. The latter was certainly the son, but it was allegiance which was the guarantee of his legitimacy. This confirms to us that blood has never justified "an elected person" except by means of a "play" on the legitimacy granted by the people. This is a show which we refrain from reproducing nowadays.

27. The first five successors to Muḥammad (peace be upon him) were so nourished by the teachings of the latter and their management of power was such that they were not questioned by their community. Yet, they did not

hesitate to dismiss a governor or a judge from his function when the Muslims of such or such a country complained about him, or when according to their own judgement, they considered the policy of the official as lacking in justice and administrative self-exigency. 'Umar, in this sense, was undoubtedly the most exigent and firmest of them all.

28. See Muhammad Hamidullah's book on the life of the Prophet (peace be upon him): *Le prophète de l'Islam*, in which he transcribes and comments upon the aforementioned constitution. New edition, 1989, edited by AEIF (Association of Islamic Students of France), Vol. II, pp.782–819.

29. We shall say a word on the question of *ahl al-dhimma* (non-Muslims in the land of Islam) without unfortunately dealing with the whole equation in this current volume.

30. The concept of man, which is born respectively from these two visions, is forcibly marked by these differences. The characteristic of man in Islam is to be the bearer of a memory; his reason, by means of revelation, is first that which derives teachings from that which he remembers. To be with God and to live with men is tantamount to remembering. Free from any absolute, the pragmatism of autonomous reason is based on construction and projection. Man makes himself in progress as well as in his capacity to master probability. This concept is the child of the scientific epoch, but remains today the point of reference in all domains of social, political and especially economic action.

31. The discourse of Muslims varies depending on whether they bring to the fore the similarities or differences. In two neighbouring countries, like Algeria and Tunisia, two thinkers will uphold from the same sources two completely opposing discourses on the question of democracy. Sometimes, however, divergences are less absolute than they appear to be, and this due, very often, to the kind of rapport that has been established with the West, rather than as a result of a deep fundamental opposition to the latter. One cannot deny, that very different opinions concerning the Islamic project do exist. These should contribute to an enriching, internal debate. Unfortunately this is not always the case.

32. We should point out that in this domain, that is the domain of ethics, which was (re-)born in the West out of the conscience of possible catastrophes, takes its meaning in other cultures, and particularly in Islam, from the conscience of the imperative of respect.

33. With regard to the idea of tolerance, see below, the chapter, "The Rights of God and the Responsibilities of Men".

34. There was, in 1981, a tentative elaboration of a "Universal Declaration of Human Rights in Islam" (*al-Bayān al-ʿĀlamī ʿan-Ḥuqūq al-Insān fī'l-Islām* or *Wathīqat Ḥuqūq al-Insān fī'l-Islām* (cf. *Islam et droit de l'homme*, Librairie des Libertes, 1984, pp.218–36). It was produced by the Muslim World Council in London with the assistance of numerous personalities from the Muslim world under the leadership of its Secretary General, Salem Azzam. This project is interesting in that it attempts to produce an audible formulation for

Western reading while clarifying in the Preface the characteristic of Islam which refers to God, His book and His Prophet. One feels, however, that there remains some important problems in formulating things according to the same canvas when concepts of man are so different. For example, in the Preface, we are reminded that "... our duties and obligations have priorities over our rights" (ibid., p.221) without any attempt to put things into a perspective which would allow the apprehension of the concept of man which implies this assertion. Moreover, the constant reference to the law (*Shari'a*) casts doubt on the possibility of respect for human rights. This is the objective which we have assigned ourselves above. Equally, there exist texts produced by the Organisation of Islamic Conference (OIC) in 1979, 1981 and 1990 under the initial title *Project of a Charter of the Fundamental Rights and Duties of Man in Islam* which later became known with the Charter of Cairo in 1990 as the *Cairo Declaration on Human Rights in Islam*.

35. See Part Two of this book.

36. Many intellectuals, Western and non-Western, have tried to date the birth of human rights in order to show that these are part of the heritage of their respective cultures. Such a debate is sterile. The Declaration of 1948 is indeed the prolongation of rationalist thought which has risen in the West since the Renaissance (some would even speak of the thirteenth century with the Great Charter of Jean Sans Tere). However, one finds in all religious traditions principles of behaviour which convey in the same fashion a reference to human rights. Islam, as with Judaism and Christianity, is bearer of a vigorous message of defence of human dignity. The mode of reflection, origins, and their histories are different and a dispute on dates would be useless. Ultimately, it is the respect of rights which is important rather than the source behind their formulation.

37. The reading of the text which we have mentioned, *The Universal Islamic Declaration of Human Rights in Islam,* is on this part, interesting. One notices there the great latitude offered to dialogue between civilisations. In a recent publication, M. Sami A. Aldeeb Abu-Sahlieh, in an attempt to give an account of the rapport between Muslims and human rights, starts by asserting that: "Being adopted by the General Assembly, the norms of human rights ensued from UNO can be considered the expression of common aspirations of all the peoples of the world." Without comprehension or clarification of the holistic system and the general concept of Islam, the author reviews a certain number of sensitive themes (his analysis remains very cursory) by referring in a more or less explicit fashion to the text of 1948. Here, thoughts and facts are reported in an abrupt manner, and this is accompanied, very often, with the irony of the one who judges others while remaining convinced of the truthfulness of the norms which are his. Cf. *Les Musulmans face aux droits de l'homme, religion et au droit politique*, Etudes et documents, Bochum, 1994.

38. Text reproduced by Ibn Hishām, I, pp.503–4. See the comments of Said Ramadan in *Islamic Law*, 2nd edition, 1970, pp.124–7 and those of Professor Muhammad Hamidullah, op. cit., pp.803–8, or his book *al-Wathā'iq al-Siyāsiyya*, 1956, pp.111–12.

39. See *Aḥkām adh-dhimma* (the legal rulings relating to the "protected") of Ibn al-Qayyim al-Jawziyya, 2 vols., in Arabic, Dar al-'Ilm Lil Malayin, Beirut, 1983. See also Abu'l A'la Mawdudi's booklet, *Ḥuqūq ahl adh-dhimma fī'l-Dawla al-Islāmiyya* (The Rights of the Protected in the Islamic State), IIFSO, Kuwait, 1984.

40. In the same sense, many constitutions of modern states reserve the exercise of supreme magistrate to a given confession.

41. Under the reign of 'Umar, General Abū 'Ubayda, unsure as to whether he could guarantee the protection of *ahl adh-dhimma*, ordered the reimbursement of sums of money paid respectively by each one. This because the clauses of the contract were no longer guaranteed on the part of the authority.

42. Yusuf al-Qaradawi goes as far as admitting the possibility of payment of *zakāt* by non-Muslims if this is done by their own free-will. Hence, a protected person would be subjected to the same obligations as the Muslims (see his *Fiqh al-Zakāt* in Arabic, 2 vols. Cf. below.

43. There exists a very famous letter from the renowned judge Abū Yūsuf which he sent to Hārūn al-Rashīd in which he forcefully reminds the latter of the rights of the *mu'āhidūn* and the obligations of power. Therein, he mentions the categories which we report here.

44. Op. cit., p.806.

45. Narrated by Abū Dāwūd.

46. Many authors, trying to prove the barbaric character of Islam, have relied on its history and revealed therein what could, in their view, be counted as valid arguments. In two recent books (*Les Chrétientés d'Orient: entre jihād et dhimmitude* and *Juifs et chrétiens sous l'Islam, les dhimmis face au défi intégriste*), Bat Ye'or presents "all her studies within the domain of *dhimmitude*". These two books do not fail to worry us and the evolution of the thesis brings to the fore objectives which are a little confused. For more than its history, it is indeed Islam that the author aims to discredit with a kind of warning addressed to all those who have a leaning to be carried away by good emotion. The Introduction (formulated across the two books) is quite plain. On the level of dogma, hence intrinsically part of Islam, "the aim of *jihād* is to subjugate the peoples of earth to the law of Allah, enacted by his Prophet Muhammad. Humanity is divided into two groups, Muslims and non-Muslims. The former compose the Islamic community, the *umma*, they hold the territories of *dār al-Islām*, which are governed by Islamic law. The non-Muslims are the *ḥarbī*, inhabitants of *dār al-ḥarb*, country of war, so named because they are destined to pass under the Islamic jurisdiction, either by means of war

(*ḥarb*) or through the conversion of its inhabitants" (p.28). Thus, *jihād*, a central notion of Islam, is erroneously presented as the dogmatic support of the inevitably conflictual attitudes of Muslims.

Reading these lines, one gets the impression that Muslims cannot live peacefully except alone or as winners. The situation of the *dhimmīs* would be inevitably felt and the author multiplies the presentation of documents which prove the horrors of the Muslim presence and the constant suffering of Jewish and Christian victims. Some positive attitudes are acknowledged here and there, but the truth the book argues is that Muslims, faithful to their points of reference and to their savants, are bent on their will to convert, kill and exploit. One must acknowledge the mistakes of history, and these did take place without any argument. But the very selective way chosen to present these events lead the reader to dangerous conclusions. Namely that dialogue with Muslims is impossible. Things are even clearer in the second book when it is a question of classifying the characteristics of the new danger of fundamentalism. It is all grist to the author's mill. It is really a good mixture in which the reader will find it difficult to distinguish that which is related to Islam or that which has come out of its perversion. Besides, all happens as if the criticism of the notion of *jihād* is sufficient to delegitimise mobilisation against the Zionist occupation. This is worrying, as is the author's other remark concerning the situation in Bosnia. The Serbs, allegedly, were the historical victims of the Muslims and the barbarity which we are assisting today has other responsibles: "The responsibles are those who, in order to safeguard their interests, attempted to impose a myth upon those who were their victims" (p.211). In other words, responsibility for the massacres, of which they themselves are the victims, is incumbent upon the Muslims because of the need to maintain untrue stories about themselves and their history. Who would not be shocked to hear that the Jews were ultimately responsible for the holocaust because of what they themselves had said, due to their election and their specificity? This is indeed a strange conclusion. The least that one can say is that this is inadmissible; Nazi actions were odious and inhumane, just as more recently Serb practices have been. Unless, that is, one wants to say, and seems to want to prove, that regardless of being aggressors or victims, the nature of Islam always renders the Muslims guilty. This is a way just like any other of siding, against the Muslims, with the Russians, Serbs, Indians and Zionists. Finally, we have to add our astonishment at the moral support of Jacques Ellul who, in his Preface, speaks of Muslim expansion and asserts: "Yet everything has been achieved through war" (cf. p.II). It is a shocking over-simplification from the pen of such an intellectual.

47. Let us recall that all studies which propose solutions that are not in themselves opposed to Islamic principles are acceptable. For it is their degree of morality

which counts and not their origin. This is especially so in matters of general legislation.

48. The great powers do not tire of praise for their will and courage to live with their time. They are "progressists".

49. Quoted in Fabienne Rousso-Lenoir's book, *Minorités et droits de l'homme. L'Europe et son double*, Bruylant, 1994, p.33.

50. In his book, *L'Europe et l'Orient*, the Lebanese historian Georges Corm has very harsh statements to make: "The public international law which takes its rapid expansion during this period encourages, besides, observations. It institutes the term of "national minority" which was hitherto unknown in the European political vocabulary ... It is only once the nation-state was installed in modernity as a superior form of the system of power that the term national minority succeeded. Yet, the term itself is absurd, since one cannot be, at the same time, both "national" and "of a minority". See the rest of the argument that Corm proposes by his pointing out the contradictions of the nation-state which did not exist with empires, particularly the Ottoman Empire, since there existed therein real pluralist space. Cf. La Découverte, pp.92–3, and after.

51. With regard to Article 27 of the international pact relating to civil and political rights which starts with these terms: "In the States where there are minorities...", France took a definitive position: "The French government states, on account of Article 2 of the Constitution of the Republic, that Article 27 does not apply as far as the Republic is concerned." This Article is properly swept aside, for France does not acknowledge itself as a nation-state, any national minority and thus the text of this Pact cannot be compelling for it. Cf. Fabienne Rousso-Lenoir, op. cit., p. 105.

52. Dominique Wolton in his *La dernière Utopie,* as also Fabienne Rousso-Lenoir, attacks this paternalism of "the progressists" who make an impasse on a major question of the end of the century.

53. Op. cit., p.82.

54. Op. cit., p.85.

55. Ibid.

56. One becomes convinced when hearing the speeches of Saddam Hussein, Yasser Arafat, Hosni Mubarak, Hafiz al-Asad, Liamine Zeroual, Ben Ali and the like that all of them continuously speak about Islam and claim to refer to it.

57. Read on this subject Hicham ben Abdallah al-Alaoui's article in *Le Monde Diplomatique* of July 1995, republished by *Le Courrier de Geneve* (11 July, 1995): "Être citoyen dans le monde arabe". The author brings to the fore the differences between Western and Arab models and presents an idea of a democratic alternative nourished by Islamic references.

58. At the time of the Prophet (peace be upon him), the communities present in Madina were basically the *ahl al-Kitāb*, the People of the Book, the Jews and Christians. Abū Yūsuf reported that when contact was later made with the

Zoroastrians of Bahrain, the Prophet said: "Let them be treated like the *ahl al-Kitāb*." The first Caliphs, and following their example, the *'ulamā'*, understood that this application can be applied by analogy to other people adhering to other beliefs. There remains, however, the problem of those not related to any religion or those who are atheists. Islamic points of reference do not refer to this case because of the context and time of Revelation. A detailed decision must be an act of *ijtihād*. Diverse positions have thus been formulated. However, there are two inalienable principles which are namely the respect of the constitution and the latitude offered in matters of private affairs. Any personal engagement which does not clash with this frame can be acknowledged. As we can see, the juridical reasoning enlarges the sphere of application by taking into consideration contemporary realities. It remains that reference to God, in an Islamic society, participates to its essence and forms the frame of reference that cannot be divided but which must rather be respected.

59. On the more general problems see Appendices I and II.
60. Narrated by Bukhārī and Muslim.

III. Economic Directives

The 1970s, with its two oil shocks, is a sad memory for developing countries. During this decade, they entered the infernal cycle of indebtedness which caused, and is still causing, innumerable catastrophes. At that time, the countries exporting oil had in hand huge sums of money which needed to be invested. At the same time, the countries of the South needed hard currency, partly to procure oil, which had then become very expensive. The balance seemed ideal; the surplus of the former could be lent to the latter and, thus, the two parties would get what they wanted. However, the countries exporting the oil called upon Western banks to operate this transfer and, consequently, set in motion the terrible process of indebtedness that we know today. Susan George explains:

"It was not until the first oil shock, in 1973, that the loans have really gone up, and rocketed up with the second, in 1979. This was quite normal since the money generated by oil had to be recycled. The countries of OPEC had the money, whereas the countries non-exporting petrol needed money, partly to buy petrol. The intermediary found was therefore the banks. We can say – and this is my opinion – that OPEC could have managed quite well in recycling its money and lent directly the money to the Third World. This way, they could have avoided offering to banks an opportunity to dispose of a weapon of absolute force. Moreover, the countries producing petrol would have been, today, in a better position."

The Muslim petro-monarchies of the Gulf – representing the vivid force of OPEC – by putting the money generated by oil in banks and letting the latter run the loan of interests to poor countries, acted in an inconsiderate fashion and forgot the fundamental principles of the prohibition of interest in Islam. Susan George reminds us of this:

"If, in fact, the member countries of OPEC were at the same time providers of energy as well as of capital for a good part of the world, they could have reinforced considerably the union of the countries of the South and enlarged their proper political influence. Giving loans with interest is severely reprimanded in Islamic law; the borrowers could have well obtained inferior interest rates." The rulers of countries with an Islamic tradition acted without any great moral concern. The debt today, coming out of this process which could have been avoided, causes the death of, on average, ten thousand lives a day. Thus, petro dollars have unexpectedly served the interests of the superpowers to which, from then on, the petro-monarchies have become linked. Susan George concludes:

"The countries producing petrol probably did not even think of recycling their money themselves. They behaved like perfect capitalists, hoping to make more money by entrusting it to professionals from New York or London. Thus, they lost a historical opportunity and opened the door to the formidable *coup* concocted by countries which were already rich. The debt, run by Western governments and their agents such as the IMF, has again weakened the countries of the South (including the member countries of OPEC). It put them in a more unfavourable situation than before the great epoch of borrowing, just as it did open the door to a real re-colonisation."[1]

It was, indeed, a historical opportunity, one which could have enabled a different, new model of economic relations to be created, one not subjected to the implacable law of interest. One would have expected even less than this from "Muslim" countries. Is the Islamic point of reference solely valid on the personal and penal level, in order to suffocate the people and severely reprimand, in the name of Islam, those individuals who dare to transgress against the law? Have we not witnessed, in this sombre, structured Islamic participation of the capitalist economy, one of the worst betrayals there could ever have been?

One must give account, today, of the horror caused by the indebtedness of poor countries as well as of the general enslavement ensuing from it. Likewise, one must take stock of the gulf which exists between those eloquent speeches which contain scattered references to the glory of Islam and the most troubled and disreputable of financial practices. Here, the hypocrisy is total.

On the international level, we find ourselves obliged to admit: there does not exist today a specific, Islamic economic model or behavioural example. All countries, from Morocco to Indonesia, are linked – tied hand and foot or suffocated – by a classical economy which intermingles the administration of interest with the excessive practice of speculation. This gulf which Susan George has pointed out is the rule rather than the exception. One may ask oneself, on account of the complexity of the parameters, whether the Muslim world has the means to suggest "another thing". The countries that have – or could have had – the means to achieve this difference have blindly launched themselves to the storm in order "to gain, quicker and quicker" while being indifferent to the dead that the machinery crushes afterwards.

We can identify, at the national level, some attempts, here and there, to create institutions and structures respectful of Islamic principles. We will, indeed, say a few words about this below, but one must admit that things are far from clear. For in the final analysis, it is not enough to add the epithet "Islamic" to a bank or a society of investment in order to achieve an alternative project.

In the 1980s, we witnessed, in Egypt, the flourishing of "societies of capitals' investment" (*Sharikāt tawẓīf al-amwāl*). These were "Islamic" because they functioned according to the principle of participation with risk, and not according to the guarantee of interest. There were honest managers, but we note that many have abused the credulity of the people. Considering the success of this operation, the Jews and Christians created, under cover, their own "Islamic" societies in order to attract private savings. Additionally, the benefits which were reported were of the order of 25% to 30%, which was certainly not in line with the rates proposed by official banks. Besides the character, not always transparent, of the transactions taking place, one may ask whether the savers had really understood the project as an alternative, or had they only been attracted by the prospect of gain. In which case, the question of the "Islamic" value of the entire enterprise is legitimately posited. The mechanism remains "capitalist" even if the forms are effectively modified.[2] One can mention many examples of "Islamic" institutions whose functioning is supposed to be at variance with the model of the classical economy. If these interesting projects exist, the particularity of vast achievements do not withstand rigorous analysis. The remaining impression is that very often the appellation "Islamic" is used to provide moral sanction as also to attract a population that is wary, today as it was yesterday, of transgressing against religious prohibitions. Such cannot be sufficient.

1.   The Moral Reference

One must repeat here, as a prelude, that the particularity of Islamic directives in economic matters is the total, permanent and inclusive link that exists between this sphere and the moral point of reference. In fact, commercial and financial transactions amongst men are encompassed and nourished by the foundation of tawḥīd, the principle of the unicity of God, and it cannot be subtracted from this relationship. In the same way that we turn towards God, try not to lie, or deceive, so in the same fashion is the rule not to steal, to always produce for the good of men and to consume good before God. It is impossible here to conceive of man as resembling part of a machine and defined, outside of any ethical quality, as a being who, carried by the search for his own profit, either produces or consumes, and whose norm of action is solely quantitative. Economic science presenting itself as positive, and which is concentrated on the study of the famous Homo economicus, is in this sense amputated in the view of the Islamic concept. Reducing man to the administration of the means, outside of any determination of finalities, is inconceivable, that is unless one wishes to confuse it with a pure thing or a simple tool. In other words, as just a link in the chain which constitutes society.

In fact, the most frequent, simple and natural economic act is always identifiable by its moral quality. Whether it is production or consumption, it is from the moral quality that man derives his value and not, in the first place, from his performance in terms of productivity, profitability or profit in the broader sense. All the teachings of the Qur'ān about the economic domain revolve around this axis. To produce evil, against the humanity of men, producing for the sake of terror or for causing a stupefying effect on the masses is tantamount to producing with loss, without any profitability before God. This no matter the extent of the financial profits achieved in the process. The same applies with regard to consumption. The latter is defectuous when it forgets itself. We find innumerable verses in the Qur'ān which link the "economic" act to the moral dimension of its finality (from the moment it is linked to the remembrance of the Creator). Here, we can identify three types of such action:

a. *Zakāt*

Zakāt is the third pillar of Islam and its essence pinpoints the importance of social participation in the Muslim universe. *Zakāt* is clearly a tax on possessions and property[3] that one should, first, understand as an obligation before God. This levying "purifies" on the religious, sacred and moral plane, the property of the one who possesses it. Thus, the link with God, with transcendence, with the remembrance of meaning and finality of life is inscribed and achieved not only in being but also in possession as in the rapport that each human being establishes with it. After the two testimonies of the unicity of God (*tawḥīd*) and prophethood; after the injunction of the prayer which founds the link between the faithful and the Creator, *zakāt*, the purifying social tax, projects the believer in the collective sphere. The latter is, thus, radiated by Transcendence and the sacred. At the same time, what *zakāt* implies is a full and ethical concept of social organisation and human relations. The person who possesses has duties, just as the one who is impoverished has rights before God as well as before men. Islam does not conceive of poverty as a normal fact of the social universe. Nor does it envisage that the treatment of this distortion be the free generosity of some towards others. This in the hope that, in a miraculous fashion, the opulence of the rich and the begging of the poor can find a point of balance. The obligation of *zakāt* places this question in the domain of law and morality and cannot be left to the discretion of each person. Social solidarity is part of faith, as it is its most concrete testimony. To be with God is tantamount to being with men; such is the basic teaching of the third pillar of Islam.

Abū Bakr, the first successor to the Prophet (peace be upon him) decided against the advice of ʿUmar to fight the tribes of the South who refused to pay *zakāt*. There was to be no compromise on a question relating, before God, to the rights of the poor, and, hence, to the responsibility of any established society. It cannot be a simple question of goodness, for it is clearly a question of justice. This notion, therefore, must be defended in each human transaction. It is something that the rich, those who have possessions, should never forget. For in their goods, as stipulated in the Qurʾān, there is "a right for the beggar and the deprived".

b.   *Individual spending*

Beyond the obligation of *zakāt* we find, in Islamic teaching, many recommendations concerning the moral scope of individual spending. The management of one's possessions cannot possibly be thought of outside the sense of being. We can delineate at least four directions which, in the Qurʾān, specify the moral scope of this spending: to please God and donate for His sake; to give right measure; to fight against egoism and hoarding; and to display some caution.

◆   Pleasing God and Donating for His Sake

The Qur'ānic Revelation abounds with this kind of reminder. We can cite here some of the most significant verses:

> ... they give food, for the love of Him, to the needy, the orphan, the captive: 'We feed you only for the sake of God; we desire no recompense from you, no thankfulness...' (Qur'ān, 76:8–9)

We find in the following two verses images which draw parallels between the "benefit" of donating in the way of God and the burgeoning life of nature which offers its goods without count:

> The likeness of those who expend their wealth in the way of God is as the likeness of a grain of corn that sprouts seven ears, in every ear a hundred grains. So God multiplies unto whom He will; God is All-embracing, All-knowing. (Qur'ān, 2:261)

and further:

> But the likeness of those who expend their wealth, seeking God's good pleasure, and to confirm themselves, is as the likeness of a garden upon a hill; a torrent smites it and it yields its produce twofold; if no torrent smites it, yet dew; and God sees the things you do. (Qur'ān, 2:265)

Faith is that intimate conviction that God sees what we do and He knows the intention behind our spending. To preserve this link with the Creator is tantamount to orientating all our financial activity towards transparency and justice. It is, beyond zakāt, donating again and again of our surplus in order to live according to our rights in unity with the rights of others.

◆   Giving right measure

It is, nonetheless, not a question of living as a hermit, or giving everything without count. It cannot be a question of impoverishing oneself in order to render justice. The real donation is that which is born out of balance while remaining conscious of both the human responsibility and the limit. The right measure of donation is, therefore, essential:

> And keep not thy hand chained to thy neck, not outspread it widespread altogether, or thou wilt sit reproached and denuded. (Qur'ān, 17:29)

> ... who, when they expend, are neither prodigal nor parsimonious, but between that is a just stand... (Qur'ān, 25:67)

To give part of one's time and goods is tantamount to giving oneself the means of a permanent engagement both for oneself, and for others. Our soul, body, and relatives have rights upon us to which we must respond. From this response will be born a real donation of oneself to others as well as to the whole of society. Right measure preserves the conditions of being at the centre of oneself in order to be better with men.

♦   Fight against egoism and hoarding

The Qur'ānic injunctions regarding this point go in the same direction and complete what we have just indicated. To neglect donation and protect one's property, to the point of burying it, is tantamount to forgetting God and attributing to the good the value of an idol. It is tantamount to counting when one should be praying and purifying oneself of the natural tendency towards egoism.

> And whoso is guarded against the avarice of his own soul, those – they are the prosperers. (Qur'ān, 59:9)

The Revelation has very harsh words to say regarding those who hoard. The evocation of the pains of the Hereafter aim at awakening people's consciousness with regard to the seriousness of an attitude which borders on idolatry and whose effect we can see every day.

> Those who treasure up gold and silver, and do not expend them in the way of God – give them the good tidings of a painful chastisement, the day they shall be heated in the fire of

Gehenna and therewith their foreheads and their sides and their backs shall be branded: 'This is the thing you have treasured up for yourselves; therefore taste you now what you were treasuring!' (Qur'ān, 9:34–5)

♦ Displaying caution

This is a constant reminder in the Qur'ān. Man is requested to find measure in that which he gives and to remain discreet and respectful of man. In truth, the way of giving is, in itself, a testimony of faith. The person who is not in need of being seen by men, knows himself to be accompanied by God in all circumstances. His caution incidentally preserves the dignity of those he has just helped.

If you publish your freewill offerings, it is excellent; but if you conceal them and give them to the poor, that is better for you, and will acquit you of your evil deeds; God is aware of the things you do. (Qur'ān, 2:271)

O believers, void not your freewill offerings with reproach and injury. As one who expends of his substance to show off to men and believes not in God and the Last Day. The likeness of him is as the likeness of a smooth rock on which is soil, and a torrent smites it, and leaves it barren. (Qur'ān, 2:264)

Such should be the attitude of men: to fight so that the right of each individual is respected and to give of one's goods silently and discreetly. This duty of caution is, despite appearances, of great importance. It imprints a distinctive mark which is, in all circumstances and at the level of each consciousness, respect for the dignity of man. It is a question of preventing evils, giving before the poor have to beg and trying not to be seen by anyone so that the poor do not have to suffer embarrassment or hide. When society does not give that which is the right of its members, the affluent among them must manifest the greatness of the morality for due generosity. The Qur'ān never stops drawing the horizon of this landscape, a landscape which we cannot afford to forget in the management of our private economy.

These four orientations imprinted on individual spending are also moral qualities which give meaning to the actions of men. We perceive without difficulty, within remembrance of God, that action enters within a sacred dimension. This because it immediately – i.e. "without mediation" – expresses the link with Transcendence. It is a carrier of a finality and a meaning. This meaning is clearly the expression *of a morality of action and, hence, of an elementary, usual and daily economic activity.*

c.   Community life

The teachings which we can extract concerning individual and communal life derive from what has just been said about *zakāt* and individual spending. It is impossible to live in autarchy, to make the testimony of faith, pray, fast and go to pilgrimage only, far from men and worrying about no one except oneself. It is worth repeating that to be with God is tantamount to being with men; to carry faith is tantamount to carrying the responsibility of a continuous social commitment. The teaching that we should extract from *zakāt* is explicit: *to possess is tantamount to having to share.* It is impossible here, in the name of freedom, to shamelessly increase one's property at the price of exploitation, and social injustices. It is also impossible to forget the interests of the entire society such that one counts only one's interests. Man is certainly free, but he is responsible for this freedom before God as before men. This responsibility is inevitably moral. In the order of this morality, *to be free is to protect the freedom of others* and their dignities.

The four practical pillars of Islam hold this double individual and collective dimension.[4] The essence of Islamic teaching sticks to this path which is drawn between two other paths, preventing the individual and his sole interests and creating a social space comparable to a jungle, regardless of any general speeches delivered thereat; or to give priority to the group and society and deny the specificity, hopes and desire of each individual by creating a structure which enchains and alienates, regardless of the plans of development undertaken. It is a difficult balance, but this project is the only one capable of responding to the requirement of the Creator who expects of man to carry *alone* the responsibility of his community life. On the economic level, this is the only path which allows man to live humanely; his nature cannot do without such exchanges. Islam reminds, through the means of all the moral energy of its message, that a human economy without duties is an inhumane economy which organises, produces, and structures injustices, exploitation and famine. No jungle on earth knows such horror.

2. General Economic Principles in Islam

Many books have been written on this subject,[5] and many Muslim intellectuals have, since the beginning of this century, presented the grand lines of the Islamic, economic model. However, it was often a question of showing the great principles and their specificities without taking the reflection further ahead. The discussion has, therefore, not gone beyond the theoretical framework. We are, today, in urgent need of a concrete strategy, thought-out solutions which are inscribed in, and by, the stages of a reform which alone will allow us to achieve a real, alternative project of an economy. For this is indeed the question. Islam, in its fundamentals, is radically opposed to the existing liberal economic order. Not because the Islamic economy will be "socialist", as has unfortunately been implied, but because, as we have shown in the preceding sections, the priority of the moral quality renders the economic activity dependent on values which are beyond it and which orientate it.

Before entering into an analysis of concrete solutions, it seems necessary to present the important principles, which we have already mentioned. These will give us a much clearer idea of what Islam can contribute to contemporary thought. Furthermore, it is possible to use this presentation as a means to opening up a debate on practical solutions. We shall though confine ourselves here to synthetically pointing out those principles which give sense to economic activity without losing ourselves in details of jurisprudence.

a.   *Tawḥīd and gerency*

We have spoken, in Part Two of this book, about the relation
which exists between the Proprietor (God) and the gerent (the
human being) in Islam. It is undoubtedly in the domain of
economy that the nature of this relation has more impact. The
teaching of *tawḥīd* is fundamental. God alone possesses in the
absolute[6] and has made earth at the disposition of men. Let us
recall the relevant verses:

> To God belongs all that is in heavens and earth. (Qur'ān, 2:284)

> Have you not seen how that God has subjected to you whatsoever
> is in the heavens and earth, and He has lavished on you His
> blessings, outward and inward? (Qur'ān, 31:20)

The idea of gerency (*Khilāfa*) gives priority to duties over
rights. Certainly, there is the original permission, but there also
exist limits that one must respect. Thus, all the elements are
signs (*āyāt*) of creation and they are, in themselves, sacred. This
remark has important consequences. All men can, as they have
the inalienable right to, enjoy all natural resources since they
have been placed at their disposal by the Creator. However, this
enjoyment cannot go as far as disturbing the natural order by
means of a savage exploitation of the elements and a disrespect
for the "signs". Ecological considerations are an inherent aspect
of Islam's philosophy of action. Enjoying the resources before
God imposes that we respect them. The Creator wants good for
men and we cannot accept the forgetfulness of this will. What is
true regarding the ecological dimension – in the sense of the
use of resources – is even truer with regard to the sphere of
production. What characterises a good production is the moral
quality of the product. The parameters of productivity,
profitability, cost, price and so forth, are nothing. These are
emptied of their sense if they are the means of production of
something useless, derisory or, more broadly, destructive. Man
must produce, quite obviously, but never solely for profit, but
rather always in balance with his real needs. We should not
omit recalling the necessity of taking account of the superior

interest of society which, echoing Divine values, fixes limits to any egoistic and inconsiderate exploitation. This is the problematic contained in the recognition of private property.

b. *Private property*

The ownership of property and possessions is allowed in Islam and is inscribed within the framework which we have recalled several times. Its use must respect the revealed moral directives and, by extension, must take into account the interests of the whole society. Included in this philosophy of being and the management of property, the right and freedom of man to enjoy his goods and to acquire properties are considerable. The principle of this acquisition is confirmed by the Qur'ān:[7]

> *To the men a share from what they have earned, and to the women a share from what they have earned.* (Qur'ān, 4:32)

The first instruction that must be drawn from this verse is acknowledgement of a property whose modality of acquisition is work. This is what has been shown by the majority of Muslim jurists. We have already spoken about the fundamental right of work, and the possible acquisition of goods derives logically from this. It can be a waged work, a work of agriculture, trade, fishing, hunting or other such kind. The only fundamental condition is that this work remains within the frame of what is considered licit (this means for Muslims that they should avoid any kind of transaction on forbidden commodities, games of luck in all their forms, monopolies,[8] interest and speculation). There exist other means of acquiring property. For example, through inheritance, capital, *zakāt* (for the poor), *waqfs*,[9] bequests and donations. We find in books of Islamic jurisprudence commentaries and detailed analysis regarding each one of these means.

The acknowledgement of property obliges social organisations to protect it. This protection is fundamental in Islamic law. In the classification put forward by the savants, which we have already mentioned when speaking of al-Shāṭibī, this protection is part of the *ḍarūriyyāt* (vital needs) in the same title as the protection of religion, person, reason and progeny. Property is, therefore, inalienable. Nevertheless, its management is subject to conditions whose absence must result in the intervention of public powers. Without entering into any great detail, we can mention those instances which require, in the name of the principle developed above, intervention:

◆ A management accompanied by corruption, theft, unjust exploitation of waged personnel, trading in illegal products, fiscal fraud (which includes payment of *zakāt*).

◆ A management which clashes with general interests and which can vary from the creation of monopolies to inconsequent wastage.

◆ Situation of national catastrophe, war or the superior interests of the community. All these clauses must, of course, be codified and form part of the legal procedures from which each citizen must benefit.

The general principle expresses itself by a kind of contract between society and its proprietor members. In exchange for protection, and well before any intervention which should be the exception rather than the rule, the proprietors owe to society a moral management of their possessions. The foundation of their social and economic freedom is not brought into question, but each one is required to respect the community in this sense. Likewise, society must encourage economic activity, and the efforts of each individual to yield a profit from his goods is part and parcel of the success of the social project. The state, in this sense, guarantees respect for the indispensable margins of manoeuvre and investment. This, at least, was the attitude of the Prophet (peace be upon him) in Madina, as it was of his first Companions. Therefore, it should also be the aim of any project which wants to take into account the nature of man in order to build a society based on an active, moving economy. In other words, the limits should be ethical. This because man always forgets moderation and the good when faced with a larger chance of gain. It is an injustice not to trust the qualities of man, as it is foolishness to turn a blind eye to his weaknesses and folly.

Demanding that men of faith preserve the moral quality of their management, the principle of Islamic jurisprudence, in matters of property, establishes two further elements which are capable of warding off excess. The first of these limitations is the obligation of paying *zakāt*. In fact, *zakāt* is a tax on wealth[10] and not only on revenue. Muslims must pay a percentage of their wealth[11] to the state every year. We have already said a few words about the religious importance of this payment[12] and of the eminent moral sense it assumes. Its scope on the level of social justice and the solidarity between rich and poor which should ensue from it is explicit. One should, nevertheless, add that *zakāt* is in itself an invitation to make work and yield profit from one's goods without any possible hoarding.[13] It is indeed this that Roger Garaudy reminds us of:

"*Zakāt*, i.e. a levy, not on revenue but on wealth, in order to 'purify it', stops any accumulation. Primitive jurisprudence, concerning this issue, excludes only the tools of work from *zakāt* (this is what we shall call today the means of production), and fixes its rate at 2.5%. This means that in 40 years (a generation) a private 'property' is entirely abolished and is returned to the community (the social fund constituted by *Zakāt* being consecrated to the needs of the community and to help the needy). No one, hence, can live an idle life solely by the inheritance of his family."[14]

The second limitation regarding property management is one of the most rigorous Islamic prohibitions in questions of social affairs. In fact, we always limit ourselves to reminding that Islam is in opposition to usury – or interest – but without going as far as the consequences of this assertion. This analysis is, however, imperative, in order that we are able to tackle, in the second phase, concrete solutions to the failings of the current economic system.

Understood within the framework of the economic philosophy which entails it, the prohibition of *ribā* carries, in itself, the exigency of thinking an alternative economy. It cannot, however, remain in the theoretical domain and, we shall see further below, that it requires very determined local engagement.

c.   The prohibition of ribā

Several definitions have been given to the term *ribā* according to whether scholars wanted to restrain its scope to the domain of economic activity or, on the contrary, expand it. The Arabic term "*ribā*" is derived from the verb "*rabā*" which means "to increase", "to grow". There are, however, divergent juridical views on the nature of the prohibition. However, the vast majority of jurists, before and now, understand it to be a question of the formal prohibition of any interest rate or usury. This because the idea entailed in the notion of *ribā* is that of an increase without a service or work given in exchange. It is an increase of capital by and on the capital itself. It is also considered that there is a form of *ribā* in situations of unequal exchange. This is "the usury of exchange" or "on sales" which relies on the famous *ḥadīth* of the Prophet (peace be upon him):

"Wheat is exchanged for wheat in equal quantity and handed hand to hand; the surplus being usury. Barley is to be exchanged with barley, in equal quantity and hand to hand; the surplus being usury. Dates are to be exchanged with dates, in equal quantity and hand to hand; the surplus being usury. Salt is to be exchanged with salt, in equal quantity and hand to hand; the surplus being usury. Money is to be exchanged with money, in equal quantity, hand to hand; the surplus being usury. Gold is to be exchanged with gold, in equal quantity and hand to hand; the surplus being usury."[15]

From this *ḥadīth* comes the idea of equality and simultaneity in exchange so that the terms of exchange between the two parties are very clear. Many other *aḥādīths* bring other clarifications which insist on the importance of the conditions of exchange. From these, jurists have concluded the formal prohibition of speculation, in all *Sunnī* legal schools. This despite many differences in interpretation on certain types of economic or financial procedure. The conclusion of Hamid Algabid, ex-Prime Minister of the Republic of Niger and General Secretary of the Organisation of Islamic Conference (OIC) is clear and juridically exact:

"Whether it is a question of usury on the loan of money or on exchanges, the meticulousness of the prohibitions and obligations, in the *Sunna,* shows that accumulation is rigorously condemned in all its forms, and that all instances, which are sometimes improbable, are 'pursued'. The transparency of that which is given in loan and that which is given back, of that which is sold and the price paid for it is an absolute rule. This is a transparency on the object itself as it is a transparency concerning the time.

"Speculation is banished as is banished enrichment without a cause, the growth of value without a legitimate counterpart (due to work, conditioning, transport, preparation…) of the thing which is an object of exchange."[16]

What appears, hence, on the strictly economic level is a double prohibition included in the notion of *ribā* from the moment we understand it in its Qur'ānic sense (increase of goods without performing a service). It is a prohibition of interest on capital and a prohibition of interest on exchanges which, based on speculation, monopoly or other "unequal conditions", is not a benefit resulting from honest trade. These are the general principles of prohibitions, and each epoch should consider the current economic practices in order to measure the degree of their appropriateness to the principles. It is clear, in fact, that the definition of *ribā* is a function of the kind of activity which is born in historical situations and *vis-à-vis* of which the field of application of its definition can be expanded.

This is what Roger Garaudy rightly points out by adding, concerning the definition of *ribā*, the priority of the moral scope of this prohibition:

"If therefore we are not looking for an economic content for the notion of *ribā* (each concerned historical epoch and social stratum has given a different one, since Mu'āwiya, founder in the 1st century of Hijra, of the Umayyad dynasty and the son of a Makkan banker, until the theoreticians of 'Islamic Banks' in the 20th century). We can, however, with enough clarity specify the moral content according to the coherence of the message. If God is the Only One who possesses, and if man is but a responsible gerent of this property, in his quality as a Caliphate, then he cannot usurp God's property in order to use it for his own profit, independently of the will of God and of the interests of the community which has priority to it. *Ribā* is, therefore, any wealth that grows without work in the service of God, or grows to the detriment of the community or other people by the exploitation of others." [17]

The insertion of this notion in the moral order, which recalls the two transcendent and collective dimensions, is of prime importance and is, without doubt, the basic objective of this prohibition. In fact, it is not a question of suffocating human activity. On the contrary, it is rather a question of rendering it just and equitable, of "separating the grain from the chaff". Progression in the order of Revelation which led to this specific prohibition is significant. The first revealed verse is allusive and spells out the moral deficit of paying interest on individual expenditure:

> *And what you give in usury, that it may increase upon the people's wealth, increases not with God; but what you give in alms, desiring God's Face, those – they receive recompense manifold.* (Qur'ān, 30:39)

This reflection is addressed to the debtors who are implicitly requested not to engage, from a moral point of view, in this type of loan. The verses of the second Revelation treating of usury speak of the Jews who had transgressed against that which was prohibited. Here, it is the creditors who are put forward, in their practice of usury, in that there is the fact of "unjustly consuming the goods of people". The notion of justice is, therefore, primary:

> *And for the evildoing of those Jewry, We have forbidden them certain good things that were permitted to them, and for their barring from*

God's way many, and for their taking usury, that they were prohibited, and consuming the wealth of the people in vanity; and We have prepared for the unbelievers among them a painful chastisement. But those of them that are firmly rooted in knowledge, and the believers believing in what has been sent down to thee, and what was sent down before thee, that perform the prayer and pay the alms, and those who believe in God and the Last Day – them We shall surely give a mighty wage. (Qur'ān, 4:160–2)

The third stage is a call to Muslims and is limited to certain kinds of practices:

O believers, devour not usury, doubled and redoubled, and fear God: haply so you will prosper.[18] (Qur'ān, 3:130)

The verses of formal prohibition are among the last verses revealed to the Prophet (peace be upon him)[19] and 'Umar noted his regret that the Prophet (peace be upon him) did not specify its total significance to the Companions. Here, things are explicit and this clearly implies that one must distinguish between good and bad practices in an absolutely moral sense. Trade which can produce a benefit is based on justice if it repeats the conditions which make it avoid transforming itself into an illegal exchange which leads to the exploitation of some by others.

Those who devour usury shall not rise again except as he rises, whom Satan of the touch prostrates; that is because they say, 'Trafficking is like usury.' God has permitted trafficking, and forbidden usury. Whosoever receives an admonition from his Lord and gives over, he shall have his past gains, and his affair is committed to God; but whosoever reverts – those are the inhabitants of the Fire, therein dwelling for ever. God blots out usury, but freewill offerings He augments with interest. God loves not any guilty ingrate. Those who believe and do deeds of righteousness, and perform the prayer, and pay the alms – their wage awaits them with their Lord, and no fear shall be on them, neither shall they sorrow. O believers, fear you God; and give up the usury that is outstanding, if you are believers. But if you do not, then take notice

> *that God shall war with you, and His Messenger; yet if you repent,*
> *you shall have your principal, unwronging and unwronged. And if*
> *any man should be in difficulties, let him have respite till things*
> *are easier; but that you should give freewill offerings is better for*
> *you, did you but know. And fear a day wherein you shall be returned*
> *to God, and every soul shall be paid in full what it has earned;*
> *and they shall not be wronged.* (Qur'ān, 2:275–81)

Usury which, in appearance, brings money and increases capital, and charity or *zakāt* which, in appearance, diminish the former, face one another. On Divine balance, on account of conscience, within the parameters of human good, things are, deep down, the opposite of each other. Usury is a loss while charity is a gain. The objective of the prohibition is indeed to set links between men in a mood of transparency, equity and humanity: "Do not wrong anyone, and you will not be wronged." It is, therefore, a question of rejecting any kind of exploitation and of encouraging equitable trade. The rich at the time of the Prophet (peace be upon him) could not but react negatively to the meaning of this message, just as they had always done in the face of any prophetic revelation, from Noah to Jesus.

> *We sent no warner into any city except its men who lived at ease*
> *said, 'We disbelieve in the message you have been sent with.'*
> (Qur'ān, 34:34)

In the same fashion, this message cannot today provoke anything but disapprobation from the most rich. This because it is, in itself, a decisive rejection of economic enslavement, financial slavery and humiliation. Its meaning does not suffer from any sprain. It is up to people to find the most adaptable system for their times, one which respects this principal pillar of the expression of an economy with an Islamic face. An economy which is inevitably opposed to interest, speculation and monopoly.

We are, therefore, in a mood of opposition to the world economic order. Rich countries, as the rich of Makka in yesteryears, cannot fail to see a danger in local or national mobilisations which aim at leaving behind the "classical economic" system. This is quite normal. However, we know today that the model of development of the countries of the North is "non-exportable". While 1.5 billion human beings live in ease, almost four billion have only the barest means of survival. The terms of exchange are unequal, exploitation is permanent, speculation is extreme and the monopolies are provocative. The prohibition of *ribā*, which is the moral axis around which economic thought in Islam is elaborated, calls believers to express a categorical rejection of an order which has respect only for profit and which suppresses justice and humanity. In the same *élan*, this prohibition imposes upon them the need to think and elaborate a model, which ought to come near to respect for this injunction. Each of the stages must be thought out in order to allow a fundamental reform and not in order to satisfy experiences which are cobbled together here and there, and which are Islamic only in function to the good conscience they instantly offer to their authors. Some of these experiences are interesting and useful without doubt, and one should take into account the horizons they have opened up. Others, unfortunately, are but a dust that blinds one's eyes and allows some states or some fabulously rich personalities, at the very moment when the quasi totality of their practices and investments are linked to the capitalist economy, to offer themselves moral sanction by encouraging a so-called "Islamic" project. Deep down, on account of the profits gained somewhere else, neither the project nor the qualifications cost very dear. Love of reputation often carries the price of the qualifications which we flout.

3. A Profound Reform

To take into account the three fundamental orientations, which we have mentioned above, requires deep reform. The principle of *tawḥīd,* which expresses the absolute property of God and which limits, in its use, the private property of each individual, all while respecting it, entails the Islamic concept of

man, this before God as well as before others. This is what Roger
Garaudy has termed "Transcendence and community". The
prohibition of *ribā* is directly born of this horizon. What should
determine human relations, before God, is transparency, justice,
goodness and fraternity. Trade between individuals is a necessity
and must be, as with all other means, subjected to values.
Production, consumption and repartition of wealth relating to
the economic domain require that we take into account
considerations other than the cold calculus which preoccupies
itself with the quantitative aspects of things. Everything, in Islam,
is opposed to this "positive" economic science which draws its
theoretical – and sometimes practical – pertinence from itself,
as a self-justified tool. This within a system which is balanced
only by calculus and which snaps at morality or human
conscience. A "science" which is lost in numbers because it
forgets God and people; it is drowned in theories because it
forgets meaning and qualities. Islamic culture calls for a total
reversal of this tendency that we are witnessing nowadays. The
fall of the Soviet Union has accentuated this phenomenon with
the hegemony of the sole economic model that "is working".
Liberal economy is in the process of subjecting the whole planet
to the infallibility of its views. The only objective is growth, the
unique success is profit and the real norm is comfort. In the
great market of competition, the freedom of some is at war with
that of others. Behind the great speeches about humanity and
liberalism is hidden the forms of a sombre dictatorship.[20]

The functioning of Bretton Woods's institutions just on their
own makes one shiver. "Programmes of structural adjustment"
imposed upon countries without development are justified by
reference to classical economy. The health of a country is
measured by its "exportable" production, and this to the point
at which nothing is left for the native populations themselves.
In the more or less long term, so they claim, and as a
consequence of the process, they will derive benefit. The terms,
however, are very long indeed.

After the "lost decade" of the 1980s, the orientation given to
respective national production, the limitation of subsidies for

the production of basic needs, the freezing of salaries – which are all measures among others – have given back to the poor their misery, and confirmed the most corrupt of dictators. The social programmes of the World Bank change nothing. Even the principle of the aid given raises questions. The cult of profit and a love for one's fellow humans does not produce a happy mixture. Aid is very often justified by political alliance and a convergence of interests rather than by a sincere humanitarian *élan*.[21] To confine economic thought to the calculus of a specialised positive science, without orientating it by means of superior human principles, leads to the horrors we know of today. Forty thousand people on average die every day because of the imbalance of an inhumane and unjust economic order. No one who has faith or conscience can sanction this state of the world. As with all religions, Islam obliges that we look for solutions and give an *élan* to the process of liberation.[22]

One must say here that very often Muslim intellectuals relate to this situation without making any reference except to their own history, their specific experiences or the studies of authors belonging to their own tradition. On the economic level, however, there exist numerous studies and field experiments from which they can derive benefit. Everything that has been produced regarding development programmes and their implementation, the level "meso" and, broadly, on an alternative economy has not yet been taken into consideration. The functioning of grass roots communities (which has so much to do with the dynamics which are found today at work in Muslim countries), that of cooperatives of production and projects of popular participation must be the subject of more in-depth studies. We find there many coincidences with the requirements of an Islamic development that is based on morality in managing affairs. From the latter we can derive an evident benefit. We should also say that a solution corresponding to Islamic norms is not necessarily suggested by a Muslim and that the strength of Islam in early times was due to its capacity to integrate any idea, organisation and progress which was not in opposition to its fundamental principles. It is imperative that we come out of our space of reference and our usual framework of analysis. Likewise, it is imperative that we start from the beginning, that is from the local plane, passing by the level of populations to that of the grass roots. There are many among those who think that it is enough to have control of the state – whatever it may be – in order to reform the entire social, political and economic organisation. Certainly, power can imprint impulsions and fix directives. However, unless it is to become a totalitarian and dictatorial regime, the state cannot make of a population that has been passive for decades, a people that is conscious of its participating responsibilities. Following the example of what we said concerning the political domain, an Islamic economy cannot be imposed overnight from above. Global thinking and strategy must determine the stages which, by reorganising the sectors of economic activity at the grass roots level, will enable the achievement of reforms. The choice of priorities is decisive. There exists nowadays numerous experiences of economic development in Muslim countries. We find, in diverse sectors, interesting dynamics, ones which have the merit of mobilising men and women in their immediate sphere of reference. We can distinguish two levels here; the local and the national on the one hand and the transnational on the other.

A.   *At the Local and National Level*

An in-depth discussion of the stages of a project at both local and national level would take a long time and would also require an appropriate analysis of each envisaged situation. We shall, therefore, confine ourselves here to showing six domains of action which have a reality in the quasi-totality of Muslim countries.

i.   To be engaged with the population

To give shape to an alternative economy which respects Islamic norms is not going to be achieved overnight through decrees imposed by a state that has become "Islamic". The mutation is long and requires thinking all levels of mobilisation.

When we discussed the social principles in Islam, we showed that the individual, in his understanding of things as well as in assuming responsibility, is the first "field of action". On the level of economic management, the priority is the same. It is a question of training individuals and groups, at grass roots level, in order that they can run their individual and communal affairs (on the local plane) in a sounder fashion.

Preparing a budget, daily buying and selling, management of the familial economy, personal and financial participation in a project involving a group, an association or a cooperative, all this is part of the Islamic training, in its broader sense. It is a question, in its daily activity, of integrating norms, values and finalities into the most basic economic action. To think of one's life along with the lives of others, to consider one's benefit in harmony with the interests of others and, of the group in general, must be done beforehand, especially at the local level.

Moreover, preference must be given to small projects which involve a limited number of people with whom it is possible to set mobilising structures in motion. We have some examples of this in the countries of Western Africa (Senegal, Burkina Faso, Mali, etc.), in the Middle East (Egypt, Jordan and the occupied Palestinian territories) and in Asia (Malaysia, Indonesia, and India, for example). At the local and regional level we find kinds of organisations which favour the complementarity of the players by means of an equitable division of labour, one which respects a balance between individual interests and those of the group. These development projects allow the population to train themselves, to become responsible and to actively participate in the necessary economic reforms. Undoubtedly, in the years to come, it will be necessary to further emphasise these local forms of action. The creation of simple economic structures – that are respectful of revealed norms – is imperative today for whoever wants to plan for the long term. On a more basic level, it is a question of giving rise to new habits of management.

Financial institutions or corporations have been created in India, Pakistan and Iran since the beginning of this century. These have, on the local level, respected Islamic principles among which, as a priority, is the prohibition of *ribā*. Muhammad Hamidullah even points out that the creation of such institutions in India dates from the end of the last century, and that the degree of mobilisation was already impressive. In 1963, in the village of Mit Ghamr in Egypt, Ahmad Najjar created a kind of savings bank. This is usually mentioned as the first experience that gave birth to the "Islamic banks" we know today.[23] It is, nevertheless, necessary to point out the popular character of this experience. The minimum sum required for saving or investment was very low and this allowed the most impoverished sections of the population to participate in it. As a result, we witnessed an unprecedented popular movement which enabled development from the grass roots level. The philosophy behind such a savings bank was to stimulate local participation. Thus eight other "banks" or "corporations" were opened in different regions. With such savings, it was possible to guarantee the internal financing of development. The socialist Egyptian power of Nasser, realising the extent of success of this experience, put an end to it in 1967, allegedly for technical reasons.[24] These projects are certainly exposed to the powers in place, especially if the former achieve an important dimension. But, it remains necessary to create regional centres of popular participation. These dynamics exist today in a number of countries, and this should be encouraged, as should the experiences be multiplied and the training deepened.

ii.   Education: an investment

One may be astonished to see education addressed within a chapter on economics. However, it is necessary to consider the fact that there is no economic development without social development. Moreover, the latter cannot take place without the education of women and men. In a nutshell, to invest in education is tantamount to giving oneself the means of restructuring imbalances in the economy.

It is difficult to involve reform at the national level, but it is imperative to lead this enterprise at local and regional levels.

There certainly exist programmes for the elimination of illiteracy and for religious education and these remain of great importance. But they are not enough. It is a question here of thinking a built-up pedagogy which allows women and men to discover meaning in their daily lives. In this, the method which was suggested in the 1960s by Professor Paolo Freire in Brazil, was of great interest. It was a question of eliminating people's illiteracy by making them conscious of their own dignity. The method's main quality consisted of opening the eyes of all students, young and adults alike, to their situation, as also to local dangers, to their participation and power to transform realities through their mastery of both written and oral language. Education was an integrated part of the social and economic content, and because of this, it enjoyed considerable success. However, military, businessmen and vested interests, conscious of the danger this operation posed, drove Paolo Freire away from Brazil, in 1964. This kind of pedagogy – which is, understandably, orientated towards education and not selection – immediately echoes the grass roots education which an Islamic engagement would imply. The latter calls, at one and the same time, to meaning (which includes in Islam the moral and communal aspects), to knowledge and to context. It is, in other respects, what the Sudanese have been trying to do for the last few years at university level. They multiplied and de-localised the sites of education by fixing in each region specific programmes which take account of the environment and the peculiar needs therein.[25]

The philosophy of such a project fits exactly with the sense of a long-term investment which should be able to dynamise society, or, according to the words of the economist Albertini, give rise to a "common fervour". It is a question of adapting training to context.

Experiences in the countrysides of Muslim countries are, in this sense, still insufficient. Certainly, the powers in place look – and they will always do so – unfavourably at any educational project which does not conform to the framework thought out in urban areas, one which will be later exported, without any adaptation, to the countryside. This is perhaps one of the reasons for these shortcomings, but one must add two further factors which can effect such a situation. These are the weight of tradition and, in a more decisive fashion, the illusion of the soundness of the modern model of selective training. Even among the most committed Muslims we find these kind of considerations accepted without any in-depth critique. However, as underlined by Albertini, the old proof of this choice is today demolished:

"Today, all the experts agree, the elimination of illiteracy among the youth should not be cut off from the entire social and economic life or from the efforts of development.

"First, the elimination of illiteracy among the youth should not be separated from that of adults, for school will have no influence unless it is supported by the whole social milieu.

"Then, it is not reading or writing alone which should be targeted. What should rather be targeted are the entire procedures that a person needs in order to fulfil his social function. The elimination of illiteracy should not be cut off from daily life, work or action in society. It should be directly linked to the daily preoccupations of individuals as well as to their future tasks.

"Finally and chiefly, the elimination of illiteracy should be in the first place a means to make a person become aware of his situation as a human being. ... The elimination of illiteracy should not be, as it has very often been, a manner of fleeing from the scene, but on the contrary a way of being inserted therein more efficiently."[26]

Such a reflection corresponds perfectly to the encompassing character of the Islamic project. Far from the calls for a development which is a carbon copy of models that are foreign to local realities, it is urgent that we train women and men who, while nourished by cultural and religious points of reference, can act and dynamise their social and economic framework. We should be able to provide for regional economic investment that which such a training necessitates and in an independent fashion and this by creating self-financing institutions. The latter exist in the Egyptian, Turkish, Indian and Malaysian countryside and cities – it also used to exist in Algeria and Tunisia before state intervention.[27] The opposition of the powers in place should not hinder the policy of taking small steps; consequent work needs to be provided in the countryside and this should be a priority. It is this "integrated education" which will allow the creation of a new social tissue which offers economic dynamics based on structures that themselves are also new.[28]

iii. The priority of agriculture

In a span of just 20 years, the degree of autonomy has regressed in the majority of Muslim countries, as it has in the entire Third World. Governments and all dominating classes had orientated agricultural production towards exportation in order to be able to buy imported goods, often luxurious (for example, cars, household goods, and the like). The International Monetary Fund and the World Bank, acting as good financial advisers, encouraged this tendency in order to allow the powers in place to obtain the necessary funds to pay off their debts as well as the interest on those debts. The visible results of this policy are catastrophic. The poor have become poorer. At the same time, the culture of acquiring imported products, often products of basic necessity, increased. This is an absurd situation which has culminated with the analysis of financial flux and influx in developing countries. Impoverished and lifeless, the latter pay more money to the North than they receive. What is to be done in order to emerge out of such a situation that has worsened year after year for the last 20 years?

All experts agree that public aid to assist the development of the countries of the South has seriously neglected agriculture. In countries where nearly 60% of the population is involved in agriculture, only 18% of the provided aid was destined for agricultural production. Governments, blinded by Western models as also by their desire to accede as soon as possible to modernity, have invested in large-scale industrial projects but allocated no more than 2% to 3% (on average) of their budgets to agriculture. We know today the dramatic consequences of these choices: chronic poverty, massive rural exodus, unbalanced and de-structured social tissue, etc. The populations of the South pay, today, the price of these ill-considered policies. While 20% of the world's population wastes 80% of the world's wealth, nearly 4 billion men, women and children have to share the remaining 20%. Still they are asked to produce in order to meet the needs of this fifth of the world's population in exchange for hard currency! Famine in the world is a question of repartition; first and foremost, it is a question of unjust repartition. Division has to do with human morality and dignity. The world economy will continue to produce misery, desolation and horror if it does not subject itself to superior values which re-orientate the activity of turning everything to one's advantage.

Re-orientating the economy means first trying to respond to the needs of those who are hungry. This in Muslim countries, as in all the countries of the South. It also means giving priority to agriculture and, in this framework, to food-producing cultivations. This against those economic policies which are sustained and imposed by the superpowers. It cannot be a question, for the time being and on account of the interests at play, of engaging in a total project of reform. It is more appropriate to achieve local adjustments at the level of the people according to their means and available financial possibilities. Economists have spoken about "integrated rural development" which adapts technologies to the social context (all while avoiding any de-structuring of the existing tissue) and which tries to take away in this dynamic all the crafts which are, either beforehand or consequently, linked to agricultural production. These modest achievements allow the inhabitants of the countryside to remain in place (thus avoiding rural exodus) and create at the same time jobs which sustain the purchasing power of farmers and small businesses.[29]

IMF and World Bank experts made a distinction, just a decade ago, between good and bad pupils. The former were countries that were minimally interventionist, having understood the soundness of total liberalism. The latter still think that the state ought to intervene in the regulation of economic affairs. The proof of this scientific analysis can be seen in the Asiatic experience where some countries, such as Hong Kong and Singapore, have presented impressive growth rates. The Asiatic model was and remains a point of reference.[30] Nowadays things have changed slightly and regional specificities are increasingly taken into account in the elaboration and evaluation of the economic policies undertaken. This includes the type of population, the level of participation, the degree of corruption, the structure of institutions, etc. Taking into account only the "liberal" or "interventionist" models is not enough. While the scientific character of expert analysis has fallen, other parameters are otherwise decisive.

At the forefront of these parameters we naturally find the dynamism of populations and we cannot inverse the actual tendency in our countries without mobilising the grass roots and making the latter aware that concrete solutions are within their reach. In Muslim countries, the Islamic points of reference could and should play a large role in the "disengagement" of energy process. This in order to give oneself the means to achieve a well anchored strategy, which aims for the long term. The example of the Federation of Malaysia is, in this context, interesting. All the while engaged in a gradual "Islamic" reform of the whole financial system, the powers that be succeeded in dynamising the grass roots through its reliance on Islamic points of reference as also by offering important margins for manoeuvre to the different states and farmers' associations.

On top of its suffering from a harsh embargo, the Sudan furthermore underwent exclusion from the IMF in February 1994. This country cannot rely on the support of any government and even less on private banks because of the relations these entertain with the great financial institutions. For the last four years, Sudan's situation at the international level has worsened. Yet, since 1991, the results of the country's agricultural policy are impressive, even in the opinion of IMF experts. The decision here was to give priority to food crops and, at the same time, call farmers to make concerted mobilisation efforts for survival.

It was a question of *jihād* – literally. It is this that Hasan al-Turabi expressed when he wrote:

"At the end of the day, and this is an essential point, neither nationalism nor socialism have been able to mobilise our societies towards development. In societies where profit and salaries are insufficient enticements, religion can be the most powerful engine of development. If we inform people that agriculture is their *jihād*, their 'holy war', they will address this problem with zeal. 'Make yourself loved by God and develop agriculture.' This slogan is in the process of making the Sudan move from a situation of food shortage into foodstuffs self-sufficiency. These words may seem strange to the ears of the rich West. But what was the role of Puritanism in America when it was a question of civilising this savage land? What was the role of Protestant ethics in the takeoff of European economies? Religion is a factor of development!"[31]

It is undoubtedly this volunteerist, agricultural policy, giving privilege to the needs of people, which is disliked – more than any violation of human rights – by the USA, the IMF and the World Bank. From Jamaica to Burkina Faso, where Sankara paid with his life, other "undisciplined" governments have already been the target of Western wrath. Nonetheless, there is no other solution for all Muslim countries, except to orientate and organise a popular dynamic based on the priority of agriculture. What the Sudan or Malaysia have decided to do at the governmental level ought to be organised at the local and regional level. The example of the Latin American production cooperatives functioning without interest and according to the principle of collective participation can be followed. This has proved its efficiency in a number of countries in very diverse situations. In Western Africa, synergies at grass roots levels have allowed decisive progress. This by giving to the people a new habit of commitment, participation and management.[32]

The teaching of Islam, in itself, carries tremendous potential for popular mobilisation. The credulity of the masses has always been played with and deceived. It is appropriate today to dispense a teaching which mixes points of reference with action

and one which also fixes priorities. Agriculture is one of them
and one has to say that among Muslims there is a dangerous
lack of innovation in this respect. Opposition to governments
cannot hinder work at the foundation. The hostility of powers,
the rich and multinational societies, are proof of this, as it is
evident that deep reform must take into consideration adversity
as also the time factor.

iv. In the cities

The most widespread notion in the West, concerning those
Muslims who are engaged in social work and alternative
economic projects, results from an archaic reading of historical
events. Intellectuals, researchers, journalists and some politicians
see Muslims, these notorious "Islamists", as having in the last
15 years nothing but a thirst for power and that they use all the
means available to them to seduce the people to their cause.
Social and economic engagement would, thus, be the loftiest
way to win the masses to their side.

This would be forgetting, however, that popular mobilisation
in the cities already existed under colonisation, and this in a
great number of countries from Algeria to Egypt and passing
by Tunisia up to India. This kind of engagement has been carried
on since independence and it is the new liberators of nations
such as Boumedienne, Nasser, and Bourguiba who stopped it
when they realised the danger it results in at grass roots level.[33]
Ibn Badis created sections of the Association of the ʿUlamāʾ in
all the Algerian territories, and Hasan al-Banna encouraged the
creation of more than 40 societies and enterprises directed
essentially at meeting the needs of the poor. It was not a question
of a simple political strategy aimed at taking over power. It was
rather a response to a moral imperative. For the struggle against
poverty is not a subject which lends itself to discussion, it does
not involve any shady deal. This because a social and economic
organisation that produces misery is an organisation which steals
dignity from men. It is as such unacceptable and does not require
never-ending politicking.[34]

Permanent rural exodus brings waves of men, women and children into the cities, thousands of them without a home or a job. If makeshift shelters are built due to the ingeniousness of those exiled, the difficulties are, however, considerably more profound when it comes to employment. Unemployment is the inhuman drama of all societies, one which is many-fold greater in the countries of the South. Nonetheless, it is not a fatality. For even in the worst situations one has seen men, women and children organising themselves and creating by means of their ingeniousness original circuits of exchange, and impressive local networks of solidarity, the whole forming an alternative economy which allows, more than mere survival, life.

When the powers in place do not have the means to launch a real economic policy which takes account of the needs of the people, when they are suffocated by the programmes of structural adjustment imposed on them by the IMF, or when the political will is absent from dictators' minds, then these solutions impose themselves. Organising the grass roots, making them dynamic by giving them the means to take the initiative and act, are urgent. However, after more than 50 years of mobilisation, the Muslims have had little interest in the economic aspect of local intervention. The 40 enterprises which were registered in Egypt during the 1940s were, to the best of our knowledge, an exception. And since the state closed them down in the 1950s, we have had difficulty thinking out a long-term strategy.[35]

That movement which allowed the creation of dispensaries for those who were more impoverished (with symbolic contributions and by relying on *zakāt*), networks of traders for selling (agricultural or craft productions), or again to install workshop structures (for example, engineering, mechanical, etc.) may still allow for the creation of small and medium enterprises which, in respect of the Islamic norm, offer jobs and amplify the dynamic. The work achieved in this sense in Dakar, Gaza, Calcutta, Kuala Lumpur and Cairo, to cite but a few examples, is patent proof. The self-financing of projects is possible if participative structures are put in place. Levying *zakāt*, contributions, profits arising from sales, generate sums of money which can guarantee total independence.

We have said again and again that Islam encourages, even requires this kind of grass roots economic engagement. Incidentally, it is part of a broader comprehension of the notion of *shūrā*, but it is more directly the first step that is required for the achievement of a sound economy respectful of revealed moral norms. Equally along this line, the creation of participating financial societies is necessary and enables gathering capitals in order to invest them in enterprises of greater calibre.

Societies of this kind already exist in Malaysia and the Sudan. Development cooperatives, of the Latin-American model, remain much less numerous (or less structured) in Muslim countries. We would, however, benefit from analysing these grass roots structures, which, deep down, totally respect Islamic principles. We should, therefore, act gradually, and look forward to creating, in the long term, alternative economic "spaces" which allow us to leave the "classical" system behind.

The prohibition of alcohol and *ribā* were achieved gradually. It was a Divine pedagogy and the jurists have unanimously retained the lesson. They have, in this sense, codified the rule of progression in stages. The complexity of today's economy requires this same procedure. This entails taking small steps at the grass roots level, steps which are sustained by a long-term strategy and which, on account of respective national realities, must orientate itself towards precisely defined objectives. On a larger scale, reflection should not limit itself to the national framework. It is a profound and general reform that must be engaged in. Islam, in the countries of the South, can, and must, contribute to the necessary change in orientation that should be imparted on the present "economism". It is a question of clearly achieving a rupture. The words of Albert Jacquard are hard but necessary and lucid:

"Liberalism *a la western* is synonymous to slavery for the great majority of men, whether they are citizens of countries of the South or relegated in the unprivileged layers of countries of the North.

"The most urgent task is not, as is done presently by the World Bank and the IMF, to deliver the impoverished to the appetite of the affluent, but rather to preserve durably the social or ecological guaranties which are obtained, often after hard struggle, by some. Then expand these guaranties to all terrestrials..."[36]

"The only criterion of success in a collectivity ought to be its capacity not to exclude and to make everyone feel that he is welcome, because all need him. Under this measure, the records of nations is very different from that suggested by economists ... Measured by these criteria, the failure of societies which are driven by economism is patent. Their technical successes are paid by an exorbitant human cost that undermines the foundations of their traditional structures. American citizens may be proud to have sent some explorers to the moon, but in the big cities they can no longer enter their own homes without trembling of fear. The French may also boast about their nuclear submarines which are capable of destroying entire cities in remote continents, but thousands of families wait several decades before obtaining a decent flat. Their children never find at school the reception which they may need. Can these find solace in knowing that "the Franc is strong"? ...

"Nowadays, the evidence is glaring; the jolts that we notice do not constitute a crisis in any way. It just happens that this is taking place at the end of a century, and even a millennium, but it is nothing more than a coincidence due to our own way of counting the years. What is important is to observe that we are living a mutation which we have caused ourselves. And this mutation is at least of equal importance to that our Neolithic ancestors have caused when some ten thousand years ago they became settled people. What happened to humanity is the result of the thoughts and acts of men. It is up to them to analyse the causes and find remedies.

"In truth, we should rejoice for living such a phase of renewal of our means and objectives. The occasion is magnificent for orientating the course of humanity towards a new direction. If we persevere in the way of economism, we can be sure of going back to the barbarism described by Aldous Huxley in *Brave New World*, and George Orwell in *1984*. To such humanity, we must know how to say no.

"Owing to this, we must do away with our most ingrained habits of thinking. Is this possible?"[37]

Such a truth is both bitter and full of hope. The Muslims rather than being delighted by the condition of Western societies (forgetting, in the process, the catastrophic condition of their own societies), must take stock of the problems and bring their own contribution to this new "phase of renewal of our means and objectives". Work at the grass roots, with the people, which nourished Islam's humane and moral points of reference, can find an echo in the ethical and humanitarian preoccupations of Western intellectuals and savants. It is indeed, as Jacquard says, a question "of orientating the course of humanity towards a new direction". All civilisations must be permanent parties, it cannot be a question of tinkering or intervention on an *ad hoc* basis.

v. The question of Islamic banks

The creation of a real economy subjected to morality and respectful of Islamic principles requires a deep reflection on the long-term means and strategies to be adopted. Here, it can no longer be a question of chasing profit for profit's sake, turning freedom into an idol which permits everything, the good and the bad, the saving and the murderous. One must in future think differently. It has now been more than 20 years, when thinking about the need to establish Islamic banks first began, that these arrangements were indeed in mind. Originally, it was a question of creating financial institutions with a primarily social character and whose principal objective was the promotion of equitable development based on participative investments respectful of the rules of Islamic jurisprudence. In the 1960s, the craze was at its peak: an alternative economy could indeed emerge from "Islamic banks".

Proof of this is the 1963 project in Mit Ghamr, Egypt. Influenced by the network of rural savings banks in Western

Germany, Ahmad Najjar organised savings at the grass roots level. He, thus, proved that popular mobilisation around concrete social projects was possible. So much so that the Egyptian state intervened. After this experience, "Islamic banks" were going to change their character. From that moment, it was increasingly a question of large institutions, often linked to states (Saudi Arabia, in particular, which took several years to accept that one of these institutions had its head office on its territory!),[38] running deposit and investment programmes, and which were always more important and far away from social action. Gerard Naulleau very rightly remarks:

"Starting from Egypt, the idea of social banks which function without interest was later taken up by the countries of the Gulf and Arabian Peninsula, and was to come back to Egypt and spread to other countries a few years later. It has, in this passage, abandoned the social philosophy which had animated the Egyptian experience and which enriched itself with the Islamic referent."[39]

The problem is really out there. It is not enough that a bank carries the epithet "Islamic" (because it avoids more or less tainted dealings with *ribā*), in order to obtain the essential objective of its realisation. It must still be part of a vast movement whose finalities, declared and achieved by stages, be the concretisation of a social dynamic orientated towards justice, equitable trade and support of the most impoverished in financial engagement. It cannot be a question of gaining as much; or more differently, it is a question of fashioning a new idea of economic management from the bottom up. As Naulleau says, and he is supported in this by numerous Muslim economists,[40] social philosophy has been lost on the way and one often contents oneself with the guarantee of the epithet only.

We have indicated above what should have been the nature of work at the level of the people. "Islamic banks", whatever be their positions, seem to loan these perspectives. One observes nowadays that they function in parallel and in relation, sometimes a very close one, with the Western economy. Reserves are placed in banks functioning with classical interest rates, and an average of more than 40% (some even suggest 50%) of investments are carried out in the West where the large financial institutions, not at all Islamic, end up getting something out of it. The justification of the presence of these banks' head offices in fiscal paradises such as the Bahamas, New Jersey, Lichtenstein, supposedly for the avoidance of laws which impose minimum interest rates on banking institutions is not enough to account for the fundamental distortions that we discover when analysing the operations of these institutions. The first of these distortions, and not the least, is of an Islamic ethical order. Far from refraining from fervour on behalf of their contracting parties, these banks fall into the trap of comparing gains and, blinded by the fictive competition which exists between the "Islamic" project and the "capitalist" model, they end up investing in large commercial dealings (*murābaḥa*) which bring big and quick money.[41]

The race for profit remains and managers, concerned with maximum efficiency, know how to find competing juridical opinions which allow them to engage in dealings which are often somewhat unclear.[42] What has, then, happened to the principles which ought to orientate economic activity? Where has the social philosophy of Islam been lost? It is sometimes retorted that Islamic banks levy *zakāt*. Are we confusing the essence of this obligation with its levying? Incidentally, one must ask oneself whether this role is really incumbent upon these "banks" according to Islamic law. It certainly is not.

In this respect, the analysis of Benmansour is without complacency:

"The achievement of economic and social development in Muslim countries was the second main objective of Islamic banks. But what of it in reality? Have they achieved this objective after 20 years of practice and after the creation of about a hundred Islamic investment societies?

"The figures which are at our disposition show the contrary. Even more serious, Islamic banks have become simple correspondents of foreign banks, and transfer money from the Muslims to Western countries."[43]

These conclusions may seem excessive, but they match the views of the well-known Egyptian economist Yusuf Kamal. The latter came to the conclusion that the Islamic banks, in their functioning, are simple accommodations, and that they betray, deep down, the teachings of Islamic morality. By giving the impression of a possible Islamic management on a large scale, in an environment which cannot lend itself to it, they delay the creation of small projects which are more viable and which are, inevitably, at odds with the classical and capitalist models.

Other critiques, particularly numerous, have moreover been directed at the Islamic banks in the more restricted sense of their functioning with regard to the precise rules of Islamic law (it is not possible for us to enter here into details about the three more widely-known financial transactions of *mudāraba*, *mushāraka* and *murābaha*). It is sufficient to say that the first two transactions especially should constitute that which is essential for the transactions of Islamic financial institutions. Certainly, *mudāraba* is allowed in Islam, but the way in which it is practised by banks resembles the fixation of interest rates under the cover of another appellation. Examples of these small differences in terminology are legion when we address the area of Stock Exchange speculation whereby, in a wider fashion, different kinds of dealings are operated with Western partners.

On a more technical level, the defenders of Islamic banks, such as Hamid Algabid, acknowledge that despite the originality of such banks there are, nevertheless, countless problems still to be tackled. The difficulties presented by the absence of juridical stuff and financial means are compounded by a viability which does not seem possible nowadays, except by short-term commercial transactions. This, in itself, represents an acknowledgement of failure of the banks' initial project, since we are far from the support that ought to have been brought to social and economic development. More than support, it should be a question of a stimulation whose absence we still notice today.

However, this is not about rejecting the entire experience that Islamic banks have allowed us to reap. We know better today those transactions which are possible on the juridical plane, just as we know what the necessary modalities for the creation of a real social dynamic are.

Incidentally, the concept of "Islamic banks" borrows a terminology which is inadequate. The principles behind the management of the economy in Islam do not orientate us towards this type of institution, regardless of the fitting-out that we may contribute to it. It is well and truly a question of turning firstly towards the creation of cooperatives or participative societies which are immediately in agreement with the social philosophy about which we have talked above. It cannot be a question, as we have said, of entering into competition with the "classical" system by showing that "Islam is the solution" because its performances are better, while running the risk of abusing individuals through substituting certain appellations with others. The question is not to compare oneself with liberalism, but rather to liberate oneself.

vi. Facing the powers

The dynamics that we have suggested have already seen the light of day in many Muslim countries. The "awakening of Islam", which the Western media associate with the actions of the most radical groups, is, in fact, perceptible in the increasing mobilisation of people and intellectuals in Muslim cities and countrysides. For more than 60 years, experience has taught us not to underestimate the opposition of powers to this social, economic, and even broadly-speaking, political work. The repression that has befallen various movements – which did not and are not using arms – has been merciless; all in the name of the superior interests of the state. One must equally avoid an excess of naïvety. Things are nowadays clear, even if they had never been for the last 30 years. Any social force, any mobilisation of identity or a religious movement which calls, in the South, for more justice and the equitable repartition of wealth will be fought and suppressed with the explicit accord of the superpowers that are respectful, within their own frontiers, of human rights. The claims of Muslim populations are, therefore, dangerous for world order and, consequently, for the interests of the rich. "Friendly governments" are, therefore, required to administer the appropriate dose of "convenient repression". So what should be done in this situation?

Some groups, being at the end of their strength, tether and patience, decided to take up arms and oppose these powers by force. Yesterday, the colonisers stole and denied these people their dignity and identity. Today, more than 30 years after independence, the despoilments still carry on, that is if they have not increased. The economy serves the rich, while misery and prisons welcome the poor. So many have reached the conclusion that there is no discussion to be had with rulers who, at the head of Muslim states, make fun of the religious injunctions of their peoples. War has been declared, and the words are virulent and often without nuance.

We understand this lassitude and this revolt, but we cannot but regret and oppose the decision to take up arms. The road remains long and the work of deep reform requires an exacting mobilisation. Today, despite repression and state terror, we must use all the spaces of freedom still existing in order to create the social and economic dynamics that we have indicated. This strategy exists nowadays in an endogenous fashion in the majority of Muslim countries. The problem lies in the articulation of these interventions around the stakes of power. The priority today is nonetheless not here. It is a question of creating and multiplying centres of popular participation in all domains, including putting pressure on, through legal means, governments and their orientations.

Certainly, the time has not yet arrived, and we can only hope that industrial investment be turned towards its integration with a development which gives priority to agriculture. However, the ability to influence these great decisions remains minimal, almost non-existent. But work on the level of trade workers' organisations, the mobilisation of workers, labourers and, consequently intellectuals, is possible and may bring long-term results. In these last strongholds of democratic representation –

in some countries only – it is possible to make a voice heard that demands a more sound management of the national economy. In Indonesia, the mobilisation of trade workers' organisations has reached 30 million individuals. The same is increasingly becoming important in Jordan, Egypt and Morocco.

Seized by the agony of liberalism, states initiate privatisation or open large sectors of private investment. Making small and medium enterprises stand on their own feet, on the basis of the local mobilisation of the people, is from now on envisageable. The means for larger mass participation is offered with the creation of jobs. These achievements are imperative and must be carried out for as long as the powers in place allow it. It is this same dynamic that must preside over the achievement of development cooperatives, societies of participation, etc. Respect for Islamic rules will be displayed by these operations' daily practices, on a small scale, and far from theoretical discourses which simplify and neglect concrete realities.

Those who have called, since the 1930s and 1940s – and then with more insistence in the 1950s and after declarations of independence – for a revivification of Islamic points of reference as well as for a real liberation from the illusions of modernity *à la Western*, must be observing our epoch with much astonishment. Certainly, they must be regretting the violence of the most radical elements, but who among them had thought that the end of this century would see their ideas rooted in each country, carried out by young intellectuals trained in the most diverse universities, finding echoes in increasingly important sections of the population. The future requires that we take account of these voices and the popular mobilisations that they were able to create. This unless we continue to shut our eyes to words and appellations which, at the heart, justify everything – support for the worst of powers, an iniquitous economic order and the most progressist discourses. Things must change. And if they do not change, responsibility for the ensuing consequences will lie with those who, in order to be clever, failed to be lucid. We cannot ask people to remain docile in the face of the indignant treatment inflicted upon them. Islam calls the Muslims to resistance, a pacific resistance for as long as it takes. But if this peace causes death, then one should expect a war that will defend life. The prelude to the Universal Declaration of Human Rights of 1948, let us recall, does not say anything different:

"Since it is essential that human rights be protected by a rule of law in order that man is not forced, as a last recourse, to revolt against tyranny and oppression."

There still remains time to avoid the worst. In the East as in the West, there are women and men who are determined to give privilege to dialogue and to defend justice. Contact should be made with the same.

B.   *At a Transnational Level*

Mobilisation at local and national levels alone cannot be sufficient at this hour of the globalisation of the economy. The game of alliances at the international level makes things more complex, and requires thinking out a broader strategy of transnational divergence. A great number of modalities, which make this possible, are nowadays available. What remains is to multiply the exchange of experience, create a united front of opposition to the present economic order and, especially, not to be mistaken about who the enemy is.

i.   National experiences

In the 1970s hopes were high when the idea of a "New International Economic Order" (NIEO) surfaced. After the recovery of the Non-Aligned Movement in Bandung (1955), a real front was at last going to emerge in order to consecrate new South-South relations. We know, after nearly a quarter of a century, what the result was. Countries of the South manage their affairs in a dispersed way, submitted to the dictates of industrial states and large financial institutions. The NIEO did not succeed and solidarity between developing countries seems to be a vain hope.

As a parallel, cooperation relating to development had to attend, for a long time, to the most urgent things first. Emergency situations mobilise almost the totality of the capacities of intervention. This without counting that these aids have not always been without political and strategic interests. For 20 years, however, reflection has evolved. Instead of these modes of aid, what is preferred is partnership and attendance towards autonomous taking charge. "Integrated projects" reflect the new ambition of creating local, regional, and even national, dynamics. Numerous experiences were, and still are, fortunate. But one is forced to notice that "aid for development" remains a simple dressing which, in order to cure some ailments, has, nonetheless, not been successful in making the countries of the South emerge from their chronic dependency. The situation is worsening and international cooperations manage, at best, several thousand distant projects which are, in view of the general imbalance, but puffs of oxygen that will not save the people from suffocation. We have even witnessed, during these last years, a political use of humanitarian action whose advocates were put at the middle of inextricable contradictions. "Humanitarian aid" has, for example, sanctioned an intolerable passivity in Bosnia and a dubious intervention in Somalia. All means are good for "aid", and this aid, in consequence, allows us to justify any policy regardless of its strategic scope. Generosity is "free"; and those who are still disillusioned are simple minded.

In Muslim countries, we have witnessed, for the last 20 years, a new phenomenon, where practically all these countries have created for themselves mobilisation movements that include within their ranks intellectuals as well as farmers and workers.[44] The transnational character of this "awakening" is, in the first instance, what frightens the superpowers who increasingly divide in order to better rule. In Washington, London, or in Paris, one pertinently knows that "the American protectorate"[45] that is Saudi Arabia does not finance these movements whose very engagement goes against its interests. But they persist in maintaining this in order to deceive public opinion about the real nature of the danger that the rich countries must face. Inspired by Islamic points of reference, this is the real front of rejection of the world order and its injustices, that is in gestation.

In order to silence these protests, the image of Islam and committed Muslims is so tarnished that, in the hearing and sight of everyone, the governments of the South are given clearance to break and eradicate those who are trying to stop their countries from turning in circles.[46] Massacres, tortures, mass executions and arbitrary arrests are the daily lot of many people. It has been understood, in short, that such is the price to pay in order to preserve Western interests. If for some, human rights are really rights; for others, one is forced to notice that they are nothing more than words.

However, and despite repression, the reality of this presence and of this current of thought is everywhere confirmed. From Morocco to Indonesia, national experiences are mostly long and mature. Some have chosen the way of arms, but the great majority have engaged in profound, long-term work. Small centres of alternative economy are being created at the grass roots far from the states' large, noisy declarations of intention: these are profit-sharing societies, small and medium enterprises and cooperatives of production which allow the people to organise themselves. In the universities, an increasing number of students are reflecting on how to open up the way to a concrete renewal that refers to the values of Islam and which is in tune with contemporary situations. The types of training in the economy are numerous and there is a gradual mastery of the tools of analysis which offer the possibility of bringing innovations in this domain. Undoubtedly, not for several decades, has intellectual effervescence reached such a scope as it has at the end of this century. One feels that one is at a turning point, at a key moment in history and that "something is happening".

In the 1930s and 1940s, just as at the end of the last century, exchanges of experience were numerous. *'Ulamā'* and intellectuals travelled the Continents and compared situations. We know of the incessant movements of Afghani, the "European" travels of 'Abduh, the study-stays of Ibn Badis and Iqbal. Just like men, ideas also circulate. Astonishingly, this movement seems to be a little blurred. Certainly, we travel and take stock of respective situations, but exchanges remain superficial.[47] We study little, and only in a summary fashion, the histories of other Muslim countries, the potential for the mobilisation of people, and the strategies that are confronted by committed movements and states. Were we to do so we would learn efficiency and the synergies would then at last be possible. However, very often it is the contrary that takes place. Conflict between schools of thought, futile animosity, the pretension of doing better and "in the first trial" and, lastly, idleness are as many realities that hinder and delay the union of forces. Different states play perfectly on their partition, and this consists of dividing and confusing. The blindness and naïvety of committed Muslims in economic and social projects lends support to these interventions. The Egyptians of the 1950s had forgotten the lesson of the Ottoman Empire's fall; the Tunisians and Algerians of the 1980s and 1990s did not sufficiently remember the collapse witnessed at the shores of the Nile. Thus goes history, from one event to another, without the experience of the first offering a better, mastered orientation to those who come after them.

It is hoped that the economic and social strategies that have been developed these last years will see a different destiny, outside their frontiers, other than that of negligence. We already notice signs of shared reflection, specific studies, even coordination between different projects which predicts a positive evolution. The transnational character of mobilisation may give rise to a new South-South link which, starting from grass roots movements, may thwart the alliance games that exist between dictatorships and superpowers. This because, ultimately, neither the Saudi government nor the Egyptian, Jordanian, Syrian, Tunisian, Algerian or any other government wants to encourage unity. What is solely important to them is to preserve their privileges regardless of the cost; 10, 20, 30 or 40 thousand dead per day is no big deal. We understand therefore their fear, and the nervous solidarity they entertain one for the other, when they see movements of intellectuals and ordinary people organise themselves in order to shake the seats of their hitherto unlimited powers. It becomes urgent that the players who are engaged, far beyond their own frontiers, contact one another in a more serious and deep fashion. It is appropriate not to neglect anything from history so as to stop falling time after time into the same trap. Finally, it is necessary to find the means to create complementary cooperatives of production and consumption. Along the same lines, exchange of experiences in the realisation of local projects (for example, the elimination of illiteracy, profit-sharing societies, structures of decision or investment) will allow, regardless of the stumbling blocks put in the way, to start from ahead. This road is certainly long, but the way already travelled cannot but fill us with hope.

ii.   A united front of interests: South–South–North

Muslims, very often, confuse the West with the Christian world and even go as far as considering, anyhow, the humanists, atheist communists, and almost all intellectuals as advocates and supporters, when they are not disguised accomplices, of the strategy of the North. If the countries of the South with Christian majorities, Western non-governmental organisations, journalists or researchers are considered at all, the atmosphere is always one of caution. According to this attitude, Islam is the enemy of everyone. Such sentiments are frequent in the Muslim world, as they are also in minority communities in the West. Such is the extent, furthermore, that the intellectual or researcher who tackles a subject dealing with Islam in a general way, with writing or saying what others have done, will immediately arouse in the minds of his Muslim interlocutors a string of questions. Is he a Muslim? What is he up to? What is he hiding? We even see particularly unfortunate scenes whereby suspicion gives way to such infatuation that it ends up by asking journalists or researchers in political science to issue a *fatwā*, i.e. to give a juridical opinion. This shows the degree of ignorance about the other and the lack of maturity which is often still the lot of Muslims on the subject of dialogue. This is so in the East as it is in the West.

It is, furthermore, equally the lot of practically all the alternative movements, so-called of "the left", in Europe and the United States. Militant Islam worries them. They were the advocates and defenders of independence; they often struggled with their socialist comrades of south of the Mediterranean; they shared the same ideals, analyses and terminology. The old advocates have nowadays become dictators or have been eliminated. Who then to support? Strong, credible popular oppositions do not speak the same language. For the latter refer to religion, morality and culture. They also refer to other words, expressions and casts of mind that are disorientating. Rather than trying to understand the meaning from within the points of reference of the other civilisation, they proceed with an apparent comparison. The awakening of Islam, in religious terms, is therefore a return to their Middle Ages. Reactions of rejection, caution and reassuring simplification do not take long to surface. It is difficult to expect anything else from committed men and women in grass roots communities in South America or Africa.[48] For some, the fear of Islam is profound and ancestral; for others, it is always a question of competition about conversion; for many finally, it is the media of the North that almost totally fashions their political posture and their analysis of the situation.

We thus have difficult relations and a deafness in dialogue, and the responsibility for this is shared. We have indicated above the established links and those to be established between different Muslim countries. Here, it should be insisted upon that bridges be built between the different experiences of popular mobilisation in the countries of the South. Anyone who has worked with grass roots communities, developing local social and economic strategies, cannot but be surprised at the similarities that they share with the Muslim experience. The points of reference and the fields of application are certainly different, but the philosophy is the same. The latter is nourished by the same source of resistance to the blind interests of the superpowers and multinationals. We have already said it, it is not a question of maintaining the complacent reality of an Islamic Third Worldism. What is true is that Islam, in that it is the point of reference of committed Muslims, is conveyed by the same exactness of dignity, justice and pluralism as that which fashions the Christian or humanist communal mobilisation. In this, therefore, relations must be multiple and exchanges of experience permanent. Since the 1940s, Muslims have increased these kinds of social integration and researches on the subject of an alternative local economy functioning without interest or usury (profit-sharing societies and others). At the end of the 1960s, the movement created by liberation theology, following, and as a relative extension of, Vatican II, went along the same lines. In both cases, what was defended was an idea of the human being, of his dignity, of his duties and rights. The texts of Cardinal Guttierez, Leonardo Boff, or the firm declaration of the ex-Archbishop De Recife and Dom Helder Camara cannot but find a favourable and supportive echo with the Muslims if they take time to study them. In the same way, the fundamental claims of the Muslims, if time is taken to know them, cannot but win the adherence of liberation theologians and of their Christian and humanist supporters. Who among them know the text and themes of the Turkish Said al-Nursi, the Algerian Ibn Badis, the Indian Iqbal, or the Egyptian Hasan al-Banna? The latter, so much criticised and so little read, and who, during a congress, was supported by three Christians who said to him: "If such is your project of a society, then we are with you." And how many other intellectuals and Muslim activists, after him, have conveyed the same claims; whether 'Abd al-Salam Yasin[49], Malek Bennabi or Abu al-Hasan al-Nadwi who, from Morocco to India, all defended the same cause.

Respective supporters ignore one another, however, with a culpable ignorance. The relations and unions of South-South, which have become impossible at governmental level, should have been multiplied at the level of theologians, intellectuals, associations, structures, and cooperatives; what covers today in development, in the language of experts, the level "meso". The dispersed centres of resistance which, further, ignore or fear one another and in which are engaged Christians, humanists and Muslims, act, finally, in a way that is not very responsible. The waste of energy, useless conflicts, maintained divisions and perpetuated ignorances that such a situation engenders are very damaging. This state of affairs serves only the interests of the superpowers. The media, dubious news, unfounded cautions, which are so much and daily denounced, end up by getting the better of our engagements when the greatest vigilance should be applied. From the Muslim side, as from the Christian and humanist sides, we allow ourselves to withdraw into ourselves to some certainties that are not communicable as also to an anathema that excludes. This despite all the discourses calling for mutual understanding and dialogue. We talk to one another but without listening to each other. In truth, an authentic dialogue between Jews, Christians, humanists and Muslims cannot but lead to a formidable common action of resistance to human folly, injustice and exploitation. What remains belongs to "salon" religion and the humanism of conference. Good sentiments, when still referred to, around meeting and banquet tables, are façile sentiments that do not honour those who end up by forgetting the human tenor of what they say, and say again and again. Understandably, they simply speak and nothing else.

Moreover, the relays in the West are not lacking. All Westerners do not support the policies of the superpowers and multinationals, just as all Muslims living in the West are not linked to the dictators of Islamic countries. Work relations and exchanges of experience should equally be increased in the West in order to launch a broader front of rejection. Beforehand, we must try to better know and understand one another as also free ourselves in common domains of action. Europe and the United States offer possibilities which are unmatched but which are still not exploited as they should be. Dialogue remains cold and timid and only basically touches theoretical or very abstract considerations, when they are not simply good mutual intentions. However, reciprocal recognition in the North, common exchange and reflection around concrete, economic, social and political questions are an important part of the dynamics existing in the South. Encounters between intellectuals, researchers, theologians and those in the field (social workers, development experts, etc.) can encourage and orientate the *rapprochement* that we hope for in the domains of misery and exploitation. One must be responsible without being naïve. Differences exist, the conflict of interests remain, the situations are complex and good-will is not enough to erase the dangers and all the differences with the specificity of objectives and hopes. We cannot expect a Jew, a Christian or a humanist, who sincerely respects Islam to the extent of concretely committing himself with the Muslims, to accept everything in Islam or of what the believers say. Similarly, we cannot ask Muslims to prove their openness of mind by a series of concessions which would empty the message they carry of its essential content. On the level of economic practices, social strategies or political orientations, some questions will remain hard nuts that are impossible to crack. Real pluralism consists of respecting what is essential to the human being who wants "to be" in his fundamental identity. The task is not at all easy; it presupposes having attained a maturity which indicates that saying, writing or doing more means wanting to say, write and do a lot.

It is urgent to create, in the West, bridges of common dialogue and action between all those who, in the name of their faith and/ or their conscience, cannot approve the present state of the world. Caution and reticence must be overcome. To assert that we are still very far away is to say little. The West is still a monster in the minds of some, and Muslims remain obscure fundamentalists for others. Here and there, however, in London, Paris and Washington as in other cities, links are being established, intellectuals are meeting each other, religious people are speaking with one another, social players are calling out for one another, and experts are together dealing with concrete problems. This is certainly being done on a small scale, but these are the first stages of an imperative, long-term work. It is the required passage for the creation of a united South-South-North front.

iii.   Not to be mistaken about the enemy[50]

It is not a question of having the same ideas, ideals or hopes. God wanted diversity; therefore, there must be pluralism and mutual respect. It is urgent to express what we reject, to define that which is for us unacceptable by engaging ourselves to do everything in order that it is not, effectively, accepted, normalised or becomes commonplace. In a world where the economic has supplanted the political, where financial and commercial interests are made a reason of state, where values are referred to only when they are not detrimental to the most obscure transactions and contracts, in such a world, we say, it is appropriate not to be mistaken about who is the enemy, and to make alliances with all those to whom the life of a person has a sense and value. The latter are those who reject murderous folly in order to defend faith, respect, dignity, fraternity and love. These are, finally, those who, driven by their convictions, are determined to disengage their whole life by accepting to face up to all dangers, sufferings and betrayals. This because it cannot be a question of "dabbling" in our struggle for more justice, citing one day the great principles in order to lose ten other days in forgetfulness and great holidays. For Muslims the Qur'ānic reminder is clear:

> Say: 'My prayer, my ritual sacrifice, my living, my dying – all belong to God, the Lord of all Being. No associate has He. Even so I have been commanded, and I am the first of those that surrender.' (Qur'ān, 6:162–3)

It is a total gift of oneself that one must consent with; and this with faith, resolve and hope:

> God has bought from the believers their selves and their possessions against the gift of Paradise. (Qur'ān, 9:111)

Here, we find this call addressed to the People of the Book in the Qur'ān. We understand, by extension, that the Torah and the Gospel require of the Jews and Christians moral and human commitments that must be accomplished in their totality in order not to be content with just calling oneself "Jew" or "Christian" without any other concrete and daily witness:

> Surely We have sent down the Torah, wherein is guidance and light... (Qur'ān, 5:44)

And We sent following in their footsteps, Jesus son of Mary,
confirming the Torah before him; and We gave him the Gospel,
wherein is guidance and light, and confirming the Torah before
it, as a guidance and an admonition unto the godfearing.
(Qur'ān, 5:46)

The circumscribed meaning of the verse which follows
expresses a call to the People of the Book to return more clearly
and profoundly to their teachings:

Say: 'People of the Book, you do not stand on anything, until you
perform the Torah and the Gospel, and what was sent down to you
from your Lord.' (Qur'ān, 5:68)

To be Jewish or Christian today presupposes a total devotion
by the person who is haunted by his respective spirituality and
by the strong moral recommendation that he finds as his point
of reference. Authentic Jewish spirituality, the true Biblical
teaching and profound Christian mysticism cannot accept the
world's status quo with its unjust societies, perverse policies and
an immoral world economy. It is here that we find the source of
union and identification of the enemy, the first enemy.

The engagement of all humanists must be of the same nature:
just good sentiments result only in nice evening parties when
they are expressed around a dinner table and forgotten the
following day. The world needs a mobilisation at all moments.
The worst enemy of men nowadays has become, both in the
North as in the South, this idleness and lassitude which will end
up, in the long run, by accepting everything. The majority of
citizens do not feel any more the need to measure their freedom
by means of a real exercise of the power that ensues from it.

The world and society are given in this present state as a finality.
Happiness, therefore, consists in finding a "good" place, a
"comfortable" one from all standpoints. In fact, the sentiment
of responsibility and the will of engagement are, we can say,
unnatural. They necessitate such an "uprooting" that is only
experienced by a few *believers*, *idealists* and *utopians*. Realism

confines to passivity; one is certainly "humanist", in a wide sense, but without much effort. Yet, as much in the North as in the South, never has the urgency for a total, organised and unified engagement been so blatant. Each human, religious, spiritual or "community" of conscience must find the means to vivify the energy of its points of reference in order to give strength and vigour to the imperative of action for good and justice. In the diversity of beliefs, the witness of sincerity lies in acting:

> *If God had willed, He would have made you one nation; but that He may try you in what has come to you. So be you forward in good works; unto God shall you return, all together; and He will tell you of that whereon you were at variance.* (Qur'ān, 5:48)

Until the day comes when we are all illuminated about our differences of opinion, there is but one possible action: doing good and fighting against whatever gets in the way of the same. The plurality of communities is presented in the precedent verse as the positive, catalysing factor of a kind of competition for justice. Today, it is as a factor of division and conflict in an indignant horror and ignorance. Our sufficiency is pathetic and inhuman. In the sense that we have meant above, the opposite of idleness is *jihād*. Passivity is indeed one of the major obstacles which must be faced by social players and responsibles of NGOs in the shanty towns of the South as in the industrialised cities of the North. Acceptance tires, forgetting the exactness of faith or justifying in conscience, is another enemy.

The awakening of consciences and the search for union must be accompanied with an increased vigilance. As long as there is no attempt, in the West, to understand the claims of Muslims relating to respect for their religion, civilisation, and culture and which, in order to do so, try to elaborate by trial and error a project of society that is proper to them; as long as this path is not engaged upon, the possibility of moving towards concrete collaborations will be delayed, and with it the hope of a transition which does not bring two civilisations into conflict. It is often the most "progressist" corners who are the most virulent towards Islam and what is often called the "Islamic awakening". Their judgements are without nuance and, sometimes, as swift and sharp as the time they have taken to study the question and listen to the players of the other civilisation. Hotchpotches are the rule. The committed Muslim is inevitably armed or viscerally patriarchal. It is impossible to imagine points of encounter, common exigencies or a similar respect for life and its values. Playing the game of the superpowers, the defender of justice, values, and humanism identifies his enemy in the civilisation that is facing him as also in the defender of this same justice, values and man. Conflict is created there where there must be dialogue, if not at least listening. The same intellectual re-routing is found among Muslims who make out of the West, as already indicated, a monolithic block which inevitably holds conflicts, and where there is not a man or woman who is not touched or undermined by moral perdition, materialism, violence or corruption. The picture is not only excessive but it is also erroneous and deceptive. It does not say anything about all the women and men who give of their time, energy and life in order to change things. It remains silent about millions of human beings who suffer from the present state of the world, people who, from loneliness to disarray, hang on to all and anything just to survive. It, finally, skips over all the rights, spaces of freedom, acknowledgements of dignity offered to citizens in the West, a simple hundredth of which is longed for in Muslim countries. These realities are to be known and acknowledged.

It is impossible to carry on with this caricaturising of the other that is armed with extreme simplifications. For sincere Muslims, just as for loyal Jews, Christians and humanists, the fight must be engaged against the reason of state and the inhumane economic strategies achieved by the USA, the IMF or by Saudi Arabia, and the Gulf states; as also against the dictatorships of Tunisia, Syria and Egypt, against social exclusions, misery, delinquency and drugs in the USA, France, Belgium or England. All this by acknowledging for the other the right to decide his faith, values and social projects; as also by a legitimate return to the living sources of his religion, spirituality, culture and civilisation. This in a total respect for his right to live his identity. To see the other only in the mirror of one's own points of reference and to judge the differences as so many deviancies is simplistic, caricaturising and dangerous. Prejudice is often worse than acknowledgement of one's ignorance. To think that one knows and to simplify things is a confession of sluggish sufficiency, and this is another enemy.

Notes

1. Susan George, *Jusqu'au cou, enquête sur la dette du tiers monde*, La découverte, 1988, pp.68–71 and after. The emphasis in the second citation is ours.
2. It is not a question here of criticising the whole of what has been undertaken. Some societies have truly functioned without interest and developed a moral attitude in the treatment of their affairs, in the choice of projects as well as in their clients-partners. Here, we are discussing the basis of such a project and pointing out the important disfunctioning that has accompanied it. See, on "the affair Salsabil" (in Egypt) and its famous societies, Abdel-Sattar's book *Qaḍiyyat Salsabīl*, Cairo, 1992, and the research carried out by Alain Roussillon, at the CEDEJ of Cairo. Dossiers du CEDEJ, *Societés islamiques de placements de fonds et "ouverture économique"*, Cairo, 1988.
3. On the translation of the notion of *zakāt*, we reproduce here a note that we have included in *Les Musulmans dans la laïcité* (p.43): "Orientalists have translated the notion of *zakāt* as 'legal charity' and often Muslims have followed in their footsteps. Yet, the formulation 'legal charity' is constrained starting from the Christian notion of charity which expresses donation, charity, to which they added its legal aspect in order to get closer to the idea that *zakāt* covers in Islam. At the origin of this formulation, we perceive the difficulty of translating with clarity the specificity of this duty which relates both to personal worship as to social engagement, in that it is an exactness before God and before the institution of the state. There was some discomfort in explaining this pillar of Islam which, by its very nature, disturbed the categories known in Christianity (and relatively in Judaism) regarding private worship, social obligation, and the sacred and the profane. The most adequate translation should be the expression purifying social tax which covers the three dimensions of the notion of *zakāt*. It is a duty before God and before man (tax); it is levied for the benefit of men and women who are members of a society (the poor and needy: Qur'ān 9:60 mentions eight categories of beneficiaries – this is the social aspect); in the conscience of the believers, it is the right of God and the poor on his property: once this part is given, his possession is properly purified. This last sacred dimension invests a social act which from the first sight looks profane."

4. Cf. *Les Musulmans dans la laïcité*, op. cit., for a presentation of the Five Pillars, pp.43–54.

5. See in particular the abundant work of the Egyptian economist, Yusuf Kamal. He exerted himself to present Islamic economics, comparing this system with that of capitalism and socialism. Moreover, he looked for concrete answers for the specific situation presented in contemporary Egypt.

6. All religions agree on the essence of this truth and all the founding texts convey this scope.

7. Some *aḥādīths* indirectly confirm the sense of this authorisation – we find for example the *ḥadīth* reported by Ibn Māja: "Your properties and your lives are forbidden." Or, again: "The properties of a Muslim are forbidden (for you to take) except if they consent" (reported by Bukhārī). We understand by the reminder of his inviolability, the reality of permission.

8. Two *aḥādīths*, at least, confirm this prohibition: "Whosoever monopolises a good in the aim of bidding higher (commits) a mistake." And: "The importer is fortunate and the monopolist is cursed" (narrated by Aḥmad).

9. A *waqf* designates the goods given to social institutions. These cannot be sold, bequeathed or inherited.

10. It is impossible to engage here, in detail, about those goods which are subjected to *zakāt*, nor examine the conditions without which this tax is not due (the real possession of the good, its quality or value, its growth, non-indebtedness, etc.).

11. According to the majority of jurists, 2.5% regarding *zakāt* on money, but the rates vary depending on whether it is a question of animals, agriculture or other things. For more details, see the excellent work of Dr. Yusuf Qaradawi, *Fiqhu 'l-Zakāt* (The Comprehension-Legislation of *Zakāt*), 2 Vols., Mu'asasat al-Risala, Beirut, 1986.

12. The Qur'ān almost always mentions together the obligation of prayer and *zakāt*. In *Sūra al-Baqara*, the injunction of prayer – which is the foundation of the whole Islamic practice – is mentioned before and after that of tax: *And perform the prayer, and pay the alms, and bow with those that bow.* (Qur'ān, 2:43).

13. There is no payment of *zakāt* on goods which do not offer a possibility of growth (means of production, for example). But, as we have seen, *zakāt* on money exists because when it is hoarded it does not bring any growth; the fact that *zakāt* is, nevertheless, levied is a clear inducement for investment and work.

14. *L'islam vivant* (Living Islam), Les belles impressions, 1986, p.74. Let us note here that the percentage of 2.5% is not unique as we have seen and that the 40 years which are mentioned in the quotation is a simple calculus which does not take into account the variable of levying. Nonetheless, the principle that Roger Garaudy disengages is clearly one of the aims of the obligation of *zakāt*. It is effectively a question of the Islamic philosophy of property and its management.

15. A *Ḥadīth* reported by Muslim. There are many other *aḥādīths* which are along the same line.

16. Hamid Algabid, *Les banques islamiques,* Economica, 1990, p.43.

17. Op. cit., p.76.

18. It is a question here of a practice of "compound interest" which was known at the time of the Prophet (peace be upon him) and even before and this consisted of paying the creditor double the initial loan.

19. He confirmed the meaning, scope and especially the importance, when he reminded us of this prohibition during the farewell pilgrimage. He mentioned the prohibition by accompanying it with a mention of the practices of his uncle al-'Abbas.

20. The book of Jean-Christophe Rufin, *La dictature libérale,* J.C. Lattes, 1994, is particularly interesting on this subject.

21. See the books of Susan George, *Comment meurt l'autre moitié du monde, les vraies raisons de la faim dans le monde,* R. Laffont, 1978; *Les stratèges de la faim,* Grounauer, Geneva, 1981; and lastly the very informative *Crédits sans frontière, la religion séculière de la Banque mondiale,* La découverte, 1994, written in collaboration with Fabrizio Sabelli.

22. It often fell to me, during meetings or colloquia, to present this point of view, which has already been dubbed as supporter of the "Third World". It is appropriate that one not be mistaken. If by supporter of the "Third World" one means the expression of a desire for justice and respect for human dignity, which is inevitably conveyed in an opposition to the policies dictated by the North, then certainly the expression has this dimension. But, in truth, the discourse of the supporters of the "Third World" of the second half of this century join the Divine injunctions which nourish all religions, and not the opposite. Islam, in this sense, calls Muslims to a determined resistance against exploitation and injustice. In the 1960s it was a question of "socialism", today it is a question of "Third Worldism" of a new "Islamic theology of liberation" or again of a "militant fundamentalism". This according to the degree of sympathy felt towards this phenomenon. It is, nonetheless, a question of returning to the message within which we find the fiercest opposition against the denial of rights as against unworthy orders. Is there any religion that teaches otherwise? Since the first dawn, all religions were "Third Worldist", that is if anachronisms do not frighten us.

23. We shall return below to Islamic banks.

24. Four years later, in 1971, the Egyptian power created its own social bank: The Nasser Social Bank of Egypt which served as a model to the great Islamic state banks that are far from achieving popular mobilisation.

25. One must make allowance for the criticisms which are showered on the Sudan. Is it really a question of defending human rights? Or is it fear of the strategic influence of this country? If it was only a question of human rights, then the criticism directed towards the Sudan should be multiplied ten-fold towards Egypt (where there are more than 60,000 prisoners of conscience) or Saudi Arabia. Yet, we hear nothing of the sort. Political and economic interests have their reason that silence justifies. Comparison is still not a

reason. It is appropriate to discern the nuance of the analysis. It is quite obvious that the Sudan is attacked today because it opposes the American and Zionist policies in the region; it also annoys the respective strategies of alliance games or the take-over of Africa. For whoever visits the Sudan, it is clear that Sudanese rulers have indeed less blood on their hands than some other Arab rulers of the area. The conflict of the South, one must emphasise, is one that has been inherited from the colonial epoch, with the British rule that divided the North from the South. In no way is it a question of a war of religion which sees Muslims opposing Christians. For the Muslims and the Christians represent but 35% to 36% of the whole population of the South; the rest is made up of animists. One must equally take account of the permanent conflicts between different opposing factions in the South. Finally, it is all the displaced people of the animist South – Muslims and Christians – who are ill-treated. Visiting camps around Khartoum confirm this. Nonetheless, one must clearly say that the present regime does not offer minimal guarantees for political pluralism, that opposition parties are muzzled and that cronyism is the rule. Muslims are called to remain vigilant, for the opposition of the United States and Israel is not enough to support the "Islamic" character of a project. Criticism of excess and injustice imposes itself; just as bringing to the fore original ideas is part of an equitable analysis.

26. Jean-Marie Albertini, *Méchanismes du sous-développement et développements*, Éditions Ouvrières, 1983, pp.250–2. The emphasis is that of the author.

27. Behind any social project dubbed "Islamist" in the West, are seen the generous hands of Saudi Arabia, Iran and lately the Sudan. The alliance game and the affirmations of the power in place are quite obvious. However, in this at least two elements are not taken into account. The first is the privileged relationship which links Saudi Arabia to the West, and, thus, we cannot see that this State would, with Western approval, finance "activists" who are so opposed to the West. As regards Iran and the Sudan, the situation is slightly different. The former has not so far engaged in social projects in *Sunnī* lands. As for the Sudan, it is so poor and has so many difficulties in implementing its own national economy that it would be very strange if it invested outside of its frontiers. The second of these elements is the endogenous character of these social activities in all countries and the capacity of mobilising funds at the popular level, chiefly, through the payment of *zakāt* (which is levied through alternative channels since certain states have neglected this third pillar of Islam) or through donations.

28. A lot of noise was made, in the Autumn of 1994, with regard to the International Conference on Population which was held in Cairo under the auspices of the UNO. The mobilisation of Muslim and Christian authorities against the propositions of the preparatory document of the Conference (as also during its progress) allowed the press to run huge titles: reactionary Vatican and Muslim Fundamentalists have agreed on dogmatic positions which oppose abortion and birth control. Yet, things were too simplified.

One must recognise, however, that the reading of some Muslims, who asserted that there was an attempt to control birth by means of abortion, was a very tendentious reading which was baseless. Thus, they have not helped to clarify the debate. It remains that a great number of those who opposed this Conference have formulated profound criticism with regard to the formulated propositions. In effect, to discuss the problems of demography without speaking about the problem of the unjust repartition of the wealth of the world, is tantamount to avoiding the real debate. The Conference tackled the effects without going as far as the causes which further implicate the superpowers and Third World countries. In this, the spirit of openness of the progressists was selective and heedless of this fact. This without counting the blunders which were repeated in the formulation. Islam is not opposed to contraception as there is no position of definitive rejection of abortion. In the latter, the juridical decision is decided case by case. It remains that fear of poverty cannot justify either contraception or abortion. The jurists base themselves generally on verse 31 of *Sūra* 17 to confirm this decision.

> *And slay not your children for fear of poverty; We will provide for you and them; surely the slaying of them is a grievous sin.* (Qur'ān, 17:31)

It remains, however, that the demographic explosion is a real threat to the running of our societies. This means that we should not formulate things of the same kind. We know nowadays that the literacy of populations, and particularly women, is inversely proportional to the rate of birth. The more women are educated the less they bear children. This datum is confirmed by all field studies. The struggle against galloping demography in Muslim lands will be the result of a vast work of schooling rather than due to the exportation of techniques which, in their precise case of use, are opposed to the Islamic concept. Education must be a priority for every state, whether of the South or the North, that is keen to prepare for the future. It remains to measure the real political will of the powers to see the people aware and mobilised. It could well be that the great International Conferences hide sombre objectives and are deceiving us about their intentions.

29. The creation, for instance, of "agricultural loans" goes along these lines. The main goal being to support small farmers by avoiding usury. Furthermore, these loans enable the modernisation of agriculture. This kind of loan is perfectly adaptable to the reality of Muslim countries.

30. We find again this point of reference quoted abundantly in the report of the World Bank: *L'ajustement en Afrique, réformes, résultats et chemin à parcourir*, 1994.

31. Article published in *New Perspectives Quarterly* (Los Angeles Times) and translated in *Liberation* of 5 August 1994 under the title of 'The New Awakening of Islam'.

32. See on this subject the interesting and optimistic book by Pierre Pradervan, *Une Afrique en marche*, Plon, Paris, 1989.

33. See our contribution, 'La pensée d'un siècle', in the book entitled *Péril islamiste?*, edited by Alain Gresh, Edition Complexes, Brussels, 1994.

34. We shall return below to liberation theology and its advocates; let us here note our astonishment regarding certain judgements. Religious people who interfere in the field of politics and profess ideas commonly linked to the centre right are treated as fundamentalists, and more or less, as extremists. The same does not hold true with regard to the religious person who defends ideas focused on social engagement, the defence of the poor and the homeless. Thus, the political interventions of Dom Helder Camara some time ago, of Father Artistide recently or again Abbot Pierre are appreciated and encouraged. They also have public sympathy. Therefore, everything leads us to believe that it is not the insertion of the religious in politics which poses a problem, but rather the nature of the religious point of reference. This "natural" nuance in the Christian sphere loses its pertinence the moment that one speaks of Islam. In the case of Islam, engaging in the defence of the poor or carrying the most reactionary ideas does not make any difference. Judgement here falls like a chopper: "fundamentalists". There is no nuance *vis-à-vis* those who do not resemble us. One would, however, benefit from measuring one's judgement and analysing in-depth the work carried out by Muslims who are engaged on the social level and who, in this process, are opposed to dictators. The latter like to depict those who are opposed to them as obscurantist bomb planters. While the great powers, being aware of the interests at play, are quick to follow and confirm the statements of the oppressive powers that they support.

    One may find many similarities between the strategies of the South American grass roots communities and the "legalist", Islamist movement. One should, furthermore, remember the policy of information put in place by the USA which, until recently, depicted all priest-workers as Marxists who needed to be fought against. The strategy is the same. However, one should not be mistaken about the enemy. During a meeting I had with Dom Helder Camara in Recife, he pointed to the laughable *rapprochement* that is made between the diabolically "Marxist" character of his engagement and the "fundamentalism" of Muslims.

35. We are not speaking here of governmental projects which, as in Malaysia or Iran for example, have tried to create a more or less happy social dynamic.

36. Albert Jacquard, *J'accuse l'économie triomphante*, Calmann-Lévy, 1995, p.79.

37. Op. cit., pp.151–3.

38. One must clarify, however, that Al Rajhi Company for Currency Exchange and Commerce (about which we are talking here) which is established in Saudi Arabia is not authorised to function as an Islamic bank. Hence, there exists no such Islamic bank on the entire Saudi territory. We should also observe that the six principal Saudi State institutions, even if they lend money without interest, place their liquid assets in the financial market and integrate interests to the accountability of their revenues, whereas all other banks function according to the classical model and are partly linked with

the Western banking network. We would be astonished to see this being considered as a strict application of the *Sharīʿa*. Once again, we seem to circumscribe this to the penal domain, when it does not justify political opposition to change. This as if the Islamic *Sharīʿa* is silent about the great economic orientations. The reading is here obviously selective. As we have already indicated, its use of petro-dollars, in the 1960s, was proof that the Saudi government preoccupied itself very little with the problems of development. The integration of its economic system into the international order and the character of its investments in the West confirm it. Saudi Arabia is an advanced stronghold of capitalist economics in Muslim lands. And this in its very centre, the land of Makka and Madina. On Saudi Arabia see the book by De Foulquier, *La dictature protégée*, and Alain Gresh's article in *Le Monde Diplomatique*, August 1995: 'Fin de régne en Arabie Saoudite'.

39. *Les capitaux de l'islam*, Presses du CNRS, Ed. Gilbert Beaugé, 1990, p.189.

40. See on this subject the recent book by Professor Hacéne Benmansour, *Politique économique en Islam*, Al Qalam, 1994. A full chapter deals in a very critical fashion with the Islamic banks. See also A'Salah, *al-Takāful al-Ijtimāʿi fi'l-Sharīʿa al-islāmiyya*, 1985.

41. We know today three principal, financial techniques which are allowed in Islam: 1. *Muḍāraba*: a contract between a person – or a bank – who provides capital to another who offers work whilst sharing risk and profit according to an agreed percentage. 2. *Mushāraka*: the participation of a contracting party – individual or bank – in the capital of a new society – in a project or direct investment – with the possibility of buying shares. 3. *Murābaḥa*: an institution buys a commodity for a person and sells it to him with an agreed margin of profit. We also know the sale called *al-salam* (a commodity delivered after payment). The banks basically practise the technique of *al-Murābaḥa*. This poses a problem, from the viewpoint of Islamic law, in the way it is practised today as also on account of the fuzziness found in its regulations. Serious liberties have been taken, through terminological side-steps, with regard to the principles of Islam. There exists another problem – which is particularly serious – regarding the objectives of these banks that transform themselves into commercial enterprises which give privilege to big-scale, short-term transactions without any other alternative strategy.

42. The banks also equip themselves with juridical councils whose members are waged. Thus, the "Islamic" rulings given are not always independent and instead serve to sanction the financial policy of the institutions themselves.

43. Op. cit., p.278.

44. It is still persistently claimed that one, two or three countries finance these "activists" from the outside, and that the real nature of their anchorage in the specific national realities is still rejected.

45. This expression is borrowed from Jean-Michel Foulquier, *Arabie Saoudite, la dictature protégée*, Albin Michel, 1995, p.125. The author quotes in the epigraph, verse 34 of *Sūra al-Naml*: "In truth, when kings enter a city,

they bring to it corruption and transform its respectable citizens into vile persons. Thus do they act" (we quote his translation as it is). The book illustrates this theme.

46. In this sense, the inhuman impassivity of Western people *vis-à-vis* the massacres in Bosnia consecrate the total success of the media enterprise in its diabolisation of Islam. As the Serb General Mladic has said: "From now on there is difficulty in getting mobilised for the sake of Muslims."

47. Many students of Islamic Studies go to Saudi Arabia or Cairo to learn their religion. Evidently, this is a very good thing to do. Unfortunately, one realises that, outside these theoretical studies, most students do not take the time to study the social, economic and political situations. They give themselves little in terms of the means of such studies. They confuse "*ṭalab al-ʿilm*" (seeking knowledge) with bookish and doctrinal knowledge alone. Such was not the case with the Prophet (peace be upon him) who, to mention but one example, asked Ibn Thābit to learn Hebrew for the sake of understanding and communication. We ought to remember this.

48. South American Protestant sects that are nowadays very widespread as well as the most fundamentalist Catholic quarters evidently do not envisage reviewing their secular judgement on the "Islamic heresy", or again, "the gentle and dangerous dream born in the mind of an Arab in the VIIth century".

49. While writing these lines, I had a profound and brotherly thought for Shaykh Abd al-Salam Yasin who is under house arrest in Morocco and who is the author of many important books. Among his French books that we know is *La révolution a l'heure de l'islam*, Carlo Descamps, France, 1990. Recently, he has written a book specifically on a very profound interest: *Ḥiwār maʿa al-Fuḍalā' al-Dimuqrāṭiyyīn* [Dialogue with the Eminent Democrats), in Arabic. Read, among others, the chapter on Democracy and *Shūrā* which reveals the scope of the spiritual teachings of Yasin. Dr. Said Ramadan reminded me that during one of his interventions in Morocco under Muhammad V, it is the present King Hasan II who, for technical reasons and with much humility, held the microphone for him for the whole of his speech. He called then to the same message and spirituality, to the same respect of Divine teaching and Islamic culture that Shaykh Yasin calls for today. Hasan II, years later, forgot part of the message, the essential part, and now places houses under surveillance.

50. This expression is certainly known. In using it here, I am thinking of my friend Pierre Dufresne, ex-editor of the Geneva Catholic journal *Le Courrier* who uses it by giving it the meaning of the struggle of all his life. He calls upon Jews, Christians, Muslims and humanists alike to work together. The common enemy is injustice, repression, exploitation and conniving silence. His engagement, in this sense, was and remains exemplary.

Part Three

Values and Finalities
The Cultural Dimension of the
Civilisational Face to Face

The Cultural Dimension

For some years now, one has noticed the daily coverage of Islam by the Western media: fundamentalism, the situation of women, freedom of speech and human rights being the subjects that are almost exclusively dealt with. Of Islam as such nothing of substance is known. Orientalists have given way to political scientists and "social researchers" who, through an almost legitimate lack of professionalism, confuse the essence of the Qur'ānic Message with the contingencies of its manifestations that are, often, its most spectacular ones. Through analysing what goes on throughout the world such as in Algeria, Egypt, Pakistan and Kashmir, they have become the helping intermediary of the media. They have become "experts on Islam". However, such a shortcut is perilous.

Deep down the debate is, thus, at the end of the twentieth century, conjured away. The world of Islam appears to us through the most repelling events and, hence, one cannot help believing that it is, fundamentally, an enemy of the West. Anything that confirms this conclusion is "true"; and anything that disturbs the superficiality of this analysis is "suspect". People "know" from now on because television has shown them "the images", radio has reported "the statements", and newspapers have confirmed "the thesis". The contribution of such or such a researcher simply consists of scientific caution in debate. Public opinion is, thus, made, formed, informed and moulded, while the political responsibles are not required to become too involved in the debate.

The specialisation of competences enables profuse advances in the respective domains of research. It is a consequent progress.

However, they become dangerous when these same domains are not clearly defined, and when such or such a researcher, who is well versed in the study of a social dynamic in a given country, within a relatively short historical sequence, allows himself to elaborate theses and formulate general conclusions which are clearly outside of his field of competence. There is, unfortunately, nowadays a propensity towards this hardly scientific type of process. It is, therefore, very urgent to return to this issue. It is the only means to produce a more in-depth analysis of what "the revival of Islam" covers today. For decades – if not centuries – this revival and new affirmation of the Qur'ānic Message transmitted by the Prophet (peace be upon him), is spoken about, announced, feared or hoped for. There is, nonetheless, little doubt that something is happening today "from Islam's side". Soon, we will have a billion and a half faithful, grass roots mobilisations in all countries, "re-Islamisation" there, or identity-based affirmation here; popular claims are increasingly heard. In the face of the West, the Muslim world is swept by a new energy, both active and reactive at the same time, which marks its specificity on a grand scale.

The West is used to dealing with sources possessing a restrained, traditional culture such as the Indians of North America and the Aborigines of Australia. These enthnicities do not endanger the supremacy of rationalist and modernist points of reference. For the first time in two centuries, and in a more "confrontational" manner, that even the Chinese or Japanese horizon could not pose, the Islamic world contests the universality of Western values either by relativising or questioning them. The question is not any longer that of enthnicities which are scattered on the face of the earth. This time, it is a question of a face to face and, there is nothing more normal than fear and tension. One may pour into one's analysis the worst, and predict an inevitable conflict – a "clash" according to Huntington – between the West and Islam which will cause wars and mutual rejection. After Communism, it is assumed that Islam will endanger the modern gains of liberty, personal responsibility and comfort. Thus, it is necessary to protect oneself from it by any means because democracies have the right to guard themselves against horrors, as Bernard-Henri Lévy has said; or because there is, here, a play of power and because "liberal dictatorship" is fed by the productions of diabolic adversity, as pointed out by Jean-Christophe Rufin. It all depends.

We can, nonetheless, hope that a real debate will take place. A debate that will offer the possibility of better knowing what Islam makes of the Muslim human being. One which will also allow legitimising of some of the claims which are so widespread today. It seems evident that we do find common values and requirements, similar orientations and identical objectives, just as it is no less evident that divergences also exist. Trying to understand, determining strong lines of dialogue and collaboration, not dissimulating irreconcilable points of reference, such seems to be the process of responsible men and women who have understood the meaning of what gerency (*khilāfa*) on earth entails as well as the nature of humanist exactness. To know Islam nowadays, despite the most shocking news which is emitted by networks that are subject to the reign of speed, is to take the time to understand its cultural dimension. The religious point of reference has given rise to a quite particular system of values, a way of being in the world and how to place oneself therein. Based on the principle of harmony and balance, the Islamic horizon has suffered great pain in living its real life, in finding its place and in fulfilling itself in Western categories and modes of being. Coexistence requires that one takes things into consideration, and then with full knowledge of the facts.

I. PROMETHEUS AND ABRAHAM

1. The West: Fire, Rebellion and Tension

Since the Renaissance we have become accustomed to thinking that the two fundamental sources of Western culture are Graeco-Roman and Judaeo-Christian. Admittedly, this "reduction" has rightly been reconsidered, and many are those historians, researchers and scientists who have reminded us of the preponderant place of the Arab-Islamic heritage in the process which, since the Middle Ages, allowed through the discovery of the writers of Antiquity the first mumblings of rationalism and liberation *vis-à-vis* clerical authority. Coexistence, encounter, exchanges between the two civilisations are not of today but Islam has participated in the evolution of Western culture.

These mutual contributions between the West and Islam have not so much effaced the fundamental specificities which exist between the two traditions and their histories. We cannot insist too much here on the basic and profound difference in the respective concepts of the sacred which, *a fortiori*, has a concrete bearing on the relationship that man entertains with the Divine. In order to do so, one has to go all the way back to Greek mythology. Coming closer to this, and trying to understand the double rapport of identification and competition which exists between gods and men, cannot be consistent without analysing the decisive and symbolic scope of the myth of Prometheus, "the great friend of men", according to Nietzsche's expression. The figure of the titan appeared for the first time at least when, for some unspecified reason, the gods and men – after numerous struggles between the gods, titans and men – were separated. In order to protect men, Prometheus tried to deceive Zeus. From this moment on, it is conflict which colours the rapport between gods and men and tension will never disappear. The latter is a component of being in the world of men (despite the mirror comportment of the inhabitants of Olympus who offer innocence to creatures). Later, Prometheus steals fire from heaven and suffers the pain of binding and eternal chastisement, condemned to have his liver devoured by an eagle. Prometheus sacrificed himself for men by defying the gods. His is the first transgression and the first chastisement.

From early on, this event was interpreted in two completely opposing ways. But, deep down, both ways acknowledge the reality of conflict, challenge and tension. For Hesiod, Prometheus had consecrated the intervention of "evil" in the world. According to his interpretation, "far from being a benefactor of humanity, Prometheus is responsible for the present decadence."[1] One notices a similarity between the scope of this act and that of Eve and Adam in the Judaeo-Christian tradition: pride is a disobedience which is, in itself, an expression of evil. The tragic poet Aeschylus, as early as the sixth-fifth centuries before Christ, presented a more "modern" reading of this myth. Here, Prometheus is a civilising hero, one of the greatest heroes. In his *Prometheus Bound*, the titan appears as the supreme initiator of crafts and sciences; he gives fire to men and delivers them from the fear of death. It is through his opposition to the master of the world, the choleric Zeus, that he offers to men the greatness and peace of the soul. It is a strange reversal which interprets challenge positively and which legitimises rebellion. The tragic dimension of the rapport between the gods and men is here evident, and the interpretation made of it, after the Renaissance, and more particularly after the Romantic Age of the last century, accentuates the expression of this tension. Prometheus is the guide and liberator in face of Divine authority that subjugates wills. Victor Hugo, in *Le sens d'Eschyle*, puts forward this "word of a man" facing progress:

> *In the immense shadow of the Caucasus*
> *Since centuries, through dreaming,*
> *Led by men of ecstasy,*
> *Humankind marches ahead,*
> *Marches on earth, passes through,*
> *Goes, at night, in space,*
> *In infinity, in the bounded,*
> *In the azure, in the irritated tide,*
> *In the glimmer of Prometheus,*
> *The bound liberator!*[2]

Humanity's march ahead, beyond the clouded epochs of obscurantism and submission, is carried "in the glimmer of Prometheus". The figure of the titan, in that it represents the expression illustrating best the rejection of an imposed Divine order and the affirmation of human autonomy and greatness, traverses the ages and fashions the complex and strained relation which exists between God (in the Christian re-reading) and men.[3] Socratic dialectic, Aristotelian syllogism, the autonomous reflection of the one and the others, are already coloured by the Promethean challenge. The idea of the separation of powers and the new relativity of morality in the practice of politics, as presented by Machiavelli in the fifteenth-sixteenth centuries, go along the same line of opposition. This when it is not a question of negating the primacy of the Divine.

This phenomenon was further amplified by scientific and technical progress. Consequently, man is unceasingly engaged in an assault on heaven (the myth of Prometheus "speaks"). As early as the nineteenth century, the motive of "the stealer of fire" is permanent. This motive is inscribed, from then on, within the Christian points of reference in the play of tension that exists between God, the Saviour and the sinner. Prometheus incarnates rebellion, rejection and the rejection of Salvation through the affirmation of freedom and innocence. His figure derives its energy of meaning from the fact that it is, at the same time, intimately linked to the notion of original sin and expresses the most radical opposition to its consequences.

It is the innocence, the creative force of the "will to be", the road of the new free man who is stimulated by existential suffering (which is a gift and not a punishment), announced by Nietzsche's prophet Zarathustra. The Prometheus of modern times thus goes to the limit of tension and conflict. The triple metamorphoses of the subjugated camel, the claiming lion, and, lastly, the innocent child cannot but lead to the murder of God. The madman who announces "the death of God" says nothing other than this. In light of the Judaeo-Christian points of reference, the innocence of the child-man-creator kills God... The fire is not only stolen but what is more is that values are transmuted: Man lives from now on in Olympus.

The young Rimbaud followed the same way. In that troubled epoch, disturbed as his century was by an impossible reconciliation between the order of Christian dogma and the scientific, industrial revolution, the poet gave a new meaning to his distress. Other poets such as Nerval, Verlaine and Goethe (who tried to yield to Biblical law) or Baudelaire (whose moral suffering was atrocious) had to live the same contradiction and tension. But Rimbaud has the exactness of not stopping halfway. The new poet, "the Supreme Savant", goes beyond tension by means of an absolute affirmation. In a letter to Paul Demeny, several motives are intermingled: Prometheus, Orpheus and Babel, all of which express the new liberation against Salvation.

"The poet, therefore, is really a stealer of fire. He is entrusted by humanity, and even by animals, he should make feel, touch and listen to his inventions; if what he brings from there has shape, he gives that which has shape; if it is shapeless, he gives that which is shapeless. It is about finding a language; of what remains, every speech being an idea, the time of a universal language will come!... The poet will define the quantity of the unknown awakening in his time in the universal soul. He will give more than the expression of his thought, more than the notation of his march towards progress! Enormity becoming norm, absorbed by all, he will be really a multiplier of progress! This future will be materialist, as you see; always full of numbers and harmony, these poems will be made to last. Deep down, it will still be a little Greek Poetry."[4]

The reference to Greek tradition is not fortuitous. To go back to one's sources is tantamount to liberating oneself from the Christian bondage. It is preferring Venus over Jesus and it is also being willing to be free in love rather than being bound in the culpability of faith. Rimbaud, having defined himself as "the one who suffers and has rebelled", reminds us that "one must be absolutely modern".

The expression of existential malaise is here more intimate than it was under the pen of Victor Hugo. But, in principle, the problematic is exactly of the same nature and has its source in the conflict which is naturally borne out in the encounter between the absolute power of God (or His Church) and the fierce will to assert man in his freedom. The Graeco-Roman and Judaeo-Christian traditions are marked by this concept of inaccessible harmony. To believe and to assert oneself, in the same breath, seems clearly impossible. Kantian philosophy, in the eighteenth century, offered a new critical geography of categories and attributions. In such a geography, the attitude of the philosopher who turns to "belief" is not situated outside the scene in which he was given birth. The same considerations are identifiable in Hegelian dialectic, in the philosophy of Feuerbach and in the socialist thinkers up to the "scientific" Marx and Engels. The theory of the three ages of Auguste Comte is the most explicit expression of this process that is fed by this conflict and which carries the hope of, and in, liberation.

Albert Camus, if he insists on the recent "modern" character of "metaphysical revolt", is conscious of its "remote origin". In a chapter of *The Rebel* – interestingly entitled "The Sons of Cain" – he begins the discussion with these words:

"Metaphysical rebellion in the proper sense does not appear in the history of ideas in any coherent form until the end of the eighteenth century. Modern times begin, henceforth, with the sound of falling ramparts. But, from this moment on, its consequences began to develop uninterruptedly. And it is no exaggeration to say that they have fashioned the history of our time. Does this mean that metaphysical revolt did not have any meaning before this date? These models are, however, quite remote, since our time likes to call itself Promethean. But is it really?

"The first theogonies show us Prometheus bound to a post, at the frontiers of the world, an eternal martyr excluded forever from a pardon which he refuses to solicit. Aeschylus increases further the stature of the hero, he creates him lucidly ('no misfortune shall befall me that I have not foreseen'), he makes him create his hate for all gods and plunges him in 'a tumultuous sea of fatal despair', and, finally, offers him to lightning and thunder: 'Ah! See the injustice I am enduring!'

"We cannot, therefore, say that the ancients have ignored metaphysical rebellion. They had erected, well before Satan, a painful and noble image of the Rebel and have given us the greatest myth of revolted intelligence. The inexhaustible Greek genius, which has greatly emphasised the myths of adhesion and modesty, knew, however, how to give to itself its model of insurrection. Incontestably, some of the Promethean traits are still alive in the revolted history that we are living. There is the struggle against death ('I have delivered men from the obsession of death'), Messianism ('I have put in them blind hopes'), and philanthropy ('enemy of Zeus... for having loved men too much').[5]

Revolted intelligence, the model of the "Rebel", the determined affirmation of man, have been produced at the crucible of a long history and have fashioned a specifically Western concept of the relation with the Divine. Fed by Graeco-Roman and Judaeo-Christian sources, it has determined the evolution of religious thought in a fundamental fashion. The Renaissance is an affirmation of this, and the centuries that followed achieved a liberation. In the West, within Christianity itself and more than anywhere else, the Promethean motive reveals its meaning: "We can also say, thus, and without any paradox, that the history of revolt in the western world is inseparable from that of Christianism."[6]

Camus's reflection has the advantage of establishing real correspondences between the differing Greek and Christian universes of reference. Before this passage he singled out the specifically Western character of this rapport with God and, in a broad sense, with the sacred:

"But, finally, is not this rebellion and the value that it vehicles at all relative? With epochs and civilisations, in effect, it seems that the reasons for which we rebel change. It is quite evident that a Hindu pariah, or a warrior of the Inca empire or a primitive man from Central Africa or a member of the first Christian communities, did not have the same idea of rebellion. We may even establish, with an extremely great likelihood, that the notion of rebellion has no meaning in this precise case. However, a Greek slave, a serf, a *condottiere* of the Renaissance, a French bourgeois of the regency, a Russian intellectual in the 1900s and a contemporary worker, if they can disagree about the reason of rebellion, they are no doubt in agreement about its legitimacy. Said differently, the problem of rebellion seems not to take its exact meaning except within western thought ...

"Revolted man is situated before or after the sacred, and is applied for the claim of a human order whereby all the answers are human, that is to say reasonably formulated. From this moment on, any questioning or speech is a rebellion, whereas in the sacred world any speech is an action of grace. It is possible to show, thus, that there cannot be for a human spirit except two possible universes, that of the sacrosanct (grace to speak the Christian language), and that of rebellion ... The actuality of the problem of rebellion lies only in the fact that entire societies have today wanted to keep their distance from the sacred. We are living in a desacrilised history. Man is admittedly not reduced to insurrection. But history today, by its contestations, forces us to say that rebellion is one of man's basic dimensions. It is our historical reality. We must find within it our values, that is unless we want to escape reality. Can we find a rule of conduct far from the sacred and absolute values? Such is the question put by rebellion."[7]

This analysis is pertinent and shows the nature of the process which led Western culture to a particular treatment of the sacred, questioning, ending up with the expression of metaphysical rebellion. Deep down, this is the affirmation of human rights[8] in the name of their consciousness, of being face to face with the Transcendence that subjected them to the absolute order of the sacred. Confident of these considerations, Camus clarifies that "the problem of rebellion seems not to take its exact meaning except within western thought." We can draw parallels from this conclusion and the elements of analysis of Marcel Gauchet who disengages, within the Christian field of reference itself, those elements which led to "the disenchantment of the world" (another way of expressing the history of desacralisation that Camus spoke of). We shall not dwell here on the pertinence of these theses. Let it be allowed us to simply point out the very specific character of this tension between the sacred and the profane, or between the sacred and rebellion, according to the terminology of Camus. This cannot be found, so to speak, in any other religion, spirituality or culture. Tension is permanent; it creates doubt which in turn gives meaning to choice. Finally, it is not up to man to choose within the sacred, but rather "for" or "against" it. Tension is, at the same time, both necessary and perilous to the heart of the sacred space. Driven to the extreme of its logic, it ends up by repudiating it. Rebellion rubs off on the not long ago serene concept of Transcendence. Curiously and paradoxically, the tragic is here inscribed and forms part of the essence of Faith.

Within the Judaeo-Christian points of reference themselves, the fact is confirmed and seen. The Biblical figure of Abraham who had to sacrifice his son is an eminent example. This is said in Genesis:

"And it came to pass after these things, that God did tempt Abraham, and said unto him, Abraham: and he said, Behold, *here I am*. And he said, Take now thy son, thine only son Isaac, whom thou lovest, and get thee into the land of Moriah; and offer him there for a burnt offering upon one of the mountains which I will tell thee of ... And Abraham took the wood of the burnt offering, and laid it upon Isaac his son; and he took the fire in his hand, and a knife; and they went both of them together. And Isaac spoke unto Abraham his father, and said, My father: and he said, Here I am, my son. And he said, Behold the fire and the wood: but where is the lamb for a burnt offering? And Abraham said, My son, God will provide himself a lamb for a burnt offering: so they went both of them together."[9]

Abraham lived the essential trial of Faith; he had to prove his love for God by preferring Him over love of his son. Tension is extreme and Abraham had to live it on his own. Upon his son's questioning, he responded in an elliptical fashion and hid from his child the truth and meaning of what he was going to carry out. This trial is tragic and its character is, therein, doubly reinforced by the infinite solitude which accompanies him, something which is attested by the kind of deception that Abraham had to use in order not to divulge anything to his son. Alone, face to face with the irrational Divine command, should he submit or rebel?

Tension is at the heart of Faith and nothing comes to appease the Prophet. This test is interpreted, by Christians and the existentialists of the last century, in light of their own history. If some chose rebellion; they, like Abraham, have chosen the tragic destiny of men of Faith who accept everything including the incomprehensible. We know well the existentialist and profound analysis which was developed by the Protestant philosopher and theologian Sören Kierkegaard in his book *Fear and Trembling* (1843). He shows that the story of Abraham carries, in itself, Christianity's fundamental Message concerning the existence of man who is subjected to the sense of sin, suffering, anguish and fear. Faith is, at best, the assumed test of anguish and inward conflict.

It is of little importance, in the final analysis, to know whether these interpretations are good or not. What should be noticed is that the decisive presence, in the texts of Aeschylus and then in the Bible but more clearly in the mentalities beginning from the Renaissance, of a tension between the domains of the sacred and the profane. Such presence had consequences on the expression of Faith. The idea of sin, culpability, suffering and Salvation by the Saviour are as many references that marked the Christian, and in a broader sense Western, mentality. This is, moreover, also the case with the notion of "the elected people" of the Jewish tradition. Whether one likes it or not, there are two poles in man which tear him apart to the point of tragic anguish. One should attach oneself to the sacred or free oneself from it. This is Camus's "All or Nothing", with the only two universes he talked about above. But as we have just seen, to say "God" is still not to attain serenity. On the contrary, the conscience of culpability gives rise to tension and suffering that give meaning to Faith. The Promethean myth finds, on a private plane, an echo in the history of Abraham as reported in the Bible: to live is tantamount to accepting distress, or liberating oneself by means of rejection. The alternative does not offer any other outlet: the Western history of mentalities imposes this reading.

2. Islam: Signs, Revelations and Submission

In showing the specifically Western character of rebellion, Camus refers only to the Hindu pariah, the Inca warrior or the primitive man of Central Africa. Perhaps he wanted to demonstrate divergences by citing such specific examples. He says nothing of Islamic civilisation which is so near and so different at the same time. Nonetheless, we do not find in Muslim points of reference a figure similar to Prometheus. Even the story of Abraham is reported in terms which, at the onset, give a particular flavour to the rapport between man and the Divine order. Certainly, there is the trial of having to sacrifice the most beloved being, his son,[10] in order to give witness of his Faith. But the tragic experience, solitude, and allusive response are absent here. Abraham speaks to his son who, having the same Faith, reassures his father, submits himself with the same kind of submission and joins his witness of Faith to that of his father:

> *And when he reached the age of running with him, he said, 'My son, I see in a dream that I shall sacrifice thee; consider, what thinkest thou?' He said, 'My father, do as thou art bidden; thou shalt find me, God willing, one of the steadfast.' When they had surrendered, and he flung him upon his brow, We called unto him, 'Abraham thou hast confirmed the vision; even so We recompense the good-doers. This is indeed the manifest trial.' And We ransomed him with a mighty sacrifice, and left for him among the later folk 'Peace be upon Abraham!'* (Qur'ān, 37:102–9)

The teachings that we can derive from these verses are many, but we shall limit ourselves to showing the strength of the supplementary Faith that the son offers to his father. There is no solitude, no figure of style and no struggle between the two loves, "both have submitted"; the son's patience echoes the intimate fidelity of the father. The trial of faith is, far from tragic tension, one of patience and acceptance. If, on the other hand, everyone has to give an account of his actions, alone; Faith is lived with the other, whose love and fraternity accompany one, appease one's heart and vivify one's conviction. Shared Faith, the brotherhood of Faith – which is the foundation of Islam – is opposed to any idea of tragic consciousness.

The reading of "signs" is exactly of the same nature. It is destined to comfort and appease. Abraham had a vision, his heart understood the meaning and accepted it. In another context, it is him who asks God to show him how He brings the dead back to life. Not because he did not believe in the same but rather "in order that his heart be appeased":

> And when Abraham said, 'My Lord show me how Thou wilt give life to the dead,' He said, 'Why, dost thou not believe?' 'Yes,' he said, 'but that my heart may be at rest.' (Qur'ān, 2:260)

Faith in God, life after death, and everything that is endowed with meaning, are not questioned: "Certainly, yes, I believe", says Abraham; it is not a question of doubt, a fortiori, in a Cartesian or existentialist sense. Nor is it about questioning Transcendence. On the contrary, what counts here is the re-comforting offered by the sign, remembrance and reminding:

> ... in God's remembrance are at rest the hearts... (Qur'ān, 13:28)

The different revelations of the Psalms, the Torah, the Gospel and the Qur'ān are so many "signs" that mark out the history of humanity. All of them are destined to orientate and appease. According to Islam, it is the human nature of man, in that he is responsible, that allows him to grasp the essence of Divine Revelation and not his quality of "being culpable" pilfered by salvation. The *tormented* nature which characterises, very early on, the experience of Faith in Christianity does not have any hold over the Islamic tradition. Adam and Eve have been forgiven, man is born innocent and his responsibility relates to the fact that he knows, according to the time and the place of his existence, how to read Divine signs and follow Revelation:

> Thereafter Adam received certain words from his Lord, and He turned towards him; truly He turns, and is All-compassionate. We said, 'Get down out of it, all together; yet there shall come to you guidance from Me, and whosoever follows My guidance, no fear shall be on them, neither shall they sorrow.' (Qur'ān, 2:37–8)

Just as there is a written book (*mastūr*), there is also an unrolled book (*manshūr*), which is the book of the universe, replete with signs, visions and Revelations. The holders of Faith see with the eyes of the heart. Creation, light, or a simple circumstance, all are a reminder, recognition and meditation. There is one particular Qur'ānic verse which has instigated numerous commentaries and innumerable interpretations. After all, it summarises in one breath all the elements that we have just spoken about. This consists of responding to the call of God and giving witness of one's Faith with others well before living a life of solitude. It is also thinking and meditating in order to know how to read all the signs. Such is the way of wisdom, when appearance wants to see therein but folly:

> *Say: 'I give you but one admonition, that you stand unto God, two by two and one by one, and then reflect; no madness is in your comrade.'* (Qur'ān, 34:46)

Enough cannot be said about how much these elements have fashioned, and are still fashioning daily, the Faith of Muslims, theologians, thinkers or simply believers. The differences pointed out in the story of Abraham are, in our mind, representative of essential specificities. The expression of tension and conflict is not, at all, of the same nature. Nor does it engage human beings, as already indicated, in an experience of doubt that is conceived as positive. Muslim thought, all along its history, does not tackle the question of tragic experience, and we can even claim that it does not know it.

The character of Prometheus, who had such an influence on the Judaeo-Christian tradition as on the representation formed in the West regarding the rapport between God and clerical authority, is absent from Islamic points of reference and traditions.[11] Regardless of the nature of the Hellenistic influence beginning from the ninth-tenth centuries, we do not find in the great Muslim thinkers any indications of a thought similar to an Aeschylian kind of interpretation concerning the rapport between man and the Divine. The question, which was posited very early on, is rather of the compatibility of the Greek theses, essentially the Aristotelian and Islamic. Abū Ya'qūb al-Kindī, who was one of the reputed translators of Greek works, Abū Naṣr al-Farābī, surnamed "the second master" after Aristotle, or Abū ʿAlī Ibn Sīnā (Avicenna), author of the famous *Al-Qānūn fī'l-Ṭibb* (Canon of Medicine) – to cite just these few – have explained, discussed and sometimes fiercely opposed the Greek theses by trying to be faithful to the fundamental Islamic teaching. Being both savants and philosophers at the same time, their object of study, their borrowed methodology, and their conclusions remained linked to their Muslim points of reference. Searching, deepening their knowledge and understanding had never meant entering into conflict with God or living the tension of doubt about Being and His presence.

The argumentation developed by Abū Ḥamid Muḥammad al-Ghazālī, in the eleventh-twelfth centuries, even though he conceives of doubt on the rational level, goes very swiftly beyond it through the acknowledgement and experience of the light of heart. At first, we can find innumerable correspondences between his thought and that of Descartes. Such correspondences certainly exist, but the frame of reference which gives the solution to going beyond doubt is fundamentally different. With the Muslim thinker, God calls the faithful to Him, He makes conviction be born in him and offers him His light.[12]

The axis of Ghazālī's thought is indeed, in the light of Islam, to harmonise the domains of philosophical reflection. In the face of Greek thought, he operates the distinction between philosophical opinion and its means. If he refutes Aristotle's metaphysics, it is because it carries postulates which oppose the revealed tenets of Islam. This, nonetheless, does not stop him from "integrating" the means. In this sense, the reasoning faculty, which "has nothing to do with faith either approving it or disapproving it",[13] carries knowledge which, in itself, is not the outcome of transgression. The latter is effective if we want to formulate rationally absolute answers. Metaphysics is of this nature but not least is science. Ghazālī's thought pursued reflection and completed it all while clarifying the importance of limits. Rational research, scientific knowledge and progress

are compatible with Islam and are not a liberation *vis-à-vis*
Divine authority. They are rather its confirmation. To think is
not at all struggling to liberate oneself from God, it is rather
coming closer to Him. There is not here a shadow of a
Promethean tone and, if by any chance, a thinker wanted,
through his own capacity, to accede to Truth, then he will find
in Ghazālī but a formal opposition to what he will consider to
be his "illness".

Historical circumstances pushed Ibn Taymiyya (fourteenth
century) and Ibn Khaldūn (fifteenth century) to take more
decisive stances concerning Greek philosophy and logic. But
the substance of their reflection remains the same. The use of
rationality, in that it allows to accede to more knowledge and to
establish legislations in tune with reality, is Islamic. There is no
need, therefore, to look elsewhere for a philosophy or a
methodology other than the points of reference and the practices
that have always taken place amidst Muslims since the first dawn
of Revelation. The process of returning to the fundamentals of
Islam (in relation to Greek or other influences) that was in a
way disengaged by Ibn Taymiyya and Ibn Khaldūn does not
amount to an absolute rejection of rationalism or logic. Clearly,
it is the affirmation that Islam (and the first Muslims proved it
by doing without syllogism for example) encompasses,
encourages and orientates, by its very essence, the exercise of
the reasoning faculty. At the time when the Western world lived
a first crisis of mentalities with the Renaissance, the great
theologians of the Muslim world were calling for a return to
the living sources of the Message and to following an
accomplished thinking by encouraging a renewal of *ijtihād*.
Reasoning anew in order to come closer to God, in the East,
was the exact opposite of a process which saw, in the exercise of
this same faculty, the greatest peril that clerical authority in the
West had to face from that time on. After, just as before, the
fifteenth century, one cannot find the expression of Promethean
temptation at any moment in the evolution of Islamic civilisation.
Based on Camus's analysis, we can say that Muslim thought has
never ventured out of the sacred space. It has rather developed

and accomplished itself within the same.[14] The cultural difference is quite evident.

On another level, Sufi traditions, having elaborated a specific terminology concerning Faith, initiation, spiritual stages, states and stations, might be misunderstood. Drawing near to, and annihilation in God have nothing to do with the experience of the "stealer of fire". It is a question of exactly the opposite. Sufi initiation is, before anything else, a study and teaching of proximity. Certainly, some great mystics have asserted to having attained such a level that their state of being human did not have any subsequent reality. The traditional teaching of Islam does not permit giving rise to such assertions, we should rather maintain a balance in our judgement. In effect, the universe of Sufism is a universe of coded language, the words have specific meanings and, if one hastens to making judgements, one may accuse such or such a Sufi of anathema, while not understanding the real scope of his message. After all, nothing in Islamic mysticism, even in its most extreme formulations, contains the sense of challenge to the transcendent Being. Renunciation, modesty, submission in exile, asceticism and contemplation are a search for spirituality and harmony. It is a question of living a tension borne out of an uprooting from materiality and not a tension of doubt.

3. Doubt and Reminder

By engaging in the discussion on a cultural dimension starting from the figures of Prometheus and Abraham, and of what they may represent in the respective histories of mentalities, we intend to show the fundamental differences. We are indeed dealing with two different universes of reference, two civilisations and two cultures. These have gone side by side and intermingled for centuries; and it seems that they are nowadays facing each other and it is imperative that we understand what profoundly characterises them. The analysis developed below should allow, evidently not in an exhaustive manner, us to go along this line. It is necessary, nonetheless, to complete this by a more circumscribed reflection on the specific types of relation with Transcendence. The cultural stake will then appear more clearly.

In his book *Biographie du XXème siècle*, Roger Garaudy points out concerning the West that: "Its principal contribution is not technique but criticism." Further below he adds:

"What Europe has contributed, from Socrates to Kant, from Kierkegaard to Marx, and from Nietzsche to Husserl, is not faith but doubt. This doubt is the trial of fire necessary to any real faith."[15]

The history of ideas convinces us of this. Since the Renaissance, the emergence of an active rationalism, in opposition to religious dogmatism, has relativised old certainties which were from that point on subject to "criticism". The Cartesian method consecrates the primacy of the reasoning faculty in establishing and recognising the Truth; this even if the latter needs "a good God" "to prove" the veracity of the first postulate concerning "distinct and clear ideas". Blaise Pascal, himself, was to use the calculus of probability in order to make the sceptic incline towards betting on God. Spinoza, Malebranche, passing through the English empiricists Berkeley and Hume, and up to Kant, all elaborate a philosophy which has, in one way or another, to build on doubt. If the Kantian critique established a leap between knowledge and Faith, he nonetheless remained nourished by the points of reference and questioning about being which agitated Western minds. He recognised doubt as an obligated stage of thought's evolution towards God. But intellectually, only postulates that are "necessary and non-demonstrable", can appease men. From the tortures of the believing conscience of Kierkegaard to the categorical rejection of Transcendence of Nietzsche; from the dialectical and historical materialism(s) of Marx to the absurd philosophy of Camus or the existentialism of Sartre; from the phenomenology of Husserl to contemporary analytic philoso-phy, existential doubt is omnipresent either to consecrate Faith or to repudiate God. Western history since the Renaissance, and after the re-reading of the Graeco-Roman legacy, has been nourished by the culture of criticism and doubt. When Roger

Garaudy asserts: "...this doubt is the trial of fire necessary to any real faith," the universe of thought which is his own and which has fashioned his rapport with Faith cannot be abstracted. To say that there cannot be faith except if there is doubt is not "audible" in all civilisations and particularly, with what is of concern to us here, in the universe of Muslim cultural stock.[16] This does not take anything away from men's sincerity of Faith, but it is here a proof of the plurality of paths which put men in the Divine presence. Religious reference, in itself, (or its comprehension), daily practice and the kind of filial transmission are as many elements which determine the expression of the religious and the sacred – as well as the totality of the symbolical universe – in a civilisation.

We can easily be persuaded that North Americans and Europeans are, nowadays, on the religious plane, children of this long history of mentalities which, since the Renaissance, has seen the critical mind encourage scepticism or Promethean temptation. The Divine presence is either doubted or repudiated; and very rare are those believers who are appeased by their Faith, and rarer still are those who practise it. When Faith is lived, it is often accompanied by a rejection of institutions, from Popes to Churches, from codified morality to religious obligations. "Modern" Faith has no need any longer for witnessing, very often we believe in private, alone and at a distance from public space whose objective seems to be making us "forget". Doubt is a faithful companion that now justifies prudence and now idleness. The modern Western world is a Godless world; conceived as such, it leaves a choice to each person to find his way often at the cost of painful, inward splits. This when it does not drive to a negligence of warnings which are devoid of questions and sometimes meaning.

Again, it still remains that choice be really given to men. We notice increasingly, with younger generations, a religious illiteracy that cannot be but worrying. Under the pretext of "neutrality of public space", religious education has disappeared or been reduced to one or two hours a week. The ensuing result is an ignorance, increasing in importance every year, of religious history and its main figures. Freedom and ignorance have been confused with one another, whereas in ignorance there is no longer real freedom. Public space, and particularly school, instead of being neutral, expresses from now on a real bias. This consists of evacuating the question of the Divine and meaning, making it an auxiliary and secondary problem. The youth of today, the adults of tomorrow, will at best doubt; more naturally, they will neglect anything that is of a "religious" character. Baptisms, marriages and deaths will exhume memories and no more. Scepticism is almost the rule nowadays and the experience of doubt, following the expression of Pascal, is the sole possible one if one decides not to forget oneself. Everything leads one to believe, in front of this scene of modernity, that we have reached, at the end of this twentieth century, the culmination of the Promethean experience. In truth, its completion is finished when the "stealer of fire" does not have any conscience about the existence of God, denying therefore that it is theft, and claiming himself to be the creator of the fire that he entertains. His doubts have no longer the necessary power to break his pride in withholding incredible scientific and technical means. In this formidable march ahead, in these successive waves of infinite progress, the eagle's torment seems to be consuming the inwards of an important number, increasing daily, of men and women who want to know what sins they have committed that inflict on them such an intense psychological and inward torture. They did not make a choice, but they are assured that they are free.

The experience of Faith in Islam is not, up until now and even with Muslims living in Western capitals, of a similar nature. We can find many Muslims who acknowledge not practising their religion as they should, but very few are those who assert not believing at all. This not because of fear of facing trouble; in London as in Washington, Casablanca or New Delhi, the answer is the same. God's existence is almost never doubted; this seems to be a natural daily given fact of men and women. In diverse occasions, even if the familial and festive character is sometimes preponderant, we have the witness of a present and living Faith in the Muslim world. For example, during the month of Ramaḍān, or during the two great feasts of the Muslim year. The Friday prayer is equally a particularly intense moment of the week. At a time when the Churches are becoming empty, and when often only elderly people gather on Sundays; the mosques are, from one side of the planet to the other, multiplying and do not cease to be filled. In the great cities of the East and the West, in the universities, in the suburbs, and in the countryside, we witness a strong identity-based affirmation going sometimes to the point of infatuation in practice. Faith was never repudiated, and now there is a will to express it more. In England, France, Belgium and the USA, identification with Islam or its discovery succeeds where repression or expensive social programmes have failed. How then do we explain this phenomenon which nowadays often scares Western people? Extremism is feared; and as there is a total absence of religious practice, wanting to practice becomes suspect, for it is already "too much".

Numerous theories have been elaborated concerning a situation that has recently come to light. But such a situation has always existed in the Muslim world when people were not allowed to freely express their religious sentiments (before the colonial epoch, during occupation and up until now). There was talk of economic reasons; poverty and misery would make the tones of religiosity be born again (such a hypothesis has difficulty in explaining the commitment of rich traders and mobilisation at the university level). It has also been explained as a question of anti-Western reaction, a will to reaffirm a denied identity (this sociological hypothesis considers the "religious" fact as secondary and finds great difficulty in tackling the spiritual dimension). Finally, it was seen as a political manoeuvre from more or less extremist manipulators trying to seize power and not hesitating to deceive the masses (this last reading does not analyse the differently engaged social categories nor the nature of popular mobilisation). It would be too simple to reject these three hypotheses with no more ado. Besides, and according to particular situations, each one of them has part of the truth in it which, even though they do not allow for an understanding of the universal scope of this phenomenon, nonetheless remain pertinent and should be taken into consideration. The economic, sociological and political analyses attempt to give account of a situation whose grasp is difficult. For a West full of doubt, the affirmation of the Islamic Faith raises a problem, and it even has aggressive tones sometimes. In general, comparisons are held with that which is known in the West. Religious dogmas (along with what they may include in terms of opposition to progress), histories and epochs (the awakening of Islam would launch an unfortunate return backwards) or again fundamentalisms (on the political level, the extreme right would be for the West what Islamism is for the East) are compared. What appeared so complex becomes, by magic, very clear. Yet, this clarity is only apparent and the simplification upon which it is founded is dangerous.

Rather than adhering to reductionist, and sometimes erroneous comparisons it would be preferable to consider things from another angle. As a result of the debates which are current today on Islam and which, almost exclusively, gravitate around the above-mentioned three hypotheses, there clearly exist differences of essence between the Judaeo-Christian and Islamic religious representations. These differences have evident consequences on the perception of the rapport with God, with sacred and religious practice. Economic or political reasons are not enough to explain the religious infatuation of populations, nor the nature of resistance to Westernisation in the Muslim world. In order to do so, one must go back to the sources of Islam to grasp the nature and meaning of the Muslim Faith. Such a discussion, absent nowadays from the multiple colloquia, is necessary. It allows us to fittingly tackle a problematic that has been amputated from its cultural dimension. For it is, indeed, a question of cultural divergences; over here, meaning was given to doubt; over there, meaning is in the reminder.

According to Islamic teaching, there exists an original pact between God and men. In effect, in the first times of creation, the Creator gathered all human beings and made them testify:

> And when thy Lord took from the children of Adam, from their loins, their seed, and made them testify touching themselves, 'Am I not your Lord?' They said, 'Yes, we testify' – lest you should say on the Day of Resurrection, 'As for us, we were heedless of this,'…
> (Qur'ān, 7:172)

There exists, therefore, at the heart of each man's consciousness, essentially and deeply, an intuition and acknowledgement of the Creator's presence. Just as the sun, clouds, wind, birds and all the animals naturally express their submission (a literal translation of the word *islām*), so does the human being have in himself an almost instinctive aspiration towards Transcendence. This is the idea of *fiṭra* that has aroused numerous theological commentaries, because it is so central to the Islamic concept of the sacred. One finds it mentioned in *Sūra ar-Rūm*:

> So set thy face to the religion, a man pure faith – God's original upon which He originated mankind. There is no changing God's creation. That is the right religion; but most men know it not.[17]
> (Qur'ān, 30:30)

A famous *ḥadīth* clarifies the sense of *fiṭra* cited in this verse: "Every new-born child is born in the state of *fiṭra*, it is the parents that make him Jew, Christian or Zoroastrian."[18]

So, there exists in man a natural aspiration towards God. Education gives him a certain historically and geographically marked form. According to Islamic teachings, the Revelation brought by Muḥammad (peace be upon him) goes back to the sources of this *fiṭra*, finds again the original *élan* of man and makes him live by the reminder. To reveal is tantamount to reminding us of the proximity of the Faith of Adam, Eve, Noah, Abraham, Moses, Mary, Jesus and all the Prophets. To reveal is tantamount to giving life to the light that lies asleep in each person's heart, one that forgetfulness put down and suffocated. Here, there is no question of an original sin, an eternal fault or a challenge to the Creator. The one who does not believe, the infidel (*kāfir*), is the one who is no longer faithful to the original pact, the one whose memory is sleepy and whose sight is veiled. In the notion of *kufr*, in Arabic, there is indeed the idea of a veiling which provokes the denial of Transcendence. Only God decides about light or veiling for human beings. The latters' responsibility lies in their permanent commitment and their intimate effort to making memory live.

It is no doubt by taking account of this fundamental characteristic of Islam that it is possible to better grasp the "religiosity" of Muslims. The idea of "an awakening of Islam" has been minutely examined for decades and what appears as "new" in the West, when all is said and done, is not so original. It is rather its visibility and scope that are today different.[19] But the integration of the religious point of reference in daily life has always existed in Muslim societies. This through language, transactions, in the sound of the calls of the *Muezzin*, in the rhythm of prayers, by the congregation of the Friday sermon, and by the month of Ramaḍān. Life is naturally marked by such an atmosphere; the sacred is in proximity. Certainly, one can see in the large cities very "Westernised" attitudes, manners and behaviours on the American model and reflexes that are very little impressed by morality. Whoever has travelled in some Muslim countries will have no difficulty in witnessing these facts. There remains nonetheless, and this is due without a shadow of doubt to the very nature of the message of Islam, the heart's attachment to religious values. Such phenomenon might seem barely comprehensible from without, but one does not understand Islam, or does so very little, if one does not take into account the emotional charge contained in the reading or listening to of the Qur'ān for example, not only in the comprehension of the meaning of verses, but also of the peculiar sonority of its psalmody. It all happens as if something is awakened in man's heart and attracts him towards the sacred dimension. It is certainly a question of this, an awakening and a

reminder coming from the depths of being. The same applies
to the sayings of the Prophet (peace be upon him), as is also
sometimes with his Companions. They have on one's heart and
consciousness an impact that nothing has come to diminish until
now. We have touched here upon one of the most fundamental
elements of Muslim culture. There has been much rambling on
about the force of attraction of the message, from North to South
and from East to West. All economic, social and political reasons
been referred to in a partially exact manner, but never has
there been discerned in this a characteristic trait, a cultural trait
of Muslim religiosity.

Such is nonetheless the case. The Muslim world is a world of
memory. Not uniquely an intellectual memory but intimately a
memory of the heart too. The Qur'ān reminds us in many
instances that it is the heart that understands:

> *What, have they not journeyed in the land so that they have
> hearts to understand with or ears to hear with? It is not the
> eyes that are blind, but blind are the hearts within the breasts.*
> (Qur'ān, 22:46)

The Qur'ānic message mixes at the same time force of meaning
and an energy of emotion; its comprehension lies indeed in
these two dimensions. This is coupled with the experience of
intimate reminder which makes Revelation seem to harmonise
itself with inward aspiration. The Qur'ānic expression "Light
upon light" expresses the idea of this appropriateness. One might
think that there is nothing more here than a vaguely mystical
and theoretical reflection. However, experience in the field will
prove this at once to the contrary. We have already mentioned
how few Muslims define themselves as atheists, and it is possible
to say that most of them, even if they happen to be critical of
some ideas or habits, have a kind of emotional predisposition
towards the message of Islam. Such predisposition expresses
itself in Muslim countries, as in the West, in a permanent manner.
It lies in the very essence of the Religion of Islam; one that
addresses as much the heart as it does reason, that takes into

account all that which constitutes man, that which makes one responsible without making one culpable, and that which awakens the consciousness of Transcendence without imposing it. If there is a tension that resides in the Muslim, it expresses itself daily in a shift between forgetfulness and remembrance, and not – or not singularly – in the experience of doubt. The Qur'ānic call and reminder awaken the intimacy of the heart's consciousness, and gives it life:

> O believers, respond to God and the Messenger when He calls you unto that which will give you life; and know that God stands between a man and his heart, and that to Him you shall be mustered. (Qur'ān, 8:24)

At a moment when, in the West, we are witnessing a profound crisis of values, a quasi general dissatisfaction with Jewish or Christian religious points of reference; when some, being thirsty for meaning and spirituality, turn to sects and other mystical groupings; at this very same time, the Muslim world is affirming a peculiar attachment to Islamic values and is expressing a permanent, daily religiosity with which the West is no longer familiar. Western culture admittedly has today "its" values which, despite the fact that they obviously do not meet the needs for meaning encountered in women, men and youth, represent a universe of reference that we are not going to question. But the Muslim world does not share that which is at the basis of this rationalism, values and points of reference. The two "cultures" are facing one another. For centuries now, we have witnessed many conflicts; but things nowadays are taking a peculiar turn as much because of the extent of populations and present dangers as due to the deep fractures that may ensue from these. We are, thus, at a crossroads.

Western intellectuals and researchers may well be able to develop the most scientific analyses, display the greatest logic and the most experimental local approach. But they will give only a partial account of the Islamic phenomenon if they do not tackle the special rapport that Muslims, whether practising

or not, have with the Qur'ānic message and with the religious
and sacred in general. There is, therein, something specific which
is not reducible to the understanding of the "religious" in the
universe of Euro-American culture. It is high time this fact was
realised. That is unless one contents oneself with theories that
present the other, the Muslim as a "reactionary" or "fanatic"
who is short of a few decades of "development". Someone "who
will evolve" admittedly, and end up "opening up" just as the
Christians have done and have, for the majority, "liberated"
themselves from the "delirium" of the Vatican. There is, therefore,
an expectation of a "cultural revolution" or an *aggiornamento* of
Islam. One should not deny that the Muslim world should
evolve, be able to respond to contemporary challenges and that,
in fact, the interpretation of religious points of reference should
be refined in order to provide solutions for actual social,
economic and political problems. The whole reflection
developed in the present book testifies to this. But this
absolutely does not mean that the Muslim world lags behind
the Western model and that it must go through the same
developments. It seems to us that we have shown enough that
the points of reference and experiences have not been the same
in these two worlds, that the modes of being in the world are
different, and that the rapport *vis-à-vis* the sacred is essentially
of another order.

Before coming to the question of the rapport between the
two civilisations, it seems to us necessary to say a word about
the fundamental axes of what we can call "Muslim Culture".

II. THE WAY OF THE SOURCE

1.   God

The preceding pages have shown that Islam offers a holistic
vision of life and human behaviour. We have also spoken above
about the notion of *rabbāniyya* which consecrates the full, exacting
and always vivified relationship between man and his Creator.
The energy and force of this link, born out of the original pact,

radiates all spheres of human thought and action. Far off from
the debates that have taken place in the West on the idea of
God, trinity or election, or the conflicts to clerical authority
posited by rationalist humanists or advocates of science, the
Islamic civilisation, from the beginning, has been nourished
with the sacred dimension and values that are linked to it. The
sacred here is not a "forbidden" domain that is closed nor is it a
privileged space of absolute dogma which imposes itself and
which no one can discuss. This as contrasted with a profane
space which offers relativity, rationality and freedom: in sum
that which is human. Nothing, in Islam, corresponds to such
categories or to this simplistic interpretation born in Western
history and which has been considered, for a long time,
applicable to all cultures.

The presence of God, the absence of clergy, and an
awareness of individual responsibility are some of the many
elements which offer, in their simplicity, a very specific idea
about the "profane" and the "sacred". Again, it is the reminder,
the remembrance of God in man's consciousness, that produces
the sacred. Thus, any action, which is in appearance free and
totally "profane", from hygiene to sexual intercourse, from
trade to social engagement, is sacred from the moment it is
nourished with the remembrance of God and a respect for
ethical limits. Abū Dharr reported, in a ḥadīth, the astonishment
of the Companions of the Prophet (peace be upon him) when
they heard him enumerating the actions that will be rewarded
by God:

"O Messenger of God", they asked, "even fulfilling one's
sexual desire is going to be rewarded?" His response was: "What
if one fulfils this desire in an illicit manner, would not one be
committing a sin? Similarly, if one fulfils it in a licit manner, one
will deserve a reward."[20]

The term ṣadaqa (charity), used by the Prophet, invests the
sexual act with a sacred characteristic the moment it is fulfilled
with the remembrance of the Divine and of necessity, in
accordance with the morality ensuing from it. The body, and
everything relating to it, is not negatively marked: the moment

that one lives in harmony with the vision which is both holistic and close to the message and that one testifies to its meaning. Here, the body, just as the spirit and the heart, partakes of the accomplishment of the human being before God. Each gesture is a sign if remembrance of the Creator illuminates it with its meaning: walking, eating, waking up, sleeping, washing and dressing, etc., are all "charity", an act of worship, thankfulness, invocation and prayer. The sacred permeates the profane that is carried by means of a vivified memory. This is a teaching that is both exacting and open, one which has been dispensed to the Muslims of the entire world. The Qur'ānic message anchors these dispositions in the consciences of today just as was the case yesterday:

> ... the hearing, the sight, the heart — all of those shall be questioned of. And walk not in the earth exultantly; certainly thou wilt never tear the earth open, nor attain the mountains in height. (Qur'ān, 17:36–7)

Man's responsibility is total: with regard to what he sees, hears, does and feels. Of all these, he will have to give account and this inward looking must arouse humility, an attitude "without insolence". Pride and sufficiency render one blind: a human being can forget himself and no longer see the signs in himself. Likewise, it may happen that the earth and mountains no longer "speak" to him and have become just "elements" for him. However, the universe, in the image of our intimacy, is full of "signs", for the one who knows how to see:

> We shall show them Our signs in the horizons and in themselves, till it is clear to them that it is the truth. (Qur'ān, 41:53)

The teaching of harmony between the microcosm and the macrocosm, that one finds in Hinduism and Buddhism, is present here as it is in numerous other verses. We have cited above a number of Qur'ānic passages which bring to the fore this sacred dimension of the universe (see Part One) and we shall confine ourselves to recalling here the following verse which caused the Prophet (peace be upon him) to cry a whole night upon its being revealed:

Surely in the creation of the heaven and earth and in the alternation of night and day there are signs for men possessed of minds... (Qur'ān, 3:190)

After having recited it to Bilāl, who was wondering about the reason for these tears, the Prophet (peace be upon him) warned: "Woe to the person who hears this verse and does not meditate upon it." This is a warning of fundamental scope: comprehension of Islam lies in the understanding of this attentive and contemplative view which is always renewed, one which knows how to see in an element the signs and struggles against the habits that neglect the same. The Qur'ānic verse that immediately follows the precedent confirms the requirement of the *rabbāniyya*'s attention:

... who remember God, standing and sitting and on their sides, and reflect upon the creation of the heavens and earth: 'Our Lord, Thou hast not created this for vanity. Glory be to Thee! Guard us against the chastisement of the Fire.' (Qur'ān, 3:191)

The universe testifies to the Divine Presence and in this the sacred dimension is omnipresent. Meditation on the world brings man to his destiny, to the sense of his life: he must give account of this. The world reminds one of the Presence of God and His Presence confirms one's responsibility. To understand the sacred is, in fact, to grasp from within the universe of human responsibility: the signs are in reach of all hearts and minds. It is in this universe that reason must move. Nothing hinders it from proceeding ahead, understanding, analysing and always pushing to search further. Nothing hinders it from doing so if not this imperative that is to always respect the equilibrium of signs and the harmony of nature. If our universe is a universe of signs, then the order of nature, the testimony of creation, is sacred and one cannot approach it without humility. This concept of the world has a direct influence on the exercise of scientific research: just like any other human action, it must respect a morality, meaning and limits.

Despite Western influences, Islamic culture is always nourished by these sacred points of reference and the ensemble of its concept of "rationality" is inscribed in this holistic perception. There exists no reason that is autonomous to the point of having no other objective except "advancing" regardless of the cost. Scientific freedom lies in harmony: to respect creation, nature, men, animals and to look for the best for the good of all human beings. Such is the responsibility of men in a universe that never operates out of "disenchantment". God made it sacred, just like life, and so will it remain until the end of time; any other consideration would be inhuman.

Such are the fundamental teachings of *tawḥīd* – the Unicity of God – and such are the consequences of the *rabbāniyya* on the cultural plane. One may be surprised, in the West, to hear and notice that the Muslim world still nourishes itself from the living sources of an exacting monotheism, one which influences daily the human being in a world of the faithful even beyond the concrete practice of religion. Some would love that Islam "progresses" and "secularises" itself by means of a real "critical" analysis of its points of reference. It seems clear, however, that the Islamic universe is not reducible to these categories. For neither progress nor criticism are rejected; but what is fundamentally contested is that it is only reason that determines the norms and fixes the good without any transcendental finality. The West needed this "revolution" in order to accede to the freedom of being able to believe, act and search. But the Islamic civilisation has known none of this and by the nature of its message it has encouraged each member of the faithful to understand, experiment and learn this while nourishing themselves with a remembrance of meaning and finalities. Science, from the moment it is a testimony of the attentive presence of conscience, is sacred. It is not at all a challenge to the Creator, it is the means of His continuing Revelation. God does not fear at all the Promethean temptation of human reason;

rather He never ceases from warning them from erring and amnesia. It is the remembrance of *tawḥīd*: the way of the source, throughout the history of men and Prophets, lies in remembrance of the link with Transcendence. Thus, are born the horizons of spirituality, the requirement of ethics and the expression of meaning and finalities.

2. Spirituality

If one takes the time to consult most of the written books, the researches produced or the quasi totality of the proposed hypotheses in the West on the "question of Islam and Islamism" today, one realises that the specifically religious and cultural dimension is taken into account only in a very secondary fashion. Little is spoken of Faith, spirituality or the concept of the world. It is always a question of analysing things in terms of social dynamics, conflicts of power or dangerous identity-based withdrawal-into-oneself. The "new" expression of the religious is taken to be caused by economic misery for some; others see in it, with the return of fundamentalisms, a "revenge of God"; while others speak of "the path of the South" which conveys the will of Muslims, after diverse stages of humiliating colonisation, to see the point of reference of their culture accede to the register of the universal.[21] Certainly, one sometimes finds a lot of good-will, some logic and coherence in these explanations. But they remain no less cut off from the dimension that appears to Muslims as being the most essential, i.e. that of reference to God and the spirituality that the former arouses.

The central notion of *tawḥīd* and the daily expression of the *rabbāniyya* have consequences on the concept of life which renders the world of Islam necessarily and irremediably resistant to the evolution and influence of Western culture. Faith and reference to God, the idea that the sacred is not uniquely in rituals, but rather in any act that preserves alive in one's conscience remembrance of the Creator, all these nourish the daily existence of women and men and give strength and meaning to their spirituality. In the entire Muslim world, one senses that there still remains a very strong imprint of the religious point of reference: this life is not the only life, each person will have to account one day for what he has done with his wealth, body and soul. Life and death have a meaning, the meaning of trial and the action of good:

> ... *who created death and life, that He might try you which of you is fairest in work.* (Qur'ān, 67:2)

These words resonate in the hearts of Muslims who remain attached to the values of Transcendence. Contrary to the idea that is widespread in the West, it is indeed hope that should preoccupy us when we observe that, despite a Western aggressive cultural invasion of our whole planet, the world of Islam asserts a Faith and values that are, by essence, incompatible with the cult of the means that has today become the rule.

Islamic spirituality engages man to live in harmony while taking into account all the elements of his humanity. Living without forgetting death, meditating without neglecting the action of good and justice, knowing oneself to be alone and living among men, nourishing one's spirit as one nourishes one's body and remaining exacting in one's search for balance. To be linked to values is tantamount to going beyond reductionist individualisms, love of goods and money and the expression of a limited sexuality towards "pleasure", a new god imposing a new cult. Monotheism and the Qur'ānic reference – the foundations of Islamic civilisation today – give a peculiar energy to Islamic spirituality: it prefers Faith over forgetfulness, being over having, finality over means, solidarity over individualism and quality over quantity.

Nothing, or almost nothing, is said about these aspects of Islamic culture because there is a difficulty in thinking that something positive can come forth from a universe that is presented through images of "bearded men" and "veiled women". This is a reductionist observation, one which is wanted by the powers that be and taken over by the media to make out that between the world of progress and that of Islam there is nothing but future conflict. One cannot free oneself from such summary conclusions if one does not take the time to deepen one's reflection and understand why Muslims are opposed to the present expression of Westernisation. For, in the final analysis, they find therein nothing of what Islam teaches them in the matter of being: they have nothing against the technical means possessed by the West. On the contrary, that to which they cannot adhere is the modalities of their use through the will of power, domination and gain. This, very often, to the detriment of the dignity of human beings.

One commits a considerable error of judgement in not retaining from Islam anything except its reactive and radical expression. From the Qur'ānic message and the traditions of the Prophet (peace be upon him) emerges values and meaning that can contribute a fruitful dialogue with all the paths that, in the West, refuse to perish on the altar of dehumanising and blind progress. The message of *tawḥīd*, invigorating the daily spirituality of millions of human beings, holds in itself the firm exactness of a human and just management of the world. Against the "hidden" polytheisms that make out of power, nation, science, technique, money, pleasure and comfort as many gods to which is devoted a publicity-based and financial cult; the affirmation of the *rabbāniyya* is a true enterprise of liberation: a spiritual liberation, if ever there was one. Islam is also this dimension; it is especially this dimension and the call addressed to the West that should be heard by all people of good-will. This not in view of conversion but rather with a concern for an engagement to unite all the forces of those who, in the name of God or their conscience, refuse the new world disorder so as to preoccupy themselves instead with values and finalities.

Saʿd ibn Abī Waqqāṣ, a Companion of the Prophet (peace be upon him), sent emissaries to present Islam to Rustam, the sovereign of Persia: the latter questioned them and they answered him thus:

"God has chosen us to bring out, through our intermediary, whoever He wills from the cult of polytheism to the worship of the unique God (*tawḥīd*), from the narrowness of this world to the vastness in this world and the Next and from the tyranny of governors to the justice of Islam."

There exists an essential, fine link in Islam between Faith and the exactness of justice: God willed that human beings do not share the same Faith; that is to say that dialogue is incumbent upon them in order to make them respect a justice from which all humanity can benefit. Just as was the case in past centuries, Islam should continue to bring a consequent contribution to the transformation of the world.

3. Morality

All that has been said in Part One of this book brings to the fore that morality, reference to good and evil, is a central domain of Islamic teaching. Yesterday, just as today, there are limits and prohibitions. Admittedly, permission comes first, but there are things that one does not do and does not allow to be done: social, political and economic liberties, as we have indicated, must be exercised in accordance with respect for certain rules. Islamic culture places morality at the origin; it is, one may say, the first object of Revelation and the latter, through its intermediary, indicates an orientation as it stipulates the principles of being in the world of men. To say that there is morality and rules is tantamount to attesting to the freedom of each person:

> By the soul, and That which shaped it and inspired it to lewdness and godfearing! Prosperous is he who purifies it, and failed has he who seduces it. (Qur'ān, 91:7–10)

To a Companion who asked him what is "the good", the Prophet (peace be upon him) responded: "You have come to enquire about the good?" "Yes", answered Wasiba. "Consult your heart", said the Prophet, "for the good is that which appeases your soul and calms your heart. Sin is that which troubles you inwardly and causes embarrassment and vexation in your heart, even if people provide you with all possible juridical justifications."[22]

Moral tension partakes of human nature. Peace of the heart or its agitation testify to the ways taken, but the choice always remains within the hands of human beings. From freedom arises responsibility: one must give account of our attachment to morality. This for ourselves, in our hearts, in the silence and solitude of our intimacy, as in our relations with our parents, brothers, friends, enemies, the stranger, the colleague, the employee, the old, the handicapped, the poor or the exiled; as also with nature, trees, forests, the air, sea and all the elements; as also, lastly, with the totality of the animal world. A tradition reports that Paradise was granted to a prostitute because she gave water to a thirsty dog: a simple gesture carrying the essentials of morality that is taught today, with reference to the message of Islam, in places as far apart as Morocco and Indonesia. This is summed up as "reforming one's character and doing good".

The principle of election in the Muslim community is not consequent upon the sole fact that its members are nominally "Muslims" without any other form of commitment. To be Muslim is tantamount, first, to living the experience of piety:

> Surely the noblest among you in the sight of God is the most godfearing of you. (Qur'ān, 49:13)

The testimony of such piety is essentially, on individual, social, political and economic planes, one of a moral nature:

> To God belongs all that is in the heavens and in the earth, and unto Him all matters are returned. You are the best nation ever brought forth to men, bidding to honour, and forbidding dishonour, and believing in God. (Qur'ān, 3:109–10)

In the mirror of nature and its order, and all whose elements belong to God and return to Him, the best community is that which respects harmony through its engagement for good and its fight against evil. The passage starts with and ends with Divine reference: the moral act is testimony to Faith, it is to man what flying is to a bird. Thus, a community, regardless of the extent of its Muslim majority, that feeds injustices, lets the latter spread and destroy the social tissue, is not "elected" at all. On the contrary, it proves each day its failing towards the exactness of the message that it claims to refer to. The Prophet (peace be upon him), however, has recommended vigilance:

"Support your brother whether he is the oppressed or the oppressor!" Some Companions displayed their astonishment: "It is understandable that we support him when he is the oppressed, but how can we support him when he is the oppressor?" The Prophet responded: "By bringing his oppression to an end."[23]

The Qur'ān and the *Sunna*, as indicated, convey general principles that pertain, at one and the same time, to both the cultural aspect of men's lives and also social affairs. These principles offer orientations which present the field of that which is possible in human action and clarify a number of limits. Thus, we find developed, throughout these sources, a concept of the world which is, all in all, the way in which the Muslims express their rapport with God, nature, other communities and which, by extension, they convey in sciences, techniques, arts and the whole social, economic and political framework. More than a religion, it is a culture and, in this case, a culture based on a system of values and nourished by morality.

It is not a question of confining, but rather of orientating. This means clearly, that in our modern epoch, it is appropriate to respect the fundamental values that are the substratum of Muslim culture and civilisation. To orientate is, therefore, tantamount to selecting among the great Western scientific discoveries that which is good for men and compatible with the values that are ours. The same approach is incumbent at the social and economic planes and up to and including artistic, televisual or cinematographical production. Respect for values always overrides the lure of gain. The selective approach is favoured by a number of Muslim intellectuals. The latter are demanding the powers that be to stop the thousands of hours of American and European programming that is screened on local channels at peak-hours. It is clear that the broadcasting and films that are "offered" by the North are not "free": cultural invasion is a clear colonisation of minds that one knows "will bear fruit" in the long run.[24] There was, in this respect, talk of "censorship" pointing out that recourse to the latter would be a return to the Medieval period with its old stench of Inquisition. Yet, it is not a question of this: to accept everything, in the name of liberty, or in a more general fashion economic liberalism, is tantamount to participating in the creation of a culture of the jungle where "everything is allowed" since it is both liked by people and is profitable. What the West has accepted for itself, other civilisations do not want to share and it is their legitimate right to "sort out" the immense production of the North; even if this means transgressing the rules imposed by the capitalism of superpowers.

The same principle of orientation must be respected on the level of the transmission of religion and culture. The damage caused by colonisation in education alone is still felt today. There are those who know nothing of their religion, those who have forgotten their history, those who no longer speak their language, and those who are torn between imported "modernity" and tradition. This is not all; in a number of Muslim countries, such as Algeria, Tunisia and Egypt to cite but the most known cases, "experts" from the North come to advise the responsibles of education on the content of programmes and pedagogy in general. In Egypt, for example, a commission was created in order to rethink the educative courses at national level and half of it was made up of American experts.[25] This is, after all, something very worrying. Hence, vigilance is incumbent and reference to the Muslim heritage requires consequent work in order to preserve the essential. Any approach which wants to uproot Muslim societies from their points of reference and original moral principles will cause splits, and withdrawals of the kind that we notice today in a great many countries. Entire sections of populations think that their governments have sold their countries and cultures to the mirage of progress and "modernism" à la Western. Such a state of affairs causes violent reactions and sometimes in contrast to what one expects: rather than assisting in the acceptance of the West, a sentiment of rejection is created and this even where there is seduction. This is not due to what the West is, but rather to the way it is presented through films, television, broadcasting and publicity. The percentage of those who understand, can, and want to identify themselves with "modern" values is minute. In this sense, the West is responsible for the way it presents itself to other civilisations: the tones of "artistic" productions that are poured out on the channels of Muslim countries give a poor idea, an unhealthy one of what nourishes the minds of the North. How then can anyone be surprised by the tensions and rejections created by such a situation?

We notice today – and these reactions towards an imported Western culture prove it – that Muslim populations have remained attached to the principles of their religion and culture. It is not possible to think of the future of these countries without making reference to the Islamic datum. It is from now on, more than a fixed point of legitimacy, an objective datum. Even governments, in order to maintain some credibility with their people, find themselves obliged to refer to it: we hear from them, and in Arabic, Qur'ānic citations, *aḥādīth*, connoted words like *Sharī'a*, *bay'a*, and the like. However, being modern, they refrain from conveying these points of reference to their Western interlocutors as they have learnt the rules of the double-face exercise, one that almost borders on the schizophrenic. Muslim ethics, on top of all social, political, economic or scientific action, determines a framework and fixes priorities. Contemporary questions are complex and it is clear that the formulation must evolve in accordance with the level of the learning progress in societies. It remains, however, that, like any other culture, reference to a holistic view of the world (here, the Islamic datum) has a decisive influence on a number of decisions pertaining to law. It is the responsibility of men, who are respectful of the Islamic Faith and concept of the world, to make the choices that are incumbent upon them. Respect for values, morality, justice, freedom of conscience, the right of each person, equality, dignity, nature and animals has an absolute and definitive priority over all other liberal and economic considerations. The Qur'ānic message on this is clear (the same message is also clear in other religious traditions): God commands it to believers.

In industrialised societies, it is the future which seems, from now on, to impose such respect upon men. The Western world, in the course of the last five centuries, has lived a revolution: the process of secularisation has not only liberated the social field from religious seizure but it has also, at the same time, been allowed to contest the soundness of its morality. Laic morality, referred to as the principle of reason, appeared from thence as a regulator. The formidable evolution of learning and techniques produced domains of specialisation in which acquired knowledge was far ahead of the reflection concerning the limits. The acquisition of means preceded the questioning on meaning: progress stimulated progress, mastery opened the doors for hope for an even more important mastery. Laic morality could not, by its essence, enable the management of this revolution. For, unlike religious morality, it is not encompassing. Being rational, it is naturally in consort with active rationality. However, we realise today that we no longer have the power to "master our mastery" of nature and techniques. Ours is an epoch of great fright whereby we are aware that "everything is possible"; that progress has developed techniques that can lead us to an even worse scenario, to the destruction of nature and men. Fundamental reflection, thus, becomes urgent and incumbent upon us all: interesting, then, that the end of the century is seeing a revival of ethics.

Committees are being formed, colloquia multiplied: intellectuals, scientists and the majority of experts are henceforth positing the question of "meaning" as regards their "means". The philosopher Michel Serres presents this new situation clearly:

"Our conquests are faster than our deliberate intentions. Observe, in effect, the cruising acceleration of our technical advances: as soon as it is announced that such or such a thing is possible, there it is achieved somewhere else, following the vertical slope of competition, mimetism, or profit, then this is considered, also as swiftly, as being desirable and even as necessary the day after that: one pleads before the courts if one is deprived. The tissue of our history is made today out of these immediate catching-ups, from the possible to the real and from the contingent to the necessary."

He further adds:

"Yes, we can choose the sex of our children, yes genetic, biochemistry, physics and other associated techniques give us all kinds of power, but we must administer this same power which, for the time being, seems to elude us because it is going too fast and, moreover, farther than our faculties to foresee it, than our capacities to manage it, than our desires to influence it, than our will to decide it, and more than our freedom to direct it. We have solved the Cartesian question: how to dominate the world?, but will we be able to solve the following: how do we dominate our domination, and how to master our mastery?... Without realising it, we are moving from the verb 'to be able to' to the verb 'ought to', as to the same actions. What an expected return of morality."[26]

These situations of limit and necessity offer a new life to the notion of "duty" and man's responsibility is total: "Becoming the masters imposes, in effect, overwhelming responsibilities, which suddenly throw us quite far from the independence which we had thought, even yesterday morning, would be a bed of roses of new powers."[27]

The return of morality and the new responsibility of men coupled with the question of survival has today imposed an ethical reflection on the West. There are many who, like Serres, have expressed the urgency of such awareness. The Astrophysician Hubert Reeves points out:

"Humanity is today driven back to take in charge the future of complexity. It is incumbent upon it to manage the formidable, but irresponsible, creative drives of nature. Under the angle "man in nature", we see, in this third volet, nature becoming conscious of the impasse in which it has engaged itself. It feels forced to go beyond itself and to quit this obsession of performances to which it has up to now confined itself. It invests in the domain of values. Through the advent of the moral sense in humans, it opens eyes and becomes responsible. Man is the conscience of nature."[28]

The scientific explanation of an evolution which will end at the presence of man gives account of this moment of necessary moral conscience:

"The human being's awareness in this vast movement of structuration of matter permits us to re-find our profound roots in the evolution of the cosmos. This vision of the world, which shows the insertion of man in the vast movement of universal organisation, can clarify in a specific fashion the moral choice of people and societies. Any strangers to the universe would have had every right to refuse any responsibility on the future of the biosphere. Inversely, the children of the cosmos are directly implicated in its future. It is up to them to take charge of the working-out of our planet. It is incumbent upon them to ensure a full blossoming of the cosmic complexity.

"This relation of man with the universe gives a double importance to scientific knowledge and to the perusal of research programmes. Not only does science tell us how the world is made, but it also procures for us indispensable documents for the preparation of files relating to moral decisions. In addition, the 'visions of the world' that result from knowledge at a given epoch influence the thought of that epoch and, as an indirect result, what we nicely call 'the spirit of laws'."[29]

Reeves' thought is nourished by the history of Western points of reference,[30] and it is interesting to note here the importance given to legislation in order to ensure the survival of the species. Science, which liberated itself from religion at the price of a fierce struggle, has today created the need for a morality. The calls of savants and intellectuals for an awakening of minds are multiplied: if the too moral calls of Mother Teresa, Leonardo Boff and Abbot Pierre are comprehensible due to their status, the stands of Albert Jacquard, René Dumont or Michel Serres have something new in them. New voices are being heard and all are mobilising themselves for values, and ethics, and a moral sense that the state of humanity and the planet imposes on us to affirm. The work and stands taken by NGOs for development have a strong moral connotation, as have the research works of Susan George, Noam Chomsky or Rudolph Stramm, the philosophical development of Andre Comte-Sponville, Philippe Forget and Gilles Polycarpe.[31] It is these same preoccupations in face of the future that drove Hans Küng to write *A Global Ethic*[32] where he clarifies: "the motto of the future is: global responsibility" by referring to the notion of the "ethics of responsibility" as developed by Max Weber at the beginning of this century. The moral question becomes incumbent with the incredible weight of responsibility.

The paths that have been so separated are now joining with one another. The original ethical reference of Islam joins the moral questioning of reason to the vicinities of limits and possible catastrophes. The nature of the questions of meaning ensuing from it is admittedly different, but the three given facts of limit, responsibility and duty enable us to establish bridges between the universe of Islamic culture and that of ethical reflection in the West. Nervous about the shocking manifestations of the other, we seem to be losing the formidable occasion for a fruitful and imperative dialogue: yet the respective contributions would enable us to shed the necessary new light, as much in order that Muslims may legislate with full knowledge of the facts as for committed Westerners who can, thus, establish relations of partnership in order to fight against scientist, technician and economist drifts.

4.   Meaning and Finality

Nothing is more feared, in the West, than reference to religious morality, and this in turn ends up by leading to no appreciation of any reference to God.[33] There are several reasons for this, as we have seen, and foremost among them one must place the concrete actualisation of the Christian message as well as the historical conflicts between clerical authority, the humanists and rationalists. The terms "Revelation" and "Truth" have been banned: those who refer to them have left behind such a memory of narrow-mindedness, closeness of thought and attitude which is often so torturous that it cannot arouse anything but opposition and rejection. It is moreover this, almost natural, posture that is adopted by intellectuals in the West, when they hear from the mouth of their Muslim interlocutors, the words "God", "Truth", "morality" or when they see them permanently refer to the Qur'ān or to the *Sunna*. Regardless of how progressist they might be, or whether they are convinced that ethics today is still necessary, they do not recognise themselves in the universe of Muslim points of reference. In simple comparison with their Judaeo-Christian tradition, they feel that this universe is still "too religious", dogmatic and stilted.[34] If, moreover, as is the case today with the majority of intellectuals, they stick to what the media report to them on the Muslim world, then they are doubly confirmed in their various stances.[35]

Thus, we notice a kind of rupture, a ditch of non-communication with human beings who, however, in their own universe, struggle for human dignity, right and justice. The words of "over-there" are not those of "over-here", and the objectives cannot be the same. The conclusion is hasty, and the apparent logic behind the reasoning is deceptive.

We have not ceased saying it throughout this present study that it is appropriate to grasp the culture of the "other" from within, by trying to understand the meaning of the terminology used in a system with a comprehensive point of reference. Extracting a word out of its context in order to judge its definition is methodologically a gross error. The new encounter between the West and Islam makes it incumbent upon us to reconsider the old certainties and to arm ourselves with more subtle and precise tools of analysis. We have the means, but we also must have the desire and intention.

The foundations of the Islamic civilisation, which revolve around reference to the Unicity of God (*tawḥīd*), give absolute priority to the meaning of life and the finality of human actions. These today are nourishing the spirituality, the hearts and minds of millions of Muslims. The relation – always sensitive – that exists between the latter and the points of reference of the Islamic culture is absolutely not comparable to that which has become the rule in the West. One can delight in this or deplore it; the facts are out there and one cannot avoid taking into account the categories of Muslim culture in the elaboration of projects of the society of today or tomorrow. Admittedly, one can, and should, fear the literalist, formal and archaic interpretation of Qur'ānic and traditional sources. Such interpretation exists and is representative of a reactive identity-based withdrawal-into-oneself encountered by some scholars, governments and social players. However, this is not, by far, the only way in which intellectuals, and the people in general, refer to their fundamental points of reference or how they would like to see them respected. The fact that they are considered of Divine origin, that they are figured as a result of reflection and rationality and that they offer orientation and principle, does not mean that they are dogmatic or totalitarian. We have already conveyed our position on this subject when speaking for example about the "deviant translations" of the notion of *Sharī'a*. Islam offers a horizon of possibles and to reduce them to radical options is wrong. One realises, *a fortiori*, that reference to the religious and the cultural allows unparalleled popular mobilisation. Channelled in an open social and political project, not necessarily of a Western kind, such mobilisation would enable the concretisation of popular participation that we are hoping for. The values of Islam call for fraternity, solidarity, respect for human dignity as well as respect for nature. Reinstated in their cultural compost, these notions find a dynamising symbolical force. These values are, by essence, opposed to individualism, exploitation, destruction of resources, the cult of technique and blind science. Will we know, in the West, how to see in Islam a safeguard against the drifts of a modernity whose evolution we can no longer control? Will the Muslims know how to make this link with God and their points of reference an advanced stronghold of the fight against injustice, destruction of the planet and "market monotheism"? Everything, absolutely everything, in the Qur'ānic message invites them to do so.

a.   *Communal solidarity*

In the majority of Muslim societies, the most active social actors in communal mobilisation are so in the name of Islamic values. Local undertakings, the networks of solidarity, the "alternative" levying of *zakāt*, the creation of dispensaries, schooling support and the elimination of illiteracy among adults, are not the work of governments and even rarely still the object of programmes of structural adjustment. Work at the grass roots is carried out in a voluntary and dynamic manner by Muslims who have understood that their commitment before God is straightaway an engagement with men.[36] In the West, nothing is often seen of this work except that which appears as a political strategy whose objective is power. This is snapping one's fingers at the fundamental teachings of Islam and that which they can awaken in the hearts and minds of the faithful. What one easily recognised in Mother Teresa and Abbot Pierre, one has difficulty in admitting for Muslims. Yet, it is a question of the same procedure, with however the difference that the Islamic point of reference, which links the individual to the community, is undoubtedly more insisting in Islam, and is even more marked by the obligatory aspect than in the Christian teaching or what it has become in industrial societies.

The sacred character of the family, respect of the elderly, support of the handicapped, partake of the order of things and cannot be the object of "concessions" in the Muslim culture. The communal dynamic is, thus, the only one envisageable because everything in Islam, from the concept of rite to the application of social affairs, refers back to the same. There is complaint in the West about increasing individualism, egoism and exclusion in so-called "post-modern" societies. The spirit of economic rivalry and competition obliterates any vague desire for solidarity: the social tissue is disintegrating and marginality is unceasingly increasing. But there is great difficulty in admitting that societies with Muslim majorities can find within their culture the means to avoid Western drifts: to refer to Transcendence or religion is not allowed at all. Yet, there exists around the notion of *tawḥīd*, and by extension in religious teaching, a holistic concept and a way of life that places fraternity, communal participation and solidarity in the first rank of the finalities of the social contract. One must persuade oneself today of the fundamental difference in the echo, in the hearts of Muslims, between a supportive call based solely on generosity and an invitation to social participation that reconciles them with their points of reference, culture and history. In the words of the Prophet (peace be upon him): "Verily God shall always come to the help of a servant as long as he comes to the help of his brother."[37]

These words resound with a peculiar force in the hearts of Muslims, whether practising or not, and are in themselves enough to set in motion supportive dynamics that no programme of development can achieve. One should stop seeing here nothing but political or populist manipulation. It is a question of a fundamental teaching of Islam and the "awakening" that is spoken about is before anything else, and in the majority, an awakening of "social Islam" one that seems to much scare the powers in place.[38] To refer to Islam is to first call for more humanity and fraternity: the Qur'ān repeats this and the Prophet (peace be upon him) confirms it; and the meaning of life lies herein. "The best among you is the one who is more beneficial to men."[39] The moral culture of Islam is, in its source, an ethics of solidarity.[40]

b. *Drugs and delinquency*

Muslim societies are still relatively preserved from the contemporary scourge of drugs. We are referring here to all kinds of drugs, that of the North (alcohol, medicine, tobacco) and that coming from the South (hashish, cocaine, heroin, etc.). The religious prohibition of alcohol and the forbiddance, by analogy, to consume any kind of stupefying substance, has played, and is still playing, an important safety role.[41] Contrary to what we can observe in Brazilian, Colombian, or in a broader sense, South American shanty towns the problem of drug consumption is not as serious in the land of Islam. Admittedly, one finds in some countries, like Morocco, the Yemen or Afghanistan, cultural habits that are taking a worrying turn; but on the whole, the problem of the youth is increasingly due to unemployment, underemployment and illiteracy.

Thus, the level of "security" of Muslim societies (obviously those that are not in a state of war) is particularly impressive. With such misery, poverty and destitution, one is astonished to notice so little delinquency, acts of vandalism or other "kinds of social violence". It is possible to walk along the streets of Cairo, Amman, Jakarta, Tunis, and Casablanca with the feeling of more security than when walking in New York, Rio or in some neighbourhoods of London or Paris. For whoever has travelled in Muslim countries, it is clear that there reigns therein a particular atmosphere which is not unrelated to religious and cultural points of reference. This fact is beginning to change due to the increasing influence of Western culture: imported films broadcast their daily lot of violent images and negative social attitudes. Drugs and their substitutes have also started for a while now to be the object of trafficking. In some neighbourhoods, one has seen, even though still in its early stages, gangs of youth in the making. The world of Islam is coming dangerously close to some delinquent reflexes known in the West.

Reference to Islam and the revival of cultural identity may enable us to fight against such a negative evolution. Religious teaching, in a broad sense, its social consequences and the atmosphere resulting from it at the communal level, are proven guarantees against the violent drifts of social fracture. It is not a question of creating a repressive society (does one have to be reminded that prevention and reform come first) whereby one prohibits, imprisons and kills "deviants". Such a narrow concept is a betrayal of the Message of Islam. As we have indicated, the principle of communal solidarity is a priority; it enables, by consequence, the fight against the use of drugs and delinquency. Indeed, Islam is also this positive dimension, even though it is often forgotten.

Yet, vigilance is incumbent. Western influence, and this is not to its honour, has very negative consequences and is causing situations that the Muslim world did not hitherto know. The loss of values, nihilism, the idea of suicide, and blind violence are many "novelties" through which cultural invasion is knitting its web. Not content with not being able to control at one and the same time the consequences of economic liberalism and social drift it is exporting a model which it does not cease to complain about itself. In this sense, television and the cinema are causing havoc: everywhere it is economic profit which takes precedence. And governments "under-tutelage" accept uncomplainingly the rules of trade. They imprison those who give everything of themselves in order to teach the youth the foundations of their identity, the rules of social participation, the meaning and finalities of a life among human beings with deference to the link with God; and at the same time, in the name of modern freedom and liberalism, they open wide the doors of intimacies to a culture without values, a culture of violence, money and falsehood. Is, then, the violence of American societies the example? Does increased consumption of drugs present any hope? Are the rates of suicide and the number of rapes enviable? Admittedly, the West is not reducible to just this; but this should not be accepted from the West.

Not everything that is given is good for the taking. The identity-based Islamic referent has proved its capacity to avoid social drifts. In front of what appears as cultural aggression, the most legitimate attitude is that which consists of an operation of selection. One should welcome everything that the West produces in accordance with human dignity, decency, generosity and learning. A culture, after all, is legitimised in commanding respect for its values. This regardless of the cost or the judgement of those who are convinced of being open, progressist, liberated and advanced. If there is no other modernity except that of the model of actual Westernisation – which is questionable and without doubt erroneous – then one must reject modernity. Islam has transmitted to us an idea of man that does not correspond to this strange "modern" specimen which cultivates the least of effort, one which is individualist and satisfies only its desires and goods. Muslim culture, by reference to the Prophet (peace be upon him), is based on the concept of the model, or moral comportment, of sociability. The transmission of learning passes through this particular dimension. The Qur'ān is clear on this:

> *You have had a good example in God's Messenger for whosoever hopes for God and the Last Day, and remembers God often.* (Qur'ān, 33:21)

In this way, the Prophet is a model as are his Companions, just as are our parents and the good people around us. So also should those who participate in a certain way in our lives through the medium of the large or small screen. Without wasting too much time on analysis, we are bound to notice that what today is presented to us has nothing to do with the way Muḥammad (peace be upon him) lived, nor for that matter Moses, Jesus or Abbot Pierre. Good people seem to be the "exceptions" who confirm the rule of absent models. The teaching of Islam cannot adhere to such a concept: the culture of reminder is far from one of commercial strategies which nourish heedlessness.

c.   *The man-woman relationship*

Much has been said about the Muslim world's confinement *vis-à-vis* sexuality and what this covers both at the personal and social levels. On this issue, it has often relied upon considerations relating to the status of women – whose sexuality is seen as being limited to following the way which will make of them mothers – female circumcision and the imposition of the veil and everything that is in keeping with it. This picture does not offer a blooming horizon; for it suggests that if there is any pleasure at all, then it seems to be reserved for men.

We do not deny that today's Muslim societies are not models of balance and well-being. Profound, ancestral links with the pre-Islamic tradition or simply local patriarchy does produce discrimination towards women. Their fundamental rights are suppressed, their education limited, the veil is sometimes imposed upon them and their role is circumscribed to the expression of maternity and housewifery. Some theologians rely on a very literalist and restrictive interpretation in order to justify this state of affairs; others balance their criticism, preferring the status quo rather than an evolution of the Western kind. Yet, the question remains: do contemporary Muslim societies present the real face of Islamic teaching on relations between men and women and their respective rights?

We have in part already raised this question when we mentioned the important movement of intellectual women who are today calling for a liberation *within* and *by* Islam. These women have gone back to an interpretation of sources and want to achieve that which is, deep down, a re-appropriation of the elements of their culture extracted from traditional interferences that have nourished alienation. For there exists in Islam, effectively, a profound concept of balance in the relation between a man and a woman which is, in the first instance, nourished by all the dimensions of being: the spirit, body, love, marriage, sexuality, social presence, etc.

The West, however, has hurriedly stopped at the "visible" expression of the submission of woman in the Muslim universe: the veil, in the end, did not but confirm what the West already knew. However, the significance of the veil is that whilst it is an Islamic obligation, it is nonetheless one which cannot be coerced upon anyone, for it is not a "sign" of religious adherence. The West's very reductionist interpretation acts like a screen to an understanding of the Muslim cultural universe. The veil should, however, rather be seen as a concrete expression of a dimension that is more fundamental in the man–woman relationship. The veil at the social level is a manifestation of the spiritual and sacred dimension of being. The gaze that a man must cast down, the hair that a woman must hide, the body that both have to protect and preserve, boil down to a Faith that takes its source in decency. It is about expressing, in our social life, that we are not a body, that our worth is not in our forms and that our dignity lies in respect of our being and not in the visibility of our appeals and seductions. Such are the rules that

Muslim culture teaches in the proximity of the sacred. The Prophet (peace be upon him) reminds of this: "There is certainly, among that which people have understood from the first prophecies, (the following message): 'If you do not feel any shame, then do as you please.'"[42]

In contrast to the evolution of a Western-like liberation, this reference to decency is still very much alive in Muslim countries[43] and it has remained a concrete expression of the call to meaning. Does this, however, mean that the exactness of decency kills love and sexuality? Certainly not, but the general concept offered by the Muslim universe gives a peculiar shape to their factuality. Islam has never acted in a way as to amputate from the human being an element of his intimacy or constitution. In Islam there is no idea of culpability in the life of the body or of any celibacy that brings one close to God. Man and woman, in their link with the Creator, are made to love, to love one another and also in order to live their sexuality. This life of the heart and body inserts them in the total harmony of creation: love, sexuality and pleasure are never detached from the meaning of life. A love without respect of being, a sexuality without love, a pleasure nourished by the sole attraction of desire or pleasure, these are as many expressions to a life that is far off from Islamic culture, and one which testifies a rupture with spirituality and Transcendence.

The achievement of this balance between love, sexuality and acknowledged pleasure passes, according to the teaching of Islam, through marriage. For man as it is for woman, it is a question of offering the other that which is protected from others. In this sense, any society has it upon itself to give to each of its members the possibility to live the blossoming of their being through marriage. We have reported above the words of the Prophet (peace be upon him) which assimilated the sexual act to the sacrality of a charity when it is conducted within the bounds of a licit marriage. In the profound understanding of this teaching, there are many scholars who have tackled, without vexation, the questions of the body and sexuality following the

example of the Prophet (peace be upon him) and that of his
Companions who conveyed clearly that it was a question of life
and that there existed indeed on the subject an Islamic art of
living. The writings of Ibn Ḥazm (tenth century), Ghazālī
(eleventh-twelfth centuries), and more clearly Suyūṭī (fifteenth-
sixteenth centuries), to cite but a few, abound with bold analyses
and commentaries on love, sexuality and pleasure.[44]

Love and sexual life is hence nourished, oriented and achieved
within a more total concept that gives it both meaning and
harmony. Before God, and while respecting the limits and
balances, it is possible and even recommended to live life fully.
The sacred allows life and life gives birth to the sacred, if only
life is made to be a remembrance of God and rights. The words
of Salman to Abū al-Dardā' were verified by the Prophet (peace
be upon him):

"You have duties towards God, you have duties towards your
own self as you have duties towards your wife: give to each their
due."

On another occasion, the Prophet (peace be upon him)
himself said to 'Amr ibn al-'Āṣ:

"Your body certainly has rights on you, your eyes certainly
have rights on you, your wife certainly has rights on you and
your guest certainly has rights on you."[45]

Holding Faith and living love is tantamount to respecting
balances and, within the bounds of decency, accepting everything
in our constitution. The man-woman relationship partakes of
this profound comprehension. Both are equal, absolutely equal
before God and they carry, each one in the same way, the
responsibility of their being before the Creator. On the familial
and social planes, this equality is achieved in complementarity:
forming a couple, giving life to a family, offering an education
which requires the participation of two beings who do not
confuse their equality with resemblance. A man is not (*not equal
to*) a woman, just as fundamentally, profoundly and intimately a
father is not a mother. All the teachings of Islam remind us of
this right of children upon their parents which is finding in the
family a harmony of sensitivities.

This notion of complementarity should not, however, justify, on the social level, discriminations. There is an equality of fact in work and social participation (from the moment that this choice has been made) which is inalienable. Admittedly, Islam fixes priorities: the familial equilibrium, being present around the children and their education takes precedence over financial considerations and personal professional success. A person should participate in the creation of a sound familial atmosphere, but it remains that the nucleus of the family is created around the mother. This is a priority, but it does not hinder, according to circumstances, the adjustments that Islam acknowledges and accepts. Thus, if a couple make the choice of the social engagement of the woman, this should be respected: not least with equality of wages to equal qualifications and competencies, trade-union rights, the possibility of promotion, etc. The facts on these points do not suffer from sexist concessions.

We can, hence, see how the Islamic teaching stresses the notions of harmony and balance. It is before anything else a total concept which influences all the levels of the man–woman relationship. To extract a domain and then criticise it out of its context is unfair; just as it is unfair to justify, in the name of a virtual ideal, concrete and daily discriminations. Muslim culture is based on decency and a respect for bodies; along with the limits, it conveys finalities and gives an existential sense to love, marriage, sexuality and desire. All these dimensions of human intimacy are part of a total vision of life which is linked to Transcendence: they are "charities" and "prayers" when they are inscribed within the way. One understands that this universe is of meaning, that this system of values, cannot be found in the kind of evolution borrowed by the West. The dislocation of the familial tissue, families that are increasingly broken (single-parent families, the ever-increasing divorce rate), the reign of a sexuality turned towards sole pleasure but which is often empty of meaning and respect, and the sale of bodies. The West, here also, seems to be losing control over its future.

At 14 or 15, youth have often seen, known and experienced it all. Everything goes so fast, just as their loves, and then they get bored. The universe often appears to them without limits: everything seems permitted in their eyes because very few adults have taken the responsibility to fix rules. This fact is so widespread that it has become a normal thing just as it seemed normal to "whistle at", in an unworthy fashion, Abbot Pierre when he asserted, during a campaign against AIDS, that the "best prevention is faithfulness". The West is not reducible to this picture, but it would, however, be hypocritical not to admit that we are living under the reign of new cults of money, sex, and pleasure in general. All the women who, in the course of this century fought a just struggle for the liberation of women and who wanted to achieve recognition of their private and social rights, equality of wages, the right of divorce, etc., would not in general identify with the actual drifts as they have materialised. A great number of people are fighting so as not to confuse the rights of woman with the image of woman that is advertised and whose body has become a trade and market product. Such a liberation is a deception and the Western model certainly carries within it alienations which leave little to be envied, this despite real progress in the matter of rights.

Today the superpowers and great commercial societies, in the name of liberalism, are inundating our planet with images and vogues *à la Western*. Show business stars, models and their private lives are reported in Kuwait, as they are reported in Rio, and Dakar. It is a question of cultural aggression, but the effects of which in terms of identity-based tension and feeling of rejection are not always taken into account. Admittedly, seduction is present, but this gives rise, in concomitance, to a very negative perception and a will of demarcation that sometimes takes violent paces. Such kind of (re)presentations from the West cannot but create ruptures between civilisations. And even if there is a share of caricature, it remains no less true in the eyes of innumerable traditional cultures, especially Islam, that the Western horizon does not seem to propose, in the facts, great projects of meaning, value and hope. So much is said about love, affection, and emancipation – to the point even of hiring experts to explain what these mean – that "one feels in all this", as Rimbaud says, "that something is missing". The Islamic concept of man, love and sexuality prevents the Muslim world from following the track of this model of Westernisation. Resistance is almost natural: the path of a different modernity is in the course of seeing daylight.

d. *Science, technique and ecology*

After several decades of confidence and hope, an increasing number of voices who criticise a technician society and the cult of progress are heard in the West. The great ideas of the nineteenth century, the great projects of our epoch seem today to be "obsolete" because of the scope of the difficulties that have been created. The hour of inventories is a time of anguish: "It is a cause of anguish to see hyper powerful techniques being used without control by enterprises who have no other law except profit, by war lords who dream of nothing but their own domination, and by bureaucrats who look for nothing except oppressive efficiency, in a world without soul, coherence or project."[46]

Serge Latouche furthermore observes:

"The drama of modern technique is not so much in the technique as it is in the modern, that is to say in society. The fact that the society born of the Enlightenment, emancipated of all transcendence and tradition, has truly renounced its own autonomy and let itself be abandoned to an outlaw regulation of automatic mechanisms in order to be subjected to the laws of market and the technician system, this society now constitutes a mortal danger for the survival of humanity."[47]

The author draws a picture of this situation without complacency. The Western model, in his view, leads to an impasse: a critique and demarcation *vis-à-vis* the idea of progress is incumbent: "Signalling that progress is at the basis of the economicisation of social life, that it is the source of economism as vision of the world and one of the basic principles of political economy, leads to the insinuation that it is a question of a profoundly Western cultural trait – indeed, to condense it is the very essence of the West as an anti-culture machine. In such conditions, a cultural pluralism would not be possible unless belief in progress is questioned, since the domination of the latter means the Westernisation of the world."[48]

This reflection is interesting and, coupled with that of many other intellectuals, it posits the major question of cultural choice: the technician thought and the idea of progress are not elements of Western culture, they are Western culture. In this sense, to speak of modernity, whether one likes it or not, is another way of speaking about Westernisation. The critique is total and it does not leave any room for the idea of a selective appropriation of the Western technique. In this, such a critique joins the position of many Muslim thinkers among whom, very recently, can be counted Munir Chafik.[49] Without going this far, let us nonetheless retain here the fixed fact of "the infernal character of the mega-machine-West". For such process has escaped any kind of regulation, and we have now "embarked" upon a cycle that has surpassed us and is causing profound social and political destruction, exclusion, marginalisation and the absence of people participation. Science brings forth science and technique justifies itself through its own progression: this is the reign of means and from now on there is no end anymore. Such is without doubt the principal characteristic of the society called "modern", "post-modern", "industrialised" and "technician". A sombre landscape, a sad perspective which led Serge Latouche to think that only the failure of the Western project can be salvific:

"The historical failure of the West, and therefore of its values which carry progress, is the only possibility in order that the question of 'good' be re-posited within human societies instead of 'how much' it has substituted beginning from Modern Times. This re-opening of the social space to the question of the good life is at the same time a possible opening to a plural society and plural humanity. Is it absurd, eccentric or monstrous to speak of an end of Western civilisation? Such an end seems inevitable not simply because any civilisation is mortal, but especially because this end can be read in the limits and failures of Westernisation. The civilisation of progress carries, in itself, the germs of its own destruction."[50]

Not all analysts have gone this far, but there are many who expect nothing from science, technique and progress. Like Serge Latouche, they call for an awakening which may lead to a reconsideration of values, ethics and the "reasoning mind". This is true of the social sphere whereby we are forced to enumerate the drifts of modern societies: the culture of technique has brought nothing of the happiness that everyone expected. On the political plane, we are witnessing, without doubt, the greatest resignation of peoples that has ever been observed. For how many are those who deplore the fact that citizenship has been emptied of its content? The more one is informed, the more one is passive: "enlightened" democracy seems to be playing with the opinion of the masses. Liberation takes the flavour of erring and for some situations, it becomes difficult not to speak of decadence.[51]

The ethical reflection that arises of these situations of limit is that scientific researches now give us glimpses of frightening possibilities whereby technical progress promises us a dehumanised universe. In the prolongation of a liberation that wanted both to defeat dogma and master nature it is now the latter that complains of men's disrespect and folly. Desertification, the greenhouse effect, the destruction of the ozone layer, pollution and nuclear energy have become the themes of ecology in vogue. Faced with "merchant logic", there have been attempts to make references to notions of respect for species and nature; but nothing has really changed. Merchant logic is indeed carried by this principle of not taking into account anything except that which is quantifiable. Weary, some ecologists have decided to convey their reflection in numbers in order to better penetrate this famous logic. Thus, they have elaborated the concept of "external cost" which is the price we pay for the consequences resulting from industrial or other activities: pollution, noise pollution, etc. The paradox though confines us to a vicious circle: a countable tinkering about the edges which does not face up to the basic problems and essentially consecrates the victory of "economism" over the ethical foundation of ecology.

On the political plane, the ecologist movement seems to be on shaky ground. For while it is critical of progress, it rarely goes as far as a total questioning of the economic system whose logic is the cause of rupture and drift. It certainly has the merit of placing at the heart of reflection the question of values; but the last decade has proved to us the capacity of the system to recuperate insofar as it has captured anew people's good feelings, is satisfied with a terminological renewal, encourages "ecological" tinkering and subjects all to its calculus of efficiency and profitability. The critique has indeed missed its target. Michel Serres, in his *Contrat naturel*, shared this intuition: his philosophical reflection tackles the question from above. Noting the rationalist evolution of Western thought, he identifies that there is an important gap in the elaboration of laws:

"One must therefore proceed to an agonising revision of modern natural law which assumes a non-formulated proposition, in virtue of which man, whether individually or in a group, can alone become the subject of law. Here parasitism resurfaces. The Declaration of Human Rights had the merit of saying 'all human beings' and weakness lies in thinking this to mean 'only human beings' or 'human beings alone'. We have not laid out any balance whereby the world enters into account, in the final inventory. The objects themselves are the subject of law and not only simple passive supports for appropriation, even if it be collective. The law tends to limit the abusive parasitism among men but does not speak of this same action on things. If the objects themselves become subjects of the law, then all the balances will tend towards an equilibrium."[52]

It seemed to Serres imperative that shape be given to a total thought which would take into account the given fact of the universe: man, society, and nature. Thus, in the course of the process of scientific evolution, at a time when progress is reaching border situations, the management of "the how", which was the work of laboratory experts, now confronts everyone's fate. Clearly, the management of the how, in the approach of the all, is a new expression of the why. Survival has forced free science to link itself with ethics.

One would perhaps be astonished to learn that on a number of points, Michel Serres' thought agrees with the original religious and cultural considerations of Islam. We are straightaway placed within a holistic vision: the universe of creation is a universe of signs whose elements are sacred because they are reminders of the presence of the Creator. The Islamic concept is, by essence, in opposition to merchant logic. It is impossible to acknowledge a self-justified science and an alienating technique. The history, conflicts and oppositions that led the West to a modernity conceived as the cult of progress are specifically Western. Islamic civilisation has known nothing of this and its teaching obliges the faithful and the community to instead draw from this "holistic thought". The very expression of *tawḥīd* and *rabbāniyya* are concrete examples of this. This is quite evidently not a gain of the reasoning mind since, from the beginning, it was the link with Transcendence that imprinted its mark. Here we do not go back to the "reasoning mind"; when all is said and done, it is impossible to come out of it.

The question of finalities is primary: quality takes precedence over quantity, as we have said. In fact, it is another way of saying that the Muslim culture is fundamentally and essentially opposed to scientist, technician, and economist logics. The notion of progress reduced to the sole parameter of productivity carries, in itself, an alienation because it is devoid of meaning. In the mirror of the relation with Transcendence, negligence results in loss:

> Be not as those who forgot God, and so He caused them to forget their souls. (Qur'ān, 59:19)

To forget God is tantamount to neglecting holistic thought and it is, in the final analysis, losing oneself in the management of the how wherein all seems to be authorised since nothing preoccupies one's memory. It is not a question, as was the case in Christian history, of opposing the evolution of things:

this is an objective fact willed by the Creator. The original pact makes it incumbent upon us to think our own mastery: this, in all time and places, must give witness to our respect of the sacred and Divine. The spirit of finality is intimately linked to the expression of learning and mastery (we would even say that it carries such an expression). More precisely, we should not be speaking of "mastery" of nature: this idea of conflict, born out of Biblical expression and the history mentalities and sciences of the West, is absent in Muslim terminology. What is important here is harmony: nature is the space of the expression of one's witness, of one's thankfulness and Faith.

We are dealing here with an ecology which is before ecology. The latter is born of the nearness of catastrophes; the former is the expression of the original pact between God and men. We can read multiple Qur'ānic calls that rely on the elements of nature: by the heavens, the moon, the sun, the night, the stars, the trees, the earth, the animals, etc., the sacred expression of nature partakes of the "link" (*religio*). The following saying of the Prophet (peace be upon him) grips one by its clarity and force on the nature of the rapport that man has to entertain with nature:

"If the Last Hour is on the point of taking place and one of you has a young shoot in his hands that he wishes to plant before it comes, then let him plant it for he will be rewarded for it."[53]

At the moment of the Last Hour which consecrates the entire meaning of existence, the faithful expresses his faithfulness by a gesture of sympathy towards the universe of signs. It is this same idea that is entailed in the recommendation of economising on water, even of a river which appears never to be wasted, when one makes ablution. The path which leads us to prayer cannot admit a rupture with the natural space.

It is an exacting ecology, if ever there was one, which questions, from top to bottom, the Western concept of the world: Islam is a culture of finalities, that is absolutely opposed to the culture of means. On the level of ecology, as on that of science or techniques, the Muslim world must make a choice. Some affirm that modernity should be rejected because "everything", in this notion, is nourished by the Western concept: it seems to them that making a selection in the vast field of scientific discoveries and techniques is a lure. Others point out that Islamic teaching is opposed to neither progress nor evolution nor technique, that Western scientific revolution owes, besides, much to Muslim savants and that, in this sense, it is quite possible to make a selection and master the integration of tools by investing them with finalities that are in agreement with Islamic ethics. It appears to us that one must take the spirit of both arguments: in order to avoid naïve considerations that make us think we can easily extract a learning or a tool from merchant logic, we should look into meticulous ways for a necessary accommodation.

To consider Islam from this angle gives another image of the role that this civilisation can contribute in its encounter with the West. At a moment when preoccupations about ethics, respect for nature, and the alienation of technician society are in the course of being developed, the presence of Muslim culture can act as an echo and a mirror. At the source of Islamic teachings, we find the exactness of values, meaning and finalities. The way of rationalism pushed to extremes finds anew that of original spirituality: rationality, through ethics, has the means to get in touch with Faith. Dialogue is possible.

It remains that those intellectuals and persons engaged in a critique of Western drifts should try to address Islamic teachings in a total manner, beyond information and manipulation, to perceive therein the elements of a culture that has positive answers to contemporary problems. Determined reference to the Islamic datum should not be considered as the expression of a fundamentalism. To state one's Faith and culture is first to state that one "is" and what one believes in. Is it not through this, when all is said and done, that one passes on a real acknowledgement of plurality in a world where unidimensionality, to borrow the old expression of Herbert Marcuse, is so feared? Let us note, however, that the responsibility of confinement does not fall solely on Westerners. For in the end, there are disturbing and shocking stands in the Muslim world, which are often justified in the name of Islam. They are of a nature that re-routes the best of intentions, such is the unconditional alignment, taken at the Rio Summit (June 1992), of all countries producing oil with the American position! Political, economic and strategic interests have their own reasons which lead to the betrayal of fundamental Islamic principles. Islam is not what the actual powers in place are making of it. Hope lies in the consciousness and intimacy of entire sections of Muslim people whose affective predisposition is still intact and whose engagement is in a position to give witness to the link with Transcendence and faithfulness to the original pact.

III.   TOWARDS A WAR OF CIVILISATIONS?

Much has been said, after the fall of the Communist regimes, about the future new enemy confronting the West: the Muslim universe, through its concept of the world and the fervour of its Islamist "militants", contests the progress of liberal society. One knows, in university quarters, the thesis of the American Samuel Huntington who announced the new era of the clash of civilisations. Islam is presented therein as a threat, and the future appears to be sombre. Bernard-Henri Lévy, retaining the elements of Huntington's analysis, observes: "What to make of this political Islam that has triumphed in Algiers and which one can with difficulty deny that it offers itself as an alternative model to the civilisation that is inspired from France and Europe."[54] After having been reminded of the words of Hobbes on the "wars of philosophies" and that of Nietzsche on the "modernity which will dominate the great religions' shock", he mentions Huntington and concludes by disagreeing with the ideologues of the end of history: "The theory of the end of history stumbles upon this indisputable fact that an increasing number of men, peoples and nations contest our definition of what is universal; they propose, even think to impose, theirs; and have taken up the torch that the Marxists have dropped."[55]

The presentation of the scene is bright and seems to be neutral as to any value judgement concerning the respective contribution of civilisations. But such is not the case. In referring to the "insipid version" of old Communism, the role of intellectuals is to resist the enemy and, therefore, to "think as one makes war":

"This moment, which always comes, whereby it is less a question of choosing between right and wrong, but rather between two doctrines that each have their qualifications and foundations – but where one of them promises nothing except servitude, desolation, and contempt, whereas the other at least allows and commands to resist the same."[56]

Islam, in claiming its social and political expression, cannot be anything except a *promise* of fundamentalism, which the West, being liberal and open, *allows* and *commands* to resist. Such crudely simplifying analysis manipulates concepts below the surface of their "media" sense, and ends up saying nothing except what is repeated, with emulation, by all the dictators of Arab countries: resisting what is presented as an "Islamist" danger which, through a will of "dangerous purity", puts in peril progress, liberty, thought, culture and humanism. Such analysis does not say anything, or almost nothing, about Western drifts, but what it does is demonstrate the culpable idleness of those minds that are opposed to anything that questions the achievements of their civilisation. It is, finally, of little importance what the latter proposes to men, it is enough to know that beyond our points of reference there exists but a "fundamentalist international" which contrasts "its purity" to our doubts and which must, therefore, be reasonably fought against. In such a frame of thinking, the Zionist project is not "fundamentalist" and must be integrated in the universe of just resistance. One can judge for oneself the honesty of such a thesis. Incidentally, readers should have known what to expect from the first pages of Lévy's book:

"What are the barbarities that will stir up the world of the year 2000; why now; why here, how can they coexist, just like in Weimar, with a time that otherwise displays such an intense love for democracy, humanitarianism, and human rights; whether it is this time or not; whether the planet where Rushdie is proscribed, where Algeria is ablaze, and where Taslima Nasreen is banned, is indeed the same one announced to us by the theoreticians of the end of history; what exactly happened with the implosion of the Eastern bloc; what has happened since – such are the questions that are at the origin of this book."[57]

The three examples cited relate to the Muslim world from where emanate the sombre odours of future conflict. Wars between "philosophies" seem to be inescapable and the West, being under siege, has the duty to resist "barbarity". Huntington and Bernard-Henri Lévy propose, before the upheaval occurs, an interpretation and make their choices. The latter at the cultural and political level, uses assertive words: "Liberty is possible only if truth is not."[58] This is another way of saying that the Western project is the only viable one. Open thought turns out to be indeed closed, and confined to an idea of truth that does not reveal its name. In other places, this is called a *fundamentalist temptation.*

Fortunately, this is not the only analysis available in the West. Some have not failed to point out the West's responsibility for the peoples of the South tuning into their own identity. Such is the case with Edgar Morin who attached considerable nuance to the historical representation of aggression and its causes: "Then, in contemporary times, and starting from old confinement, secularised Europe and the Islamic world had anew shut themselves off from one another; Islam revitalising itself in its resistance to the Europeanisation of morals which corrupt the identity of Muslim peoples."[59]

The history of the encounter between civilisations, as this author reminds us in other passages of his book, was full of *rapprochement* and conflict. The end of the century reveals a reciprocal sentiment of aggression. One should not try to hide the state of this situation. Understanding is difficult, tensions and rejections are frequent and the future seems to be leading us to serious rupture. This is certainly the case, but it is still not a question of presenting a superficial and simplifying scene of "goodies" and "badies" by prophesying a total war against the enemy. The theses of Huntington and Lévy have, moreover, their parallels in the Muslim world. Incidentally, these feed into one another and, each reinforces itself with its alter ego. The real danger is indeed out there.

One must, nonetheless, go further in the analysis and look for very concrete areas of dialogue, encounter and common achievement. We have indicated a certain number of these in this present book. As soon as one recognises the achievement of Western culture, admits that reference to Islam is inescapable in the Muslim world, and one is ready to accept the concrete consequences of plurality, then one can go beyond gut reaction, find interlocutors and build the future. Such is not the case today. We are living a borderline situation, one attendant with a profound nervousness, whose causes and scale must be understood and analysed in order to hope for more serene tomorrows.

1. Attraction-Repulsion

Seen from the viewpoint of Muslim countries, relations with the West are quite complex. On top of religious and cultural considerations, one must take into account a particularly heavy historical legacy and sentiments that are not always clear or mastered. Attraction, to the point of fascination, exists next to the most radical rejection. The first requirement, therefore, consists in putting things in their proper order.

a. *Seduction*

A great many Muslims living in countries of the South share, with all inhabitants of the Third World, a kind of fascination for Western progress in the broader sense. One is sometimes astonished by, and one may even mock the contradictions in Muslims who seem so attracted by that which they claim to reject.

However, nothing is as natural as this state of affairs. The West presents an attractive visage when one considers the standards of training and breathtaking competence, the incredible technical performance, the respect for the human person, a very comfortable daily existence, permanent spare-time activities, and the freedom of morality. Whoever, in the Third World, is not, even slightly, attracted by this universe is not a human being. Such a scene does not say anything though about the fractures of intimacy, solitude, and the distress that is engendered by a Western lifestyle. The objective is, indeed, not to show any of it. When one encounters Western culture through publicity, broadcasting, films or a short stay, then it is impossible to measure the human and psychological consequences of this modernity. *A fortiori* everything, in the discourses and achievements through which the West presents itself, is destined to put ahead the modern, progressist, in vogue and liberated character of this culture. The Western lifestyle feeds itself by and through seduction in order to awaken man's most natural and primary instincts and desires: social success, will-power, freedom, sexual desire, etc. The recent evolution of the morals – as also the principles – of the liberal economy, which are little linked to moral considerations, has led to the situation that we know today with an inflation of violence, money and sex.

At first sight, seduction cannot not be. But even if analysis does not take into account anything except the standard of university training, scientific and technical progress and social and political liberty, one is obliged to acknowledge that the West has reached, in these domains, incontestable and enviable standards. In fact, one straightaway realises the complex character of such a relation. These latter objective facts seem as if they are carried by the force of this real attraction because it responds to a natural impulse in us. It is, however, difficult to admit because these facts run counter to the moral and religious universe. Such is indeed, incidentally, the consequence of Westernisation. Exercised seduction gives rise, at the same time, to a fierce resistance. Conveyed in the form of a paradox – but which is not in the final analysis – one can point out that the Western mode of being holds, in essence, the germs of a formidable tension: in the world of Muslim points of reference, the elements of its seduction are the main causes of its rejection.

b.   *Identity-based reaction*

Therefore, the rejection is profoundly natural. Faced with the torrent of images and information coming from the North – in which all seems to demonstrate that there is little preoccupation with God, the soul or good and evil – reaction can be fierce and violent. Such a reaction is indeed exactly of the same measure to the potential danger undermining the norms of identity. It is not rare to hear (in speeches whose objective is to protect oneself from Western drifts) caricatures accusing Western culture of the worst observable evils. But here there is a lack of nuance. For there is a light-hearted intermingling of consideration for the Jewish and Christian religions with reflections of a strategic, political and economic order, the whole being enveloped in an ordered attack on the surrounding "immorality". The West which we are still confusing with the universe of Christianity, finds no favour in the statements of some Muslim theologians and thinkers who assert their Muslim identity in opposition to the United States and Europe. They are Muslims against the West, and all their reflection is fed by this cast of mind.

This kind of attitude, which is emotional and immediate, exists and remains understandable regardless of its primary character. However, we cannot justify its excesses. But such is not the position of the majority of intellectuals. They are, certainly, opposed to the Western cultural invasion and refute the colonisation of minds and morals that are being imposed today, but their position is not, in itself and solely, of a reactive nature. They first insist on asserting their religious and cultural adherence and on seeing the latter respected in countries of Muslim majorities. They are for Islam and not against the West: the difference is huge in that the assertion of the Muslim universal is not achieved here through the negation of the Western universe, but rather through the acknowledgement of plurality. Their statements, directed towards the North, go along the same lines: to admit the Islamic point of reference is tantamount to accepting the legitimacy of identities outside rationalist and liberal logic. Does the West have the means of and will for such an acknowledgement? The heart of the debate lies here, that is unless one considers that any identity assertion that does not respond to American and European universals is, in itself, anti-Western. In which case, it is the West alone that is creating for itself enemies and digging, without mediation, the trenches of conflict.

c.   *What interlocutors?*

In such a game of complex relations, it seems difficult to establish a serene dialogue. One is tempted, in the West, to make contact with a third category of intellectuals. The latter are those who have accepted reference to Western norms, just as they have accepted and reproduced them. They think like "us", they speak like "us" and they criticise the same follies. Moreover, they have this advantage, this enormous advantage, of being from "over there". If their conclusions resemble ours, then it is sufficient confirmation of the soundness of our analysis. Trained, or not, in European universities and fed by Western culture, these intellectuals are, in the final analysis, little representative of the world to which, in appearance, they seem to belong. It is not enough to call oneself Ahmad, Tahir, Khalida or Malika in order to represent the majority tendency of Muslim culture in its Moroccan, Algerian, Berber or Touareg specificity.

Some people are offered, in Europe, a legitimacy which is often not verified in their countries of origin. Of these, there are those who do not speak Arabic, who have not, so to say, sojourned in their countries for decades, those who have received less than 1% of the votes in regional elections, those who support dictatorships, or those who denounce the same in order to gain fame. And the West applauds because it "understands" what is being said: *a fortiori* these intellectuals repeat what the West wants to hear. The media multiply the interviews that are as many confirmations of what one already knows, as they are future further proofs.

The situation is complex and strained, but one cannot insist too much on warning against easy solutions, like those which consist of looking among "the other" for "an other" who resemble us. It is high time that the plurality of cultures and opinions are dealt with. To refute cultural invasion is not, once again, tantamount to being anti-Western. It is rather an opposition to the rapport of force and to the will of hegemony of the symbolic universe of the West. It is an opposition not to its being but rather to its manner of being. It is this manner of being that expresses itself in the attitude we have just indicated and, which consists of selecting discourses in the function of their acceptability and conformity to one's own norms. It is about a dialogue of cultures that are truncated and false; it is about inviting the other in order to speak amongst ourselves. This is what has already been done to the North American Indians and it is a perpetuation which is striven for.

To accept diversity, when approaching the Muslim world, is tantamount to taking into account the differences in points of reference, sensibilities, histories and projects. It is also about making contact with intellectuals who, all the while knowing Western "universal" values, make a step, not backward but sidelong, in order to express their Faith, lifestyle, concept of man and life in their own manner. Attempting to find them is tantamount to studying their languages, analyses, and the internal logic of their discourses in light of their own sources.[60] One quickly realises that, despite the difficulty that their expressions present to Western ears, their legitimacy is otherwise more real than many of those intellectuals whose statements comfort idle and sufficient minds. The first step is undoubtedly that of living a small intellectual revolution that entails ceasing to suppose that the USA and Europe are culturally advanced and others are trailing. In this domain, to claim, or simply to think oneself, to be ahead is another way of imposing oneself.

Incidentally, one quickly finds identical values, common hopes, expectations and possible synergies. Coexistence is, nevertheless, achieved at the cost of this effort of understanding and the search beyond caricatures. The present book intends to contribute to the exigency of clarification in this dialogue. To say things clearly is not tantamount to conceding; rather it is making accessible for the other one's own cultural universe and identity in order to better walk along together. Together, but with real respect for diversity and not under the banner of a "multicultural" future which confuses plurality with an eclectic folklore whereby no one recognises himself, except the one who, already, has not assumed any identity.

2. Speeches and Facts

Listening to the speeches of presidents and directors of international financial institutions and heads of great multinational institutions, one may think that our epoch is entirely preoccupied with respect for human beings, their rights and those of nature. But the facts deny the generosity of such declarations. For never have the cleavages been so important with their procession of poverty, misery, drugs, delinquency, corruption and bloody regimes. Relations between the West and Islam suffer from this discrepancy that ought to be, from one side as from the other, analysed for what it is.

a. *Human rights, democracy and freedom*

Revelations of dubious procedures and corruption in the political quarters of the USA and Europe have disgusted more than one person.[61] Many are those who do not trust politicians and parties who say one thing and do something different, and who seem to be only interested in power. Such an atmosphere drives one to resignation. To compare situations, one may ask what ought to be the reactions of the people of the South regarding the speeches of the powerful of this planet about "human rights, democracy, and freedom". What trust to put in them when they see them, for reasons of economic interest, collaborate with the most ignoble, terrorist or corrupt regimes? Saying such beautiful things, and then doing or allowing such dark ones.

Human rights are referred to in a selective fashion according to the objective alliances that one has with such or such a dictator. Democratic façades are supported which, from Tunisia to Egypt, suffocate their peoples and oppositions with daily repression. Nations are put under embargoes, simply because they were unfortunate enough not to yield to the dictates of the Americans or Europeans. Conversely, there is an impressive haste to welcome the oil-producing monarchies who, under tutelage from the likes of Saudi Arabia and Kuwait, apply totalitarian and shameful policies. We know it, and we see it confirmed daily: it is raw materials, products and arms that have a price. The right of a man, his choice and freedom can be sacrificed on the altar of interest or, in the words of the French ex-Interior Minister Pasqua, in the name of the superior reason of the state.

Humanitarian aid, itself, in all its forms, is subject to the reality of "strategic interest". The share of votes of the industrialised countries in the World Bank Group (the World Bank and IDA) represent more than 60%; the decisions concerning the projects to be achieved are linked to the interests of the economic policies of the superpowers. A poor and disobedient country has one extra defect in surplus. Is there any human being on earth who still has any illusion to the contrary? Turabi, in the Sudan – just as Sankara during the hopeful epoch of Burkina Faso – can bring to mind all the political prisoners and the reality of conflict in the South; this is of little importance. That his regime is less repressive than Saudi Arabia is of no importance. Oil and geo-strategy decide who are friends; the poverty of the Sudanese who are subjected to an embargo has no "value". One can multiply the example of this too oriented aid to development, for one knows the American policy on this matter with the famous P.482 Article which stipulates the "conditions" required in the matter of food support.

The principle of human rights, the notion of democracy and the ideal of freedom are, in practice, emptied of their content. Just as in the Athenian epoch – a model? – one is content, more or less, to ensure its concretisation only for a small number – in industrialised countries – and play according to a variable geometry "outside". The pressure exercised on the people is terrible, but there is a cure and the most militant NGOs find themselves, sometimes, taken over by the policy of the powers in place.[62] Who then to trust? Sitting comfortably around a table at a colloquium or in front of the television, some reproach – admittedly with reasons – the people of the South's, choice of violence. But they quickly forget the devastating character of the violence and the denial of rights that they suffer as a consequence. Duverger has spoken about the "external fascism" of modern superpowers: whom they are reproached to have, at least, resisted? Imposing such an order on the world and to carry on using notions such as "human rights" and "democracy", is tantamount to giving a lie to the words and to revealing hypocrisies.

b.   *Western contradictions*

We have, in many instances, reminded readers that the policy of the superpowers is not founded on principles but rather on interests. A good reading of events starts from the following question: for whose benefit is this? The problem of values and rights is secondary. At a time when civilisations are facing one another, in a universe that is becoming increasingly narrow, as we are reminded by Huntington,[63] relations of a strategic and political nature and conflicts, even in minor appearance, take the way of symbols and signs. The least that can be said is that it is difficult to remain very optimistic.

Muslim peoples do not any more have any great illusion regarding Western "good" will. The good Muslim today is not the most moderate one – we have learnt to convey the meaning of words. Rather, he is the most rich or the most strategically useful. If he happens to possess both qualities and that, in spite of everything else, he is a little traditionalist or a dictator, then a blind eye will be turned. Economics decides the degree of political honesty: one has to resign oneself to this. One has without doubt not measured, in the West, the real symbolic scope of four events which have marked Muslim consciousness on a planetary scale. The end of our century, in view of the contradictions and two-geared policies of the West, sees an acceleration of situations that are pregnant with tension. Religious and cultural identification is nourished, amidst nervousness, by obscure political management whose inventory one day ought to be made.

i.   The Gulf War

The allied operation, after the invasion of Kuwait on 2 August 1990 by Saddam Hussein's army, has marked minds in the Muslim world. The "discrete massacre", according to the title of Claude Le Borgne's book, of the Iraqi people comes close to 300 thousand dead with an embargo which, today, continues to kill daily the most poor, plus the incredible armed mobilisation with, in addition, the American presence in Saudi Arabia, all have contributed to Muslim enlightenment. They were lied to, just as the whole Western world was lied to.[64] Who, then incited Saddam Hussein to invade Kuwait? What was the role of the then Ambassador April Gilespie? Was the real strength of the Iraqi army not known? Why have the Americans decided to leave the dictator in his seat? Such are but the apparent questions, mere cynical hints; we know better, henceforth, the intentions of the "saviours". The Americans have reinforced their presence in this sensitive zone. As policemen, from now on, they will "protect" and submit to their order the very "open" sympathising monarchies. In addition, the "new regional order" needs Saddam Hussein. As pointed out by Paul-Marie de la Gorce in *Le Monde Diplomatique*, Hussein is useful: his presence justifies the embargo and the cessation of the production of Iraqi oil maintains the flows to a level that is profitable to American and Saudi resources.[65]

Moreover, the "permanent" presence of danger allows the sale of significant arms ($19 billion in the 16 months that followed "Desert Storm", $14.5 billion of which were to Saudi Arabia alone).[66] Such sales continue as do the revelations, at regular frequency, about the most crazy intentions of aggression that are allegedly blossoming in the mind of the dictator of Baghdad. And the American forces mobilise themselves accordingly.

American hegemony was total, falsehood permanent, broadcasting alienated and the theatricalisation masterly. Decisions came down like lightning, the UN was put under tutelage, the Security Council instrumentalised, and the world watched a worthy operation of the defence of the rights of peoples. Who then was deceived? What aroused the bitterness and disgust of a number of Western intellectuals and journalists, has awakened consciences, fervour and anger in the Muslim world. We know today what motivates the generous interventions of the West. Can we blame any person who feels in himself the expression of a violent drive in the face of so much cynicism? Within the limit of what is humanly bearable, man's cry and his despair remain human. It is time that the people of the West became aware of the responsibility their respective governments share in the spread of violence on a planetary scale. The Gulf crisis has participated in the enterprise of rupture and clash between the Muslim world and the West.

ii.   Bosnia

What to say, in comparison, about Bosnia? In the interval of only a few months, the fierce determination of the allies, the UN and the whole "civilised" world gave way to procrastination, never-ending discussions, superficial disagreements, the betrayal of promises and the desertion of Muslims when the most terrifying information and images were broadcast to the entire world. What serene reading of these events, so close to each other, can one today legitimately make? Between a massacre for economic interest and political resignation, what lesson can one keep?

Western people are astonished, shocked, even horrified by the events of ex-Yugoslavia.[67] One understands this. One should understand even better the impatience and revolt of Muslims throughout the world. On the one hand, they held it against their governments whom they called to give account of their passivity. They saw themselves suppressed as was the case in Saudi Arabia and Egypt where demonstrations of support were banned. They observed the West and put to it a question which is both simple and meaningful: would the reaction have been the same if it was not a question of "Muslims"? Responding in the affirmative would be to discharge, all too quickly, the implicit presupposition of such an interrogation. In the eyes of a great number of Muslims, Bosnia appears as tangible proof of the fact that a clash is going on and that the West is, clearly, at war against Islam. One may speak of simplification, a thousand and one analyses and theories can be referred to, one can explain and explain again, but one will not be able to convince them. Nothing, in light of the objective data surrounding the conflict – ethnic cleansing, arms embargo, non-protected "safe havens", the Russian position, strategic interests and the conniving passivity of Europe and the USA – fundamentally contradicts the thesis.

Night after night, Friday after Friday and Ramaḍān after Ramaḍān, we increasingly hear the enchanted, revolted and radicalised statements of intellectuals and *Imāms* calling for a profound awareness about the dangers of this end of the century. Bosnia is a sign; it is a question of not becoming blinded.

As the Bosnians have rediscovered their "Islamicness" in horror, more and more voices are making themselves heard that want to awaken identity-based adherence, Faith in God, religious practice and concrete commitment. Bosnia – has this been realised in the West? – had the effect of an earthquake. Identity assertion, born out of the spectacle of such disaster, is often reactive, nervous and, unfortunately, given to conflict. Can it be otherwise? Incidentally, one understands that to be serene in such a state is tantamount to being blind.

Beyond terror, rapes, and the dead, Bosnia is in the course of causing immeasurable damage. If it is here a question of one of those "peripheral conflicts", one must admit that it is playing its role perfectly. The fact is that from now on it is firmly imprinted in memories. There are many, those Muslims, who assert that they will not forget. They should not be the only ones. Western people should demand from their political authorities some account regarding the world they are building and the future they are preparing for their children. All this leads us to believe that we are in the process of gathering the elements that will naturally cause the fracture. In this sense, one should not be mistaken about the significance of the docility of Muslim powers. Being subjected to economic interests, their silence is similar to the silence of servants. They do not represent the nature of discussions and the force of popular resentments. For the majority, there is a conviction that the West does not like Muslims. Who has got the means to prove the contrary?

iii.   Algeria

Undoubtedly, it has been forgotten that there were the beginnings of a democratic process and elections at the end of 1991. After the carnage that followed the *coup d'état* and the cancellation of the electoral process, a certain number of intellectuals acknowledged that the military intervention should have been denounced with more clarity and force. For in the final analysis, one cannot call for something and its contrary at the same time: wishing democracy for the entire African continent and opposing the results when one finds them inconvenient.

Incidentally, the simplification of political data has been without comparison in Western discussions of the Algerian situation. In a voluntary way, or only apparently, the Islamic Front of Salvation (FIS) was identified, without any nuance, as a movement of the deprived, led by populist and obscurantist leaders who made use of the credulity of the poor to establish a hard-line "Islamic State" based on a medieval interpretation of the Qur'ān and the *Sunna*. As Hitler was elected, so was the FIS. History having taught us not to make the same mistake twice, intervention was, therefore, incumbent. This is a strange comparison, when all is said and done; a crude comparison, to say the least, that lies about history as well as about the content, form and legitimacy of the "Islamist" movement in Algeria. One may disagree with the theses announced by the responsibles of the FIS – disagreements do exist within the Front itself and, more broadly, between Muslims – but one must exact from oneself an in-depth analysis and objectivity. Little was made of such requirements in the West with its support, in the name of freedom, of an absolutely Machiavellian, dictatorial, torturer and terrorist power. France and the USA should, one day, make an assessment of the massacre of people that their policy of support, apparent or hidden, sanctioned.

Making the economy of an in-depth historical analysis leads to errors of interpretation that are almost the lot of the majority of researchers nowadays. Everything started in 1979 after the Iranian Revolution. Before this, the Islamic point of reference is considered absent. The conclusions are simple and evident. In Muslim countries the "madmen of God" benefit from the conjunction of two elements: the presence of the Iranian model and a social crisis due to poverty. There is nothing religious, spiritual, identity-based or cultural – hence nothing legitimate – in the "Islamist" movements. It is, therefore, uniquely a question of an expression of the will for power in a difficult socio-economic context. It is enough to economically "stabilise" the societies in question in order to contain the blind mobilisation of the "deprived", a new expression designating the "casualties" of the 1960s. The latter are to Muslim society what the extreme right is to industrialised society. Children of misery and revolt, they are forthright, intransigent and dangerous. This is, in sum but without any exaggeration, the analysis that is produced, on a great scale, in the West and which justifies a policy of support for the most terrible governmental crack-downs. Yet, a double error of interpretation is committed here, helped in this by the dictators who present themselves as the first bastions of resistance and safeguard for Western interests. First the degree of people's adherence to the Islamic point of reference is badly appreciated and, then, there is no differentiation between the kinds of intervention on the social and political scene.

The case of Algeria is patent. The names of Ben Badis, Sahnoun, Ibrahimi and Bennabi have been forgotten. The social work carried out since the 1930s "in the name of Islam" has been neglected. Lastly, it was thought, for a very long time, that the Algerian war against the French had no religious connotation, just like Paul Thibaud who asserts:

"The 'Western disguise' of the élite which was produced by colonisation and then exacerbated by the recourse to vulgarised Marxism has induced us into error. Thus, the religious factor had been dissimulated by the leaders of the FLN ... This difference between the way in which a people was seen, in which his own élite conceived it to be and the reality of what was brewing underneath explains the brutal rupture between Algeria and those who, in France, have fought for its independence: there was an error in the object."[68]

This history is not that of an Algerian, terrorist action. It is rather a history of the thought which has fashioned generations of intellectuals who engaged in a work of religious, cultural and, broadly-speaking, identity-based claims. It is easy nowadays to bring to the fore and denounce the violent actions of some "fantasised" youth. Denunciations are, certainly, incumbent, just as should be denounced the imprisonment and torture inflicted on hundreds of intellectuals the day after an election, before the taking up of arms and, prior to any radicalisation. All the educated and level-headed responsibles were subject to roundups and/or executions, and the field was left free for another kind of intervention and armed resistance. Must one say it and repeat it again? It is the repression of the power in place which, purposely, created the armed violence of some small groups. This to a point whereby it is legitimate today to say that the most precious, objective allies of governmental policy are its most extreme opponents. To put it plainly, the presence of a "very agitated" GIA – one obviously infiltrated – allowed Lamine Zéroual to refute the Rome Agreement and to organise presidential elections in the midst of all the upheaval.[69]

Who is happy nowadays about what is going on in Algeria? Apart from the dictatorial powers of all Muslim countries (who see their policy of firmness justified) and the superpowers (who find arguments so much for their strategic support as for their disturbing economic relations), nobody can find therein cause for delight. The drama is daily, and one would like to see this violence stop quickly. Does this mean that the question will be sorted out once the hypothetical returns to calm? Nothing is less sure. Again one should take the exact measure of the dynamics present in Algerian society, and cease indulging in hotchpotches. By listening only to the actual eradicators of the power in place, Khalida Messaoudi or Malika Boussouf, one risks reproducing yesterday's errors. Namely not to give legitimacy except to those who "speak like us"[70] and, by extension, to classify all the others in one and the same category. The latter are terrorists, fanatic fundamentalists and the "bearded" who are all dangerous to the West. The fact is clear. The idea of moderation amongst "Islamists" is a "fraud" to use the word of Charles Pasqua, the ex-French Interior Minister. Such an interpretation of events is a product of the most perilous blindness. The Islamic referent has a legitimacy with all the categories of Algerian society which are not sufficiently evaluated: academics, politicians, entrepreneurs as, also, all the people. Whether one likes it or not, one will have to interact "with" Islam. The degree of the superpowers' lucidity and of the power in place will have a certain influence on the nature of mobilisations to come. But in denying history, refusing the religious and cultural points of reference and considering nothing but geo-strategic and economic interests, one creates states of tension and rejection. A Muslim is not anti-Western, by nature. However, from the shameful treatment to displayed arrogance, he can become so. The West seems to be doing its utmost to create such a reflex.

Muslims, even those who did not support the position of the FIS, see and observe every day the media campaigns which, in the West, revolve around the Islamic question. The opportunity is given – permanently – to the same people who seem to be legitimised, on account of their origin, to speak "the truth" about Islam. They see also the simplifications, blindness and silent conspiracies. Algeria has, admittedly, been a sign among others of selective interpretations, orchestrated lies and sustained conflicts. But Algeria is today the birth-place of a culture of reciprocal mistrust. Would the West let the world of Islam decide its own fate? Will Muslims declare a merciless war against Western civilisation? Such fears are, from now on, legitimate as are the fractures real. This makes it incumbent upon us to deepen the scope of our analyses, to engage in a dialogue on the essential by accepting to make contact with "new" interlocutors who, in order to refer decisively to their religion and culture, are no less open to discussion and do not perceive their relation with the West in terms of confrontation. Such intellectuals and politicians do exist. They abundantly fill the prisons of Muslim countries or are suffering terrible pressures. In terms of popular representativity, they have a legitimacy that is more important than the powers in place. In the West, little is made of their elimination through imprisonment, torture or execution. With a certain cynicism, those intellectuals assassinated in Algeria and elsewhere are counted, but those who count – in the literal sense – are only the ones who think in a Western manner. It is an inequitable calculus which shows the long way that remains to be travelled in order to engage in a debate "of equal legitimacy".[71]

iv.   The Palestinian territories

One would have hoped to see just agreements, and also an equitable peace. There is none of this, and recent history proves that the strategy of "agreements" makes of these but a stage of programmed capitulation. Alas! In the West it is asserted that "this" peace is better than any war. If, *a fortiori*, Yasser Arafat has accepted the clauses, then there is no need to deepen the critique. Such is a strange conclusion indeed. Can Arafat do otherwise if he wants to keep his power and his legitimacy? His personal fate is from now on linked, imprisoned, to this process. Many high officials have criticised and left him but the "democrat" continues to advance while recognition of his people's rights shrinks away.

When the *Intifada* erupted in December 1987, the Palestinian cause had a very weak international audience. It was images of Israeli repression against children who were throwing stones that, suddenly, reversed the tendency.[72] Overnight, the Palestinians on the inside gave Arafat's struggle a new credibility. Strong in such a reversal of the situation, the PLO – encouraged by the Americans and its allies in the Near East – engaged itself, in 1988, on the path of conciliation. It accepted the state of Israel, accepted the idea of dividing lands as also Resolution 242. Arafat was assured that peace, and his state, could not afford to make any more concessions. However, Shamir and Bush both remained stonily indifferent. It was then that the Gulf crisis and the Iraqi invasion of Kuwait happened. Arafat's support for Saddam was to prove a culpable political choice. With the tacit agreement of the USA, the Gulf countries cut their financial support for the PLO, which was soon in a state of suffocation. It was in such an inextricable situation, forced to accept the majority of Israeli demands (bilateral talks, kind of representatives...), that the Palestinians engaged in the peace process in October 1991 in Madrid. For two years, negotiations were bogged down while, at the same time, repression raged in the occupied territories and the implantation of colonies was never as important as it was since 1970. With the passing weeks, the credibility of Arafat fell to such a point that increasing voices demanded a restructuration and democratic elections within the PLO. Losing his representativity, let down by his financial backers and cornered by the White House, Arafat had no choice, and his political fate was from then on linked to the peace process. From the American and Israeli sides, the cause was well understood.

Already personally protected by the Israeli Mossad since 1992, the Palestinian leader prepared his political salvage behind the scenes. The secret negotiations of Oslo – Arafat participated without his legal advisors who had all resigned – were his last chance. He did not hesitate to grab it. He was obliged to sign an Agreement that dealt with only 2% of Palestine, that did not mention Jerusalem and made of the "occupied territories" from that moment on "disputed" territories; that granted "administrative self-determination" while speaking of a "redeployment" of Israeli forces and not of a "withdrawal"; that did not mention the "right of return" and that, lastly, imposed upon the PLO the denunciation and cessation of violence, consecrated the creation of a security force of 35 thousand Palestinians entrusted with taking over from Israeli occupation forces: to put it plainly in order to become a kind of interior police on behalf of the Israeli state. The latter, as pointed out by James Baker, save for its recognition of the PLO, "has not given anything": no clause referred to the cessation of Israeli repression, not even the follow-up to the peace process. Besides, Rabin never made any reference to it if not to affirm that "Jerusalem is the eternal capital of Israel". It was a strange Agreement.

The international community was bombastically delighted about this peace and it must feel worried today because of the renewal of violence that it perceives as being solely a manifestation of Islamic fanaticism. This agreement seems to hide, nonetheless, some of the most frequent stands in Western policy in the region. Furthermore, the USA, Europe and the UN share a great part of the responsibility for the excesses that we see today. For in the final analysis, since the end of the 1940s, there seems to be an ostrich-like policy at play. This beginning with the creation of the State of Israel – which made the Palestinians pay for European anti-Semitism and allowed the division of "Muslim countries" – passing through all the decrees of the UN that Israel, backed by the unconditional support of the USA, has not respected, up to the recent agreements that make of an old "terrorist" a man of peace. The only objective behind all this is defending Western strategic interests regardless of any consideration relating to the basic rights of people. These interests are from now on threatened by popular mobilisations that must be, everywhere, suppressed.

The West is today distributing terms as to the submission of one or the other to the new international order. Saddam, yesterday's friend, is the "demon" of today, the Afghan "resistants" have become "terrorists", "the throwers of stones" have become "extremists" and, lastly, Arafat, the cornered terrorist, is the new "friend". Who are the partners of this peace? It is those who are at the top of the list of governments violating human rights: all are engaged in discussions with the State of Israel which was in 1992 second on Amnesty International's black list. These leaders are also responsible for the escape of Arafat, the old mythical figure of the Palestinian struggle who today increasingly owes his survival to "friendly" governments rather than to the will of his people or the members of his government.

Will there, at last, be any talk about these peoples? In the entire region, the heavy weight of dictatorship and repression is merciless. Is there anything left to hope for from the powers in place or from the West? The peoples have serious doubts. In Gaza and the West Bank – as in all neighbouring countries – there is mobilisation and struggle. At the same time when the superpowers and the media are distributing removable labels, whether "madmen", "extremists", or "fanatics", without any other nuance, all those – and they are the majority in the Muslim World – who desire a real peace, which is other than this unjust peace, are considered as dangerous "opponents" to Western policy. Violence endures, bombs here, jam-packed prisons and torture there. The international community is, by supporting an inequitable process and by not assuming its responsibilities regarding the question of Jerusalem, reaping what it has sown. The Palestinian people see their rights denied and the Muslim conscience cannot be satisfied with an imposed silence on the question of running Jerusalem.

Those who are today opposed to the peace agreements are not all mad.[73] These demand that their rights be fundamentally recognised and that the real questions be put, as much on the level of political rights as on the level of religious recognition. Zionist forces, being the result of a colonial project, are forces of occupation. The USA and a great number of governments have given considerable support to the Israeli policy and continue, today, to be accomplices of its intransigence. There is very little in the way of content for the recognition of the right of Muslims regarding Jerusalem and the right of Palestinians to their land. The political fate of Arafat, symbolical as it is, has but a very relative interest. It is today appropriate to prove, beyond speeches, that dialogue in equity is possible with the West (or with the State of Israel: an advanced stronghold of its strategic policy in the region).

This conflict remains a subject of tension between the West and Islam. For Muslims, the dispute remains heavy: the blind support for the Zionist state has created much suspicion; likewise, the collaboration that the Israeli Secret Services entertains with diverse governments (first amongst which one should count Egypt, Algeria, Morocco, ...)[74] makes the facts particularly complex. The encounter between civilisations is difficult.

c.   *Muslim confinement*

Muslims are not outdone when it comes to the gap existing between speech and fact. Such "double" talk is not rare. Without entering into detail, we can bring to the fore two intellectual attitudes, or postures, which are unfortunately all too frequent nowadays.

◆   **Idealisation and simplification**

How many are those *'ulamā'* and intellectuals who do not intend to present the ideal Islamic society by referring to a thousand proofs taken from the history of civilisation? Islam, is a model of justice, goodness and fraternity whereof there are no problems since it is the way that has been commanded to us by God. It is, therefore, enough to go back to it in order to create a new society of the future. Incidentally, it is not necessary to preoccupy oneself with actual social problems, for Islamic points of reference will see to them. To a student who asked how the political and social organisation, in Islam, can fight against unemployment and inflation, a university professor responded: "In an Islamic society, there is neither unemployment nor inflation since everything is well organised." Such answers which mix the ideal with oversimplification are dangerous. It gives the impression that Islam is a panacea to be applied without any great difficulty. Admittedly though such idealisation and simplification underlies a great number of "Islamic" analyses today.

Admittedly, we believe that God has revealed the Qur'ān and that He has sent Prophets; certainly, we think that we ought to stick to these points of reference and be faithful *rabbāniyyīn*, not neglecting the pact, the link, with Transcendence. Certainly, we are determined. However, this does not mean that we should be satisfied with expressions such as "there is nothing but...", and "it is enough that...". If the expression "Islam is the solution" can serve as a slogan, it should nonetheless not hide the stages, the inescapable difficulties, the innumerable pitfalls which will accompany, hinder or oppose social reform. Societies with Muslim majorities are today going through very profound and complex structural and moral crises. The exact measure of such crises should be taken by referring to realities and not only to quotations taken from the sources.

Many Muslims, when they are questioned by Westerners, confine themselves to purely theoretical considerations and refuse to take into account the actual situation. Besides, some of them perceive and feel the legitimate question of their interlocutors as their manifestation of an opposition to Islam. All happens as if, feeling on edge, the person who does not at once share our views is an enemy. Simplification of the terms of conflict proceeds from the same idealisation of the project. Critical debate is difficult.

We have heard many general discourses on Faith or humanism being dissolved in political projects that have become totalitarian and repressive. Examples of this are legion in the West as in the Muslim world. It is appropriate, therefore, to remain vigilant and critical towards our respective societies. The Muslim world today is very far from respect for its own points of reference. To recover from paralysis, to reconcile itself with the universe of meaning that is its own and to achieve social, political and economic adjustments will take time as it requires permanent evaluation: changes are achieved at this cost. Opposed to the Western drift, the scene of the "Islamic ideal" is a nonsense. To present the broad orientations of the Qur'ān and the *Sunna*, to explain our culture and to concretely and modestly engage, after that, and in a strictly pragmatic way without great theories, such is the appropriate way.

◆ The silence of minds

When Muslims speak among themselves, they are inexhaustible in criticism of their co-religionists and, more broadly, of the catastrophic state in which the *Umma* finds itself. Complaints and rejections are the rule. The least that can be noticed, from Morocco to Indonesia, is a feeling of bitterness, malaise and deep disenchantment that is shared by a large majority of the people. The *affective* inventory is negative.

We can certainly understand this, for there is nothing delightful in that which we can observe today. Yet, what is more vexing is the fact that the affect takes precedence over a real, precise, in-depth, critical and uncompromising analysis of the causes of these fractures. The Muslim world, for the one who can see, is still lacking intellectual exactness. Very limited in number are those voices that go to the limits of honest analysis, that refuse to say something and then keep quiet when they see its contrary being applied, that denounce events, governmental policies or silent conspiracies.

If we reject primary idealisation and simplification, the only solution seems to us to be the awakening of a critical conscience and mind that are at the source of Islamic teaching. That we are – very naturally, one must confess – questioned by Westerners or by statements made during debates within the Muslim world, rigorous analysis must be part of our Islamic training. Besides, it is this mind that we kill in many schools in the Muslim world whereby children are drowned in deadening programmes of learning that leave them the choice of repetition, cramming or failing.[75]

We are, nonetheless, in a state of emergency. It would be too difficult to emerge from the actual upheaval without making a precise analysis of the causes and responsibilities: from the illiteracy of people to the betrayals of the powers in place whose hypocritical policies one must denounce at the cost of one's life perhaps – but this is the passage obligated by reform. Keeping silent is tantamount to being an accomplice, it is "betraying God, His Prophet and all the Believers" according to the exacting expression of the Prophet (peace be upon him). On the geo-strategic level and at the level of economic policies, some Muslim countries participate and collaborate in an immoral management of the world and are implicated in some of the most dubious dealings and trades. All this must be analysed, rigorously described, stated and then denounced. It should, of course, be denounced in a constructive manner, but also loudly, clearly and intelligibly. We cannot reproach Westerners for their "double language" and turn a blind eye to our own. We cannot criticise at will American permissiveness or delinquency and then, always, remain silent about the hypocrisies of Saudi power, the Tunisian horrors or the blind violence committed in the name of Islam. Yes there are some voices that express themselves, but these are very few in number.

One does not protect oneself from one's enemy by concealing from him, and by hiding from oneself, one's defects. On the contrary, it is appropriate to be completely aware and clear about one's own shortcomings. Those who consider the West as an enemy feel that any criticism directed at Muslims is a kind of dishonest compromise especially if it is enunciated in the presence of Westerners. Keen to appear "unwavering", they forget themselves. Yet, to elaborate a critical denunciation in no way means making an "alliance" with the West. It is before anything else remaining faithful to the Message of Islam which, above all, imposes justice and equity. We have reminded readers enough of this. Besides, it seems clear that we are opposed to the economic and strategic policies of the West, and this does not mean that the West, in itself, is the enemy. There exist a great number of intellectuals, journalists and researchers who have a genuine concern for understanding and who need to hear, read and refer to an honest and well-thought-out discourse and bring to the fore, without complacency, the gaps and betrayals in the Muslim universe. This, unless we want to persevere in a confinement that neither the Qur'ān nor the *Sunna* have prescribed.

3. Fears and Hopes

It would be naïve to anticipate better tomorrows and a serene future for our planet and then maintain a blind eye on the real state of the world and on relations between the West and Islam. We cannot agree with Huntington's analysis or Lévy's simplifications, but still one must nevertheless be clear. We are at a crossroads and our epoch is decisive. Tension is noticeable, and no day goes by, in the West, except that there is reference to Islam, Muslims, and the "fundamentalist danger". We are justified in fearing the worst: the clash between civilisations is not only *theoretically* possible, but we can also say that the signs of potential rupture are visible. This reality must be kept in mind, just as one must take full measure of the dangers that are in store for us at a time when being a Muslim, a practising Muslim, is almost a defect in itself in Westerners' minds. They have heard so much talk about the "Islamist" or "Islamic peril" that this universe appears to Westerners to be suspect, cumbersome and hostile. The fracture is as much in people's minds as it is in the geopolitical and economic stakes at play.

a.   *Fears*

The subjects of fear are not lacking and the coming decades will undoubtedly accentuate some deep divergences between the two civilisations. The most evident element is without any doubt that of the difference in the status of religion in the two respective societies. Western culture, that has done so much to liberate itself from dogmas, now has difficulty in grasping the presence, or return, of "the religious". When such a phenomenon touches circumscribed and confined ethnic groups, then there is no reason to fear a disruption. But when it is a question of Islam, the facts are different. In terms of numbers, influence, strategic stakes, a rapport of force and on account of the historical legacy, religious manifestation in the Muslim world does not have the same objective consequences as for the West. Admittedly, there is affirmation of a "concern" with regard to "extremisms", but what seems to be underlined by all analyses is that the religious reference poses a problem. Acknowledging God and then wanting to give to one's life the sense of Faith poses a problem of "order" to many American and European minds, this is *a fortiori* more so when it is a question of entire sections of people who express, thus, their identity. The affirmation of *Tawḥīd* and Transcendence shakes the foundations of the liberal universe.

Such is the second object of the tensions that concern in very explicit fashion the hegemony of Western culture. All the progresses (from sciences to techniques), the acknowledged rights, the achieved process of secularisation, the so-called "universal" values find themselves faced by a symbolical universe which, in fact, relativises their scope. The Islamic civilisation, with its reference to the Qur'ān and the traditions of the Prophet (peace be upon him), with its concept of the world and human beings, and with its history, is not reducible to the cultural, terminological or semantic categories of the USA or Europe. Admittedly, there were attempts from the North to drown the capitals of the South under a torrent of Northern products; but one realises that the people – from intellectuals who are Western trained to the most poor – react in a sharp manner the moment that the elements of their "intuitive culture", to use François Burgat's expression, are mentioned. They remain deep down, and in a peculiar way (as we have indicated at the beginning of this chapter), attached to Faith in God, their Religion, their civilisation and their culture. It is true that the posture varies in accordance with the level of training and education. The most uncultivated quarters giving rise to kinds of identification which are sometimes forthright or violent, whereas we find, in university quarters, more refined and elaborate postures.

Everywhere, however, one should acknowledge the decisive reach of the religious and cultural point of reference. This fact appears as a factor of opposition to Western hegemony; and incontestably it is. For the first time for centuries, the culture of science and progress finds itself in a position whereby it is contested. Tension is, therefore, legitimate.

We should notice the same apprehension at the political level. There is awareness, for some years now, about the transnational phenomenon of so-called "Islamist" mobilisation. It was thought that it was a question of manipulated groups here or there by some states that, from Saudi Arabia to Iran, financed "fundamentalist" activities. Serious analyses have today dropped such simplifying considerations. If, in effect, armed mobilisation is the act of some small groups, political oppositions referring to Islam have a very important popular legitimacy and this in countries of Muslim majorities. One acknowledges that there exists today many Muslim countries that adhere to Islamic (or Islamist) political demands formulated by oppositions that reject violence and want to follow legal means. The powers in place know the strong representativity of these movements and play on hotchpotches in order to stop their participation in real democratic consultations. Such a phenomenon is noticeable in the quasi totality of Muslim countries. What was thought to be the awakening of "deprived wasters" has turned out to be a very large movement of intellectuals (many of whom have studied or lived in the West), with an important popular legitimacy that is opposed to the powers in place as also to the Western policy of support for dictatorships and the unjust management of resources. The alliances, South-South, around Islamic points of reference are from this moment on achievable. The superpowers are clearly aware of this, just as they also know that many interests are at play. In order to justify their policies, they have used the strategy of demonising: Islam is a step backward, committed Muslims are obscurantists or suspects, women suffer the worst kinds of discrimination, etc. The repertory is well known: behind this description, this image, are hidden important stakes and pernicious intentions. It is a question of justifying policies of influence and dubious support, instigated wars, and violations of forgotten rights and all kinds of endorsement. At this time, we should acknowledge that the strategy of the superpowers has borne fruit but controlling its consequences is far from certain. The phenomena of radicalisation that has been nourished, encouraged and on the basis of which such or such political decisions are explained, promises uncontrolled skidding and tomorrows of confrontation whose greater part of responsibility lies with the West.

In this enterprise, one cannot insist too much on the decisive, and sometimes dangerous, role of the media. The mastery of information on a huge scale is a formidable power which is devolved today upon some agencies, of Western majority, and which quite obviously presents a certain point of view of the state of the world. The image, the succinct commentary and speed have taken over text, in-depth analysis and holistic comprehension. Simplification and caricature have become the rule at a time when there is an urgent need for nuance and reflection in the face of complexity. The media, thus, forms public opinion and nourishes fears.

Today it is television that makes "a subject", and it is often in relation to the latter that the public, including university quarters, become agitated, pronounce itself or "think". Everyone knows it, and each person suffers the consequences, but only a few succeed in disengaging themselves from the pressure and oppression of the media, in order to formulate and elaborate an analysis that is free from tension and subjects that are "in vogue". For it is Islam, Muslims, and the nervousness that relations engender, that are the phenomena in vogue; "trendy" subjects and clear-cut conclusions are thrown around with phenomenal speed. One ends up by no longer "knowing" that Islam is a Religion, a spirituality, a universe of meaning and a concept of life. Not any more, for the images have shown it (we have seen it, therefore, we know), and the commentator has implied it, Islam is before anything else "a danger". If Sufism still benefits from some "favours", it is in short not exactly Islam. Being remote from the world, it does not disturb anyone. Some journalists, one must salute them, try to go to the limits of analysis: being committed, they understand what is at stake and feel that something is being hidden, that the reality is not what is being said and that there is often a collision between Western powers, multinational societies, the producers of arms and the dictatorships of the South. The case of the great media tools whose shares are owned by arms producers are not rare. Their interpretation of the world is not innocent and their engagements are not fortuitous. Some journalists, researchers and intellectuals refuse the cynicism of these interested positionings. At a time of fear, withdrawal and rejection, they are opening a horizon of hope.

b.   *Hopes*

Hopes do exist if we show some good-will. The present book aims to show that numerous preoccupations are shared between theologians, intellectuals, and more broadly, Western and Muslim peoples. Without minimising the differences between the religious points of reference, the cultural foundations and the social, political and economic dynamics, the women and men of good-will find convergent domains of action that, more than dialogue, must allow common stands and engagement.

In the Muslim as in the Western world, one encounters individuals, thinkers, and governments that are satisfied with the present state of the world and who try to justify such or such a policy through a reference to the Islamic tradition, or the liberal ideal; this without being afraid of sanctioning horror and the worst betrayal to the revealed Message or to any egalitarian principle. Such people exist and they are many. By contrast, it is also possible to get in touch with women and men who have a conscience and exactness of another type and whose first quality is intellectual honesty and lucidity in the face of what is proposed to us as the "order of the world". We have spoken, above, about the creation of a

South-South-North front: it must be acknowledged that all the conditions necessary for its achievement are present today. So, we should take time to establish links and aquire the means to better understand one another. A fruitful encounter can be achieved at the cost of such an effort.

The vivid forces of opposition to frantic and aimless "scientism", "economism", "technician society" and "progress" who, from intellectuals to scholars, express themselves and struggle in the West, can find in the Muslim world partners whose existence they do not even suspect. The exactness of the points of reference, values and finalities that founded the Islamic culture around the notion of *tawḥīd* echoes, in these times of crisis, the Western questioning on meaning and ethics. It is not a question of having the same answers; plurality, as we have said, is an objective fact of creation and the state of the world.

It is rather a question of creating a front of resistance to a liberalism without a soul, one which considers as natural that the order of the world imposes "sacrifices"; that there must, therefore, be some who are "sacrificed". After the hope of "developments" of the 1960s and the 1970s, we have entered an era of "cynical realism" whose main trait is not to spare any illusion. Such fatalism, resignation, this sombre colonisation of minds is the real peril that the West should face: no other danger threatens it in so profound a fashion; neither communism, Islam nor "the barbarians". The movements of mobilisation in the South, carried by Faith and/or the will to refer oneself to man or humanism, can be allied to these latter voices that, in the North, call for awareness. Energies must come together, encourage and enrich one another.

Without doubt the first domain of action should be social. Islam cannot accept a world whereby societies suffer such fractures. Many are those social players who, in the same fashion, cannot admit the serious dismantling of societies. Collaboration could be very concrete and it goes without saying that the relations established between Muslims living in Western societies and those of American or European stock should facilitate the encounter. The road is difficult and it is appropriate not to indulge in complacent optimism; each day brings its disappointments with regard to the relation-ships which are entertained by the two civilisations. The door is narrow, but whoever is nourished with Faith or deep conviction knows that to live is tantamount to taking up such a challenge.

We are assisting in the West a return to the question of meaning. The revival of ethical preoccupations, the scope of economic questions, and awareness about the limits of progress and growth prefigure the advent of a new era. There are also signs that new forms of religiosity are multiplying: sects, mystical groups, conversions, the important presence of oriental traditions especially Buddhism, etc. The youth express new needs; metaphysical and cultural preoccupations are brought in line with current tastes. The times are changing. Observing "extreme mobilisations", some have wanted to see in this a "revenge of God". However, it seems that in the whole society of men, there is an expression of "something" that is lacking. We can, without great effort, appreciate such a phenomenon. Some would delight in it as some would deplore it, it all depends. It remains that the order of the world, the actual drift and the daily injustices necessitate an urgent reaction. If the actual malaise and crisis can engender a sudden burst – just as artists derive the same from suffering their inspiration – then we can hope that the remedy will be born out of the evil itself. Maybe then we will accept turning towards other religious and cultural horizons in order to discover a universe of positive meaning, invigorating ethical exigencies that, in respect of plurality, can contribute to the changing of the world. A civilisation that is still nourished by such a sacred spell of the world, that is morally exacting, ecological by essence, humanist through Revelation, present and significant in the intimacy of more than a billion beings; such a civilisation, say we, partakes of the dynamism of the future. They will be pacific if we master the tendencies to demonise; they will be conflictual if arrogance, sufficiency and falsehood persist.

Being linked to God, wanting to give daily meaning to the *rabbāniyya* is tantamount to striving for peace. It is, in the same *élan*, resisting all injustices and lies. A peace based on injustice and falsehood is not peace. It is rather a resignation of conscience. With different civilisations, we cannot content ourselves with pretences: equity is an imperative and transparency a duty. We would hope that consciences become a little more enlightened before catastrophes occur. Our hope lies in minute and meagre signs. Our responsibility is never to give up. Our Faith invigorates our trust and our patience in action:

In the Name of God, the Merciful, the Compassionate

> *By the Afternoon! Surely Man is in the way of loss, save those who believe, and do righteous deeds, and counsel each other unto the truth, and counsel each other to be steadfast.* (Qur'ān 103:1–3)

In plurality, it is appropriate to acknowledge and never forget the sense of our trial, regardless of who we are or where we come from.

Notes

1. Mircea Eliade, *Histoire des croyances et des idées religieuses*, Bibliothèque historique Payot, 1989, 3 vols., Vol. 1, p.269 [English translation, *A History of Religious Ideas*, 3 vols., tr. Willard R. Trask, The University of Chicago Press].
2. Victor Hugo, *Les contemplations, Au bord de l'infini*, Livre de poche, 1972, pp.477–8.
3. The figure of Prometheus takes on quite a significant sense from the Renaissance onwards. The identification of "two" liberations is almost natural: the Church and the mirror of Olympus that were challenged.
4. Arthur Rimbaud, *Oeuvres complètes*, ed. La Pléiade, p.252 (passages underlined by Rimbaud).
5. Albert Camus, *L'homme révolté*, Gallimard–idees, 1977, pp.43–4 [Translation into English by Anthony Bower as *The Rebel*, Hamish Hamilton]. Camus's reflection on the question of God, tension, contradictions, rejection and rebellion is developed in this book as well as in *La Peste* whose characters perfectly illustrate doubt, suffering and the difficult face to face of human intelligence with the Divine. We have here a perfect example of Promethean legacy. The influence of Dostoevsky and *The Brothers Karamazov* is patent. Ivan's tormented,

tortured and conflictual reflection cannot but collide and be opposed to the transparent mystic Aliosha, the anti-Promethean figure *par excellence*. The reality of existential conflict is not brought into question, even if Camus identifies himself with Ivan and Dostoevsky had a confirmed inclination towards the faith of Aliosha. Let us note that Blaise Pascal, even being a Christian author if ever there was one, had as early as the seventeenth century, described and discussed this tension of faith. *The Pensées* is an accomplished expression of this, and it is under his pen that we find the description of the three orders relating respectively to the sensual people, the savants and the sages which will later orientate the "modern" themes of this Russian author. This is to say that Christian thought has been profoundly influenced by Promethean legacy and Greek tragic, this if it had not stimulated it itself.

6. Op. cit., p.45.

7. Op. cit., pp.33–4.

8. Camus points out: "Rebellion is the act of informed man, who possesses the consciousness of his rights." Op. cit., p.33.

9. Genesis, 22:1–2 and 6–8.

10. According to the Islamic tradition, it is a question of Ishmael (Ismāʿīl), the eldest son born to the servant Hajar and not Isaac (Isḥāq) son of Sarah. The Bible acknowledges Ishmael as being the eldest, which makes very strange the expression: "Take your son, your unique Isaac whom you love."

11. Iblīs, the demon or Satan, is certainly, according to the Qur'an, the transgressing *Jinn*: he was proud and refused to obey and submit. However, he does not repudiate what he knows and sees; he does not try to contest Divine power, for he is clearly submitted to the same. If he likes to deceive people it is with the consent of God Who, at the same time, offers men the means to guard against this deception.

12. Ghazālī's *al-Munqidh min al-Ḍalāl* (Deliverance from Error), French translation by Farid Jabre and awkwardly rendered as *Erreur et délivrance*, Beyrouth, 1969 (English translation by M. Watt is included in *The Faith and Practice of al-Ghazali*, Oneworld Publications) includes explicit passages on this question and the *Mishkāt al-Anwār* (*Le Tabernacle des Lumières*, tr. Deladrière, Seuil, 1981). [There is an English translation by W.H.T. Gairdner, under the title *The Niche for Lights*, New Delhi, 1991, but the French translation is more reliable and far superior] is an imperative complementary reading in order to understand the frame of reference to this debate. Revelation is inescapable and necessary for the accomplishment of Faith. See equally the thesis *Une critique de l'argument ontologique dans la tradition cartésienne* by Hani Ramadan, Publications Universitaires Europeennes, Peter Lang, 1990, pp.219–35.

13. *Deliverance from Error*, op. cit., pp.22–4.

14. Again one should clarify that the sacred is not of the same nature as that which we encounter in the Judaeo-Christian tradition. This consideration is at the centre of the cultural debate and we are forced to return to it below.

15. *Biographie du XXème siècle*, éditions Tougui, 1985, p.384.

16. Roger Garaudy converted to Islam after a long evolution which he qualifies as "natural", as is here his reference to the notion of "doubt" which is explained by the fact of the origins of his thought. His long experience and his participation in the biggest political and philosophical debates of this century make of him a philosopher of reference in understanding the Western world. His critical reflections are as interesting to Muslims in that they call for re-finding the living forces of "early Islam".

17. The most famous commentators of the Qur'ān and the 'ulamā' of different Islamic sciences have given different interpretations to this notion of "fiṭra". Some have spoken of "human nature", others about "natural religion" and many have translated it as "Islām". In truth, it is possible to find a common ground for all these "interpretations". In the Muslim concept, the order of nature is testimony of the submission of all the elements to the Creator (submission that is Islām in the first sense); man is part of this order and his natural aspiration towards God prolongs and confirms in him this submission of the universe. Order is to nature what fiṭra is to the human being. It is the (natural) fundamental expression of the acknowledgement of the Creator, of acceptance and submission (Islām). This harmony expresses the original, essential Islam, that the Islamic Revelation in the seventh century has come to confirm and elaborate in worship and social affairs. Thus should be understood: "There is no change in the creation of God. This is the unalterable religion."

18. Ḥadīth reported by Bukhārī and Muslim.

19. The recent and important presence of Muslims in the West as well as the multiplication of "religious" resistance movements have hit American and European consciences. This is in itself a proof of the lack of knowledge about Islam and Muslims as such. The expression of natural religiosity has not fundamentally changed. What is "new" is its committed and demanding social and political structure. On the subject of the Muslim presence in France see the interesting book by Jocelyne Césari: Être Musulman en France – Associations, militants et mosquées, Kartala, Paris, 1994; and on the theme of the presence of Muslims in Europe see, Jørgen Nielsen, Muslims in Europe, Edinburgh University Press, 1992.

20. An extract from a ḥadīth narrated by Muslim.

21. This is the central axis of François Burgat's analysis whose gist relates to the political dynamics of Muslim societies (see L'islamisme au Maghreb, re-edition Payot, 1995, and L'islamisme en face, op. cit.). If, on the strictly social and political planes, the theses formulated have a pertinence, one is obliged to note that this author eludes the religious and spiritual dimension, and that he tackles the cultural question only in terms of references of mobilisation face to face with Western values. This is the theory of "rocketing stages" where the Muslim world passes through three successive stages of struggle against colonisation: political, economic and, today, cultural. An analysis of the themes of reference of Muslim intellectuals, within a long historical sequence,

demolishes such a theory. Similarly, we find among committed Muslims (the "Islamists"), who have not passed through the political left or nationalism, analyses that are far from a reactive cultural expression. They speak of God, refer to Islam and its spirituality, develop principles of social, political and economic morality for what it is in their own tradition. Such a cultural dimension would profit from being studied as it is in itself and not only "on the surface", where it is referred to only in order to explain political dynamics. Our long hours of discussion with François Burgat, after all, have not ceased: we are thankful to him for his concern for analysis and for his will to remain close to the field. His books have the merit of giving an account of a situation that is particularly complex. We should retain his non-traditional interpretation of the "Islamist" movements, his clear denunciations of power plays in place and the usefulness of his questionings of modernity as seen from the West.

22. *Ḥadīth* narrated by Ibn Ḥanbal and al-Dārimī. Another *ḥadīth* which runs along the same lines is narrated by Muslim: "The good is good character; sin is that which troubles you inwardly and which you do not like other people to find out about."

23. *Ḥadīth* narrated by Bukhārī and Muslim.

24. See on this subject, *inter alia*, the work by Serge Latouche, *L'occidentalisation du monde*, La Découverte, Paris, 1989, and that of Jean Ziegler, *La victoire des vaincus*, Seuil, 1987.

25. A consequent work of research on these questions was carried out by intellectuals in Egypt. A series of brochures (eight to date) were edited under the title *al-Ghazwa al-Fikriyya fi'l-Manāhij al-Dirāsiyya* (Cultural Invasion in Educational Syllabi). Each brochure deals with a conspiracy (*mu'amara*) in a given domain: language, morality, history, the institution of al-Azhar or others. The main editors are Jamal ʿAbd al-Hadi and his wife Wafa M. Rifʿat (in Arabic), Dar al-Tibaʿa wa'l-Nashr al-Islamiyya, Cairo, 1992.

26. Michel Serres, *Éclaircissements, entretiens avec Bruno Latour*, ed. François Bourin, 1992, pp.249–51.

27. Ibid., p.252.

28. Hubert Reeves, *Malicorne, réflexions d'un observateur de la nature*, Seuil, 1990, p.162.

29. Ibid., p.179.

30. See in particular the last part (the tenth) of his book *Malicorne* (pp.167–84): His reflection is interesting in that the enunciated categories and the kinds of conflict concerning science and religion pertain to the Western history of ideas. The philosophical scope of the debate is of much interest to the Muslim world.

31. See *L'homme machinal, Technique et progrès: anatomie d'une trahison*, Syros alternative, Paris, 1990. A sub-chapter is entitled 'L'ablation du juste et de l'injuste', but this entire book revolves around ethical preoccupations at a time when "Technique" has become a new god.

32. Hans Küng, *Projet d'éthique planètaire, la paix mondiale par la paix entre les religions*, Seuil, Paris, 1991 [translated into English as *A Global Ethic: The Declaration of the Parliament of World's Religions*, SCM, 1994).

33. Speaking about "republican" ethics in *L'homme machinal*, op. cit., the two authors felt obliged to clarify the following: "This ethics is not animated by any absolute truth, no metaphysics commands it and no transcendence overhangs it" (p.29).

34. During a discussion with my friend the sociologist Jean Ziegler, he acknowledged the soundness of Muslim identity-based mobilisation, pointing out while half-amused, half-vexed and greatly frustrated that: "This affirmation is religious, what can you do, it is just so..." Such vexation is understandable, and one must salute amicably his probity.

35. There is nonetheless an element which does not fail to surprise us: some intellectuals and researchers have developed an impressive critical arsenal with regard to the techniques, sciences and media manipulations. They are inexhaustible on the social, political and economic mechanism of manipulation and stunning of public opinion in general. Yet, these same intellectuals, in their approach to Islam, fall into the same trap they denounce, and reduce the Islamic question to problems in vogue. They define, without making an in-depth analysis of the manipulation of the powers in place, all Muslims engaged in opposition as potential fanatics. They listen and applaud, without detecting what is politically at stake, the statements of Khalida Messaoudi; they engage themselves, without grasping the cultural stakes underlined by the impacts of the media, in supporting Taslima Nasreen and Salman Rushdie. It is not a question for us to criticise those who are engaged in causes which they consider to be just; rather, it is the real degree of critical analysis which interests us here. Some events often reveal unavowed objectives: the question in vogue gives a repulsive image of the Muslim world. Who then benefits from this? Where are the intellectuals who are ever supposed to call for vigilance in order to avoid political manipulation?

36. The concept of supportive engagement in Islam is intimately linked to the idea of personal responsibility which is a fundamental fact of Islamic teaching. Nothing of what has been said about the so-called *fatalism* of Islam corresponds to its message.

37. *Ḥadīth* narrated by Bukhārī.

38. The non-governmental Islamic associations and independent institutions working in the field have the people's confidence and this worries the powers that be, who would love to put these dangerous "activists" in the same "fundamentalist" bag. In Egypt, for example, during the earthquake of 12 October 1992, state aid was contemptible in comparison to that of the "Humanitarian Relief" Association (*al-Ighātha al-Insāniyya*) that received the majority of individual donations, so much so that the government ended up banning all donations outside its own services.

39. *Ḥadīth* (*ḥasan*) narrated by al-Dāraquṭnī.

40. An original analysis, and sufficiently rare to be pointed out here, has been presented by Alain Campiotti in an editorial entitled "*L'islam travaille dans nos têtes*". Therein he presented two theories of reference (Huntington and Etzioni) and thought to perceive in the project of "communal recovery" of "militant Islam" a (beneficial?) influence in the "heads of Americans and Europeans." Cf. journal: *Le Nouveau Quotidien*, Lausanne, Switzerland.

41. It is of course not the case in the British, French or American suburbs. The permissive social environment changes the facts: the rates of drug consumption (alcohol and stupefying substances) is proportionally the same among Muslims and British, French or American youth who live in the same social context.

42. Ḥadīth narrated by Bukhārī.

43. Even if, in most capitals, Western influences are being felt through films and imported cultural habits and *vis-à-vis* which we can list three kinds of reaction: a total identification to Western "liberated" modernity; a split between the culture that one holds and the modern mirage that attracts one; and a contemptible rejection of a universe that does not seem to have values any longer. The first category includes a minority of youth. Due to complexes of culture or a feeling of inaccessibility, the rule is rather a ravaging split or an intransigent rejection. Right away, it seems that a profound culture will have to defend itself in tension and conflict.

44. See *Ṭawq al-Ḥamāma* of Ibn Ḥazm (French translation under the title *Le collier de la colombe*, Créadif livres, Paris, 1992), and the last part of *Iḥyā' 'Ulūm al-Dīn* by Ghazālī. See also the interesting work of Malek Chebel, *Dictionnaire des symboles musulmans*, 1995, Albin Michel.

45. The two ḥadīths, with different variants, are narrated by Bukhārī and Muslim.

46. Serge Latouche, *La mégamachine, raison techno-scientifique, raison économique et mythe du progrès*, La Découverte/M.A.U.S.S., Paris, 1995, p.41.

47. Ibid., pp.21–2.

48. Ibid., p.203.

49. As far as we know, only one of his texts has been translated into French: *L'islam en lutte pour la civilisation*, al-Bouraq, Beyrouth, 1992.

50. Serge Latouche, ibid., p.216.

51. On this subject see the excellent work produced by "Synthèse Nord-Sud" supervised by Roger Garaudy, its Director of Publications. Articles of synthesis, critical reflection and fundamental information and questioning constitute the content of seven issues so far published. Among these, Issue No.3 is about "The Decadence of the West" and No.5 is about "The USA, avant-guard of the West".

52. Michel Serres, *Le contrat naturel*, François Bourin, pp.65–6.

53. This ḥadīth is narrated by Aḥmad. Calvin had an answer similar to the meaning of this tradition. Asked what would be his last action before the end of time, he expressed that he would wish to plant a tree.

54. Bernard-Henri Lévy, *La pureté dangereuse*, Grasset, Paris, 1994, pp.42–3.

55. Ibid., p.44.

56. Ibid., p.48.

57. Ibid., p.12.

58. Ibid., p.264.

59. Edgar Morin, *Penser l'Europe*, Gallimard, Paris, 1990, p.40.

60. The conclusion of Burgat's book *L'islamisme en face* (cf. above), goes along this line. We can count on the fingers of one hand, for example, the European intellectuals and researchers who have real and in-depth contact with the men of the field from the so-called "Islamist" opposition. Knowledge of the dynamics is in measure to such contacts: the gaps are today important.

61. See the excellent dossier of *Courrier International* of 8–14 December 1994 (No. 214): "L'Europe a les mains sales." The hidden transactions of parties and politicians and the games of alliance are analysed in many countries and the situation holds sway. Cf. also above: les dossiers Synthèse Nord-Sud of Roger Garaudy.

62. See the interesting study of Jean-Daniel Muller, *Les ONG ambiguës, Aides aux États, aides aux populations?*, l'Harmattan, Paris, 1989.

63. We have already referred to his article: 'The Clash of Civilizations', *Foreign Affairs*, Summer 1993. Huntington's thesis, as already seen, is questionable. It remains that many elements of reflection are brought out and deserve particular attention. His reflection on the demarcation line of conflict gives food for thought, as does his discussion on the contest of interests, values and power of the West.

64. See the excellent Canadian documentary *Les mensonges de la guerre du Golfe*. The example analysed – the so-called murder of babies taken out of incubators – can be multiplied by ten with regard to the whole operation. See also: *Les mensonges du Golfe*, ouvrage collectif, Reporters sans frontières, Téléram, Radio France, "L'Arche de la Fraternite", Paris, 1992.

65. The Saudis are amongst the fiercest opponents for lifting the embargo on Iraq: the Iraqi people lost the status of brotherly people when it became a question of accountancy and appropriateness to the economic policy of the USA.

66. We should remember that the Americans were paid to carry out this demolition (by the petro-monarchies mainly, but also by the Japanese and German governments). Lastly, we should note that it is Western entrepreneurs (in order: American, British and French) who had the privilege of securing the first reconstruction contracts.

67. One remains, nonetheless, a little perplexed with regard to the participation which was reduced to demonstrations for Bosnia. We remember the words of the chief of the Serb military forces in Bosnia, General Mladic, which asserted that the American and European public opinion would not accept that their soldiers would come to die for Bosnia in order to save "Muslims". What to say also of the passivity that reigned during the massacre of the Chechnean people?

68. See the very instructive issue of *Esprit*, *Avec l'Algérie*, January 1995, *Le combat pour l'indépendance algérienne: une fausse coïncidence*, interview with Paul Thibaud and Pierre Vidal-Naquet, op. cit., p.148.

69. Holding elections in the actual circumstances are untenable and indefensible. The power in place is looking for a legitimacy that cannot be given to it today. It has spread violence and death amidst the people and fed into radicalisation. There is insufficient good reason to hold an election.

70. André Glucksmann, in an article in *Le Figaro* of 18 April 1995: "Deux femmes flammes", indulges in such simplification. The only legitimate discourse, in his eyes, is that which subjects the Algerian reality to Western categories. His view is very questionable and the conclusions dangerous.

71. One would benefit greatly from reading Pierre Guillard's book, *Ce fleuve qui nous sépare, Lettre à l'imam Ali Belhadj*, Loysel, 1994.

72. Let us recall the words of Bernard-Henri Lévy where he asserts in his *Questions de principes* that the Israeli occupying force were "stoned": victims they were; and victims they remain: the aggressors are incontestably the Palestinians. Engagement for justice is, sometimes, very selective indeed!

73. The analyses of Jean-François Legrain are interesting and cast new light on the debate: See *Les Voix du soulèvement palestinien, 1987–1988*, CEDEJ, Cairo, 1991, as well as his contributions in *L'Etat du monde 1995*, La Découverte, Paris, 1995. See also the article by Alain Gresh, *Le Monde Diplomatique*, September 1995, where the author reviews the situation and the question of Palestinian occupied territories. He identifies the state of general deterioration that has occurred since September 1993, the date of the agreement between Arafat and Rabin. The deadlock in negotiations caused by the Israeli government, impoverishment, colonisation, unemployment and the totalitarian nature of the power established by Arafat, with the tacit help of the Israelis who do not look unfavourably at the development of a Palestinian entity which is absolutely undemocratic. Alain Gresh quoted the words of Shimon Perez, in *The Financial Times*, presenting the broad line of the last project concerning autonomy: "The agreement leaves in Israeli hands 73% of the (occupied) territories, 97% of security and 80% of water." Can one be any clearer than this!

74. Such information is now known and verified.

75. From this point of view, school programmes in a great number of countries are worrying. In Egypt, Saudi Arabia as in the whole Maghreb up to India, teaching does not respond to the requirements of development or to analytical intelligence.

Conclusion

A Triple Liberation

Nothing in Islam is opposed to modernity and we can firmly state that the Muslim thinkers and *'ulamā'* (savants) who are opposed to this notion and to the idea of change and evolution that it covers often confuse it with the model which is current in the West. Clearly, they confuse *modernity* with *Westernisation*. Thus, they justify an attitude versed in traditionalism and forms which are sometimes sombre and rigoristic, and which presents Islam as opposed, by essence, to any social or scientific progress. Hiding behind the "drifts of the West", they deduce that faithfulness to the Message is achieved by an "absolute" and definitive interpretation of the sources.

The first two Parts of this work have shown that this should be otherwise. For a deep comprehension of the Revelation, in its letter as in its orientation, is imperative. All Muslim reformers never ceased to remind us of this. The Qur'ān and the *Sunna*, the fundamental sources of the *Sharī'a*, which always require renewed interpretation in order to respond to the needs of the time and place, are reduced to explaining the meaning of the views elaborated by the *Faqīhs* (jurists) of the first centuries. Yet the latter did not try, in matters concerning social affairs, but to formulate answers in tune with their time.

This stilted conception of religious fact is heavy in consequence and this, first, because it rests on a double distortion. On the one hand, it operates a dangerous shift in meaning as to the comprehension of the domain and the dimension of the sacred. On the other, it defines the horizon of Islam by opposition to the West. The risks of rupture and non-dialogue are thus multiplied because, as a consequence, one has considered the reality of differences (of a theological or historical order) as proof of an inescapable conflict. Yet, everything in the history of societies and religions should lead us to depth and nuance.

Muslims have themselves, therefore, to discover the challenges of their time. Nothing in Islam is opposed to individual engagement, social reform, to progress and well-being. On the contrary, one of the principles of *Uṣūl al-Fiqh* is to consider that all social reform and scientific progress that bring an improvement in the lives of men are permitted if they do not betray, in their actualisation, the sense of the general orientations offered by the sources. The general orientation remains and the steps taken on the road are in accordance with the contingencies.

This is indeed the central axis of the Muslim concept of a possible modernisation. It is a remembrance of the point of reference, Revelation and a reminder to men of the finalities of life in respect of creation, men, animals and nature. At the same time, this reminder imposes upon them a real commitment in the society of their time. The remembrance of sources, if it is stilted, betrays what it claims to defend. Only an awakened, living remembrance, which links Revelation and reality, is a faithful one. Faithful in that it makes faith the light of life; one which makes one *see* in order to better *orientate*.

Muslims are formally demanded to find this challenge; to preserve, in their daily life as in their project of society, both remembrance of the points of reference and the capacity to act, reform and build. To be believers and pragmatic, this is the first liberation that is hoped for and which many Muslim 'ulamā' and intellectuals have defended, sometimes at the cost of their lives. The powers in place have often, and very quickly, perceived the danger of this type of dynamic and renewal of religious thought (*tajdīd*). The reformers are a living denunciation, even in the name of religious points of reference and without using arms, of their repressive and dictatorial order. Their social thoughts as well as their political engagement find real echoes amongst the people and rulers are swift in demonising their "too radical" opponents with the express complicity of "friendly Western powers". The same process was used with the theologians of liberation in South America. When communism was the enemy, their community work was presented as being the result of dangerous "Communist, red priests". We must remember this. Nowadays the allied objective of dictators and the world order imposed by the USA is the radical minority of Islamist movements. The latter presence justifies all suppression and denial of freedom. The tendency that is intellectually open, politically legalist and a majority party is the one that is feared most because it is opposed in a well-thought-out, convinced and reasonable manner to state terrorism and the world order that justifies it. We are shown an aggressive enemy whose presence, sometimes fabricated, justifies the suffocation of another, one whose real discourse is made sure not to be understood. It is a cynical strategy but how efficient when, *a fortiori*, it is doubled with a policy of division whose only aim is to smash into pieces possible unions on the ground.

In the face of such a strategy, one has the choice between withdrawal into one's own identity and this may be mixed with a violent reaction, or a continued, transparent and exacting affirmation of a conviction which takes its source in faith and is actualised in a commitment to reform things in depth. At the same time, it is appropriate to warn against an anti- and pro-occidentalism which is devoid of any analysis. The second liberation which, in our view, should enable us to unfetter ourselves from the mirages of Western technology and the modernist ideology which underlies it should not confine us to a nervous rejection of the West that is from now on demonised *by reaction*. One must take things into consideration; think the finalities, select the means and derive benefit from experiences at all levels. It is at this cost that Islamic modernity can avoid the crisis that the West is today going through and whose process of modernisation ended up by instrumentalising everything. Here, many means have dissolved the conscience of finalities and one finds oneself left to suffer individualism, exclusion, blind scientism as well as growth and savage productivity. Islam accepts progress in that it is one of the measures of time, but it makes of faith and conscience the tools of balance and limits. This because there is no justice without balance and no humanity without limits.

This is indeed the meaning of social principles, political orientations and economic directives about which we have spoken above. It is a question of orientating and not imprisoning. Human reason, in its autonomy, will try to remain *faithful* to this orientation. Everything that it produces in terms of tools, techniques and knowledge is in accordance with the finality to which it subjects them. Thus, it is not a question of opposing progress, television, computer science or the like. What is the object of contestation is the manner in which these are used in a kind of amnesia of values, points of reference and meaning. It is the image of this science "which ruins the soul", when conscience dies. The modernity of Islam puts the principle before the tool, orientation before the limit and the conscience of ends before the fixed fact of catastrophes.

The third liberation is of this order and is essential. Camus maintained that the man, in the image of the philosopher Kierkegaard, who calls upon God gets through to another register other than that of rationality. He "makes a jump", powerless and anguished; he *adds* an answer to the concrete emptiness that lucidity is faced with. In Islam, the aspiration towards transcendence is original and natural. It is part of the human being to the point of qualifying as blind or dead anyone who does not live faith. Here, not to see except through reason is tantamount to amputating oneself. This is an abnormal state for one who is suffering an illness. In the Muslim universe, the rationalist subtracts, he steps backward and his apparent lucidity is veiled. Evidently, the concept of man, the lucid man, is here radically different and the third part of the present work attempts to show this. Yet, at the end of the century, Islam and other religions have the responsibility to make humanity accede to another logic other than that of market interests. Regardless of the respective concepts of different religions, the world is manifesting every day the need for a new lucidity which sides with finalities, values and, more broadly, meaning.

The awakening of Islam may bring a contribution, hitherto unsuspected, to a real renaissance of the spirituality of the women and men of our world. Again one should avoid presenting the encounter between Islam and the West under the terms of a conflict, but see it instead in the perspective of mutual enrichment. In the face of a civilisation that maintains everyday its attachment to its faith in a unique God, prayer, morality, spirituality in daily existence, the West will benefit in looking, and finding, in its own religious and cultural points of reference the means to react against the sad economist and technician drifts which we are witnessing. Does it have the means? Can it go beyond this stage of nervousness and rejection of everything that is not itself? The question deserves to be posited. Muslims doubt this sometimes; some foresee an inevitable conflict whilst others have trust in God and dialogue. All agree, however, in asserting that the future depends on our present engagement. Our daily spirituality must be nourished by the exactness of justice. This is the ultimate liberation that founds fraternities; to be with God and to live with men.

Appendices

Appendix I

The heart present in life in order to live at the heart of the Presence

Current events conceal the spiritual dimension of Islam, even though it is essential. In a world wherein "to be" is becoming increasingly difficult, religions must take up together the challenge of the heart and meaning. But this does not seem to be the essential; the preoccupations, the fears, that Islam inspires nowadays make us forget, if not conceal definitively, its specifically spiritual dimension and the essential horizon of faith. Such is the extent that there is a distinction between "two Islams"; one which is favoured by a large Western public, "the Islam of mystics", inclined to interiority and meditation; and "the other Islam" which, in its visibility, nourishes all the tensions. Love of the former justifies rejection of the latter.

Yet, this is tantamount to forgetting that Muslims quench their thirst from the same source and that the first mystic of Muslim history was indeed the Prophet Muḥammad (peace be upon him). His attitude, his frequent seclusions, and his nights of prayer remind us that faith is, first, a disposition of the heart which is, deep down, the real conscience of the believer. According to Muslim tradition, there exists an original pact between the Creator and men. In the heart of each person, there is a spark which is at the same time the testimony and expression of Transcendence. Mircea Eliade agrees with the same concept when he asserts that "the *sacred* is an element of the structure of conscience". Indeed, it is a question of this, and it is for this reason that spirituality is, in our heart, it is at the heart of life.

We find in the Qur'ān this reminder: "O you who have attained to faith, respond to the call of God and of His Messenger when they call to that which gives you life, and know that God places Himself between man and his heart." The call of faith and spirituality gives life, a new life that is strong with an inward disposition. It is exactly a question of conversion. The conscious heart feels and *knows* God's proximity. In that case, all the elements, the universe, human beings, animals and plants become, beyond their materiality, "signs" reminding of the Presence. "... *nothing is, that does not proclaim His praise, but you do not understand their extolling*" (Qur'ān, 17:44). It is the heart that sees and understands the signs and praises. The element which is a sign becomes sacred. There is here a fundamental ecology which is of another nature and which precedes political ecology born out of the conscience of limits.

This spirituality conveys a way of being in the world. There is prayer, which entails a solitary thinking of our destiny; fasting equally, about which Ghazālī said that it finds its completion in "the fasting of the heart"; there is pilgrimage that Muslims come to live at the Centre, nourished by the unity of a faith held by millions of beings. There is above all the search for balance and harmony whose challenge is not to want to deny anything of what the human being is. Both body and spirit, living for the over-here and hoping for the over-There. How to find the way of an engagement in meditation and of a social action in seclusion? How many are those who have been lost, drowned or isolated themselves? Spirituality is this trial.

Muḥammad (peace be upon him) recommended engagement in the fight against injustices with all his being. At the same time, he called for being on this earth "as a stranger or passer by". He sought the path of balance, of the "just middle" which is the peculiarity of spirituality with a human face. This is tantamount to being in this world, never accepting the unacceptable but, at the same time, not forgetting the sense of finality. Knowing how to be in what one does; and in order not to lose oneself taking the way of the sources, protecting one's remembrance, one's heart and conscience behind an inwardness and solitude from which are born dignity and the force of the Reminder.

The message of Islam is carrier, first, of this spirituality. Awakened and conscious, the heart has the means to avoid the traps of consumption without finality, of an individualism without warmth, of a defence of interests without justice. In a nutshell, the traps of a life that has no life. It was all made too early and too fast, cunningly making us, egoist consumers. On this point at least, and on this point above all, the Jewish, Christian and Muslim traditions have to pull together. To all of them it is reminded that the body cannot be without the spirit, and the spirit will be lost if it loses the heart.

Appendix II

The great current problems of Islam and Muslims

How many are those Muslims who complain about their situation, regret the passing of former times and notice with bitterness the scope of the damage caused? How many are those who are discouraged by divisions and conflicts, and are disgusted by daily betrayals and horrors? How much to trust in God in order that, finally, things change?

The picture is, in effect, sad indeed. From one end of the earth to the other, Islam is the object of the worst type of publicity, very often, due to the fault of the Muslims themselves. What is to be done? Here it seems to us important to try to delimit some of the most tricky problems of our epoch and, at the same time, evaluate the stakes of responsibility.

Poor and without education

In observing the map of the world, we realise that most Muslims live in the southern hemisphere in conditions, which are often dramatic. In effect, 85% of the 1.5 billion faithful are poor, and 60% are illiterate. It is a reality that we know intellectually but without really considering its more or less long-term consequences. Giving back life to an open Islam that is in tune with its time will require that we take on two of the greatest contemporary challenges: providing for basic needs in the matter of nourishment and dispensing basic education to all children, whether rich or poor. There is through this a response to the most elementary rights of men that everything, in the letter and spirit of the Qur'ān and the *Sunna*, refers us to. It is a priority, and Muslims would do well not to reverse the order; a project of society cannot see the light of day if three-quarters of its members still receive help.

Behind the dictators

The scope of the task requires a general mobilisation of all social players. It requires above all the manifestation of a firm political will from the governments in place. But, for the time being, one is obliged to notice that almost all countries with a Muslim majority are under the yoke of dictatorships or regimes which do not know the changeover of political power. Here and there, there is perfect derision of the people and/or their participation in social or political debate. Monarchies, bourgeoisies of state and military despoil the wealth of their population by making them pay the cost of their life-styles, and of heavy expenditures in armaments or for strategic alliance. The powers impose their institutional, social or economic policies with an iron hand, often, in agreement with Western powers, the International Monetary Fund and the World Bank. Everywhere the people suffer from the injustices of governments that, for the majority, have chosen repression as a means of interior policing, terror and torture in jails, or summary executions. Little is made of the case of the people. It is difficult, in these conditions, to hope to take on the challenges that we have indicated. The brutality of the governments in place is a threat to the life of all those persons or movements that want to try to remedy the deficiencies of these same powers; there is thus not a great choice. Today, only quasi clandestine grass roots mobilisation seems to yield results, but this seems not quite enough.

As long as a door is not open so as to leave the aspirations of the people expressed, nothing can be hoped for from these dictatorships and their horrors. Therefore, this is the third expressed priority: to mobilise energies in order to free Muslim countries from their oppressors. This without violence and if possible by means of every legality. At the same time reminding the West that it will not be possible for it to continue to insist upon democratic ideals inside its own frontiers and associate itself, outside, with the most bloody regimes in order to preserve its interests. Denouncing these hypocrites must be the task of all persons who chose the exactness of justice, whether they are Muslim or not.

A nervous reaction

One can never stress enough the importance of the above three factors in the reality of the Islamic world today. One way or the other, they influence the manner in which Muslims live and portray their adherence to their faith and culture.

This is quite obvious with regard to the essential popular discourses. Suffering from a daily denial of rights, they launch analyses that are often aggressive, inflammatory and nourished by a heavy resentment towards a West that is judged, without nuance, as being egoistic, hypocritical, arrogant and sure of its values to the point of being willing to impose them on all. The discourses coming from the South echo the statements that are heard in English or French suburbs.

The intellectuals, in claiming their Muslim identity, refer in their turn to the entire repertory of the events of history, proving that the West is leading a real war against Islam. A war that each day brings us additional confirmation of it. Thus is understood the support given to Israel and to the most sinister dictatorships as well as the permanent economic and cultural colonisation of the lands of Islam. If one adds on top of all this the massacres in Iraq and Bosnia, the conniving silence about Algeria and the "humanitarian" intervention in Somalia, where can one find counter-examples to this felt "war"?

There is no doubt that all these interpretations contain part of the truth. But it remains that very often the affective charge takes the upper hand over objective and considered analysis. Many Muslims – living a daily existence of misery and shame or suffering the worst vexations – have no longer the means to make nuances. Thus they cry out their rejection of a West from which they expect nothing. One must remember that the most shared sentiment among Muslims of today is without doubt contained in this sentence: "They do not like us." Whether this is true or false, what is important is that this impression lies at the heart of the majority of anti-Western "reactions". We are dealing purely with an affective mood.

One must certainly understand "from where" people speak when they speak (their situation, their history...) in order not to be mistaken by the tone or the literal sense of the discourses. However, it remains that one cannot take stands without nuances that will lead to a dialogue of the deaf whereby two rejections co-exist. It is the responsibility of Muslim intellectuals not to engage in the same mistake. They have a duty to produce in-depth analyses, strong in rigour, precision and nuance that are imposed by a will to reform Islam and the Muslim world today.

We lack concrete reflections and projects that distinguish between what we reject and what we want to build, between the rejection of Western interference and the domain of possible exchanges. We also lack thinkers who know how to say, without aggressiveness or compromise, what kind of society we want in a positive manner without inscribing their project as being in opposition to a West that is often caricatured or ignored. Ones who are even willing to receive Western criticisms without stopping at a supposed hostility in order to measure (with all objectivity and a minimum of intellectual probity) their pertinence, soundness, clumsiness or error.

How many Muslims pour out daily on their co-religionists the worst kind of terms, complaining about their ignorance, cowardice or the bad image they give about their religion. These same Muslims also tend to dig in their heels the moment a Westerner dares to issue the slightest reserve about Islam and Muslims. This happens almost instinctively because it is *him*, the Westerner, who said it, as if being a Westerner is a sufficient *shortcoming*. One must guard against this tendency and this is not the least of our difficulties today.

The question of women

One of the most evident stumbling blocks between the West and Islam is undoubtedly the question of women. The West's insistence on bringing about debate on this subject makes

Muslims suppose that there is an unwholesome and, inevitably, hostile intention. It could be that this holds true for some, but this cannot in any case justify our displayed deafness concerning the expressed questions and criticisms. This because in the final analysis one must acknowledge that the situation of women in many Muslim societies causes a real problem. This is not only with regard to Western values but equally in the light of points of reference that are strictly Islamic.

This because a well-understood Islam cannot justify the discriminations that are in place in Muslim countries (mainly Arab countries). Neither can it justify that the Maghreb countries have one of the highest rates of feminine illiteracy in the world, that a real juridical existence for women is not acknowledged in some states, that they are not allowed to drive a car in Saudi Arabia or that one legitimises a claimed Islamic legislation by a questionable code of personal statute (betraying in its formalism, and on account of the broken familial structure there where it is applied, the spirit of social justice in Islam). All these facts, which have an objective reality, are to be acknowledged, first, and then denounced in order to apply an Islam whose authenticity is concretised as a priority in the achievement of true programmes of social reform.

It is not a question of betraying the fundamental precepts of Islam, quite the contrary. A veiled, practising woman has inalienable fundamental rights the least of which is to live in a society which allows her to blossom. Such a society is yet to be born, and energies must be committed to giving it shape.

The ways of a renewal

How can one today manage to mobilise the efforts of Muslims in the project of changing our societies, making them more just and true to the spirit of Islam? It is appropriate first to promote a new breath in the Muslim consciousness. Since the last century, scholars have taken turns in standing and calling for a rebirth of the Islamic civilisation through a return to the fundamental sources of the religion that are the Qur'ān and the *Sunna* of the

Prophet (peace be upon him). They insist on going beyond the historical quarrels of interpretation in order to promote a reading of the sources that is in tune with our time.

Thus they distinguish between the *Sharī'a*, the way of legislation, and *fiqh,* the work of interpretation applied by the jurists, in order that the Muslims free themselves from the quarrels of different schools and return to the essential in the message of Islam. The Qur'ān and the *Sunna* give but the broad lines of legislation and the jurists, each according to the needs of his time, have carried out a work of interpretation and promulgated laws that are respectful to the spirit of the basic texts. They have carried out a work of men for the men of their time and the results which they have reached, while one has to respect them, should not be sacralised.

This distinction between *Sharī'a* and *fiqh*, once assimilated, requires that we Muslims, of this end of the twentieth century, take a bearing on our social affairs (*mu'āmalāt*) and produce a *fiqh*, a legislation appropriate to our time and which is inspired from the fundamental points of reference.

It is high time to start up a broad reflection, one which takes into account the concrete realities of our societies; that the scholars ('*ulamā'*) and experts of diverse domains of social and political action, as well as those of the economic and financial fields of investigation gather and work in unison in order to establish the priorities and perspectives of a society which, in its order and objectives, comes as close as possible to the Divine recommendation of justice.

In order to do so, we must go beyond our quarrels about the details and commit ourselves to a profound reform of mentalities that, only itself, can enable a radical transformation of our societies.

To be absolutely liberated

The order of the world is far from ideal. 18% of the world population squanders 80% of the earth's resources. After the confrontation of the two blocs during the Cold War, the superpowers, multinationals, and international institutions are today maintaining an order that has shifted the field of conflict. The North and the South are now face to face. The awakening of Islam (just like liberation theology) is confronted with the monstrous take-over of economic liberalism and the reality of the market. And the peoples, just like the opposing intellectuals, see themselves suppressed by governments that are little concerned with justice and representativity. What is to be done? Which political strategy should one adopt today?

Some have made an inventory of failed attempts and have decided to change the order of things by the use of arms. These people have lived repression, torture and the cynicism of dictators. In some instances, they have seen members of their family humiliated, raped or killed. Violence cannot, certainly, constitute the substratum of a real change of social orientation nor is it acceptable. But it happens that this violence has a history which makes it human, too human unfortunately.

Yet, the challenge of all sufferings should be taken on by organising at the level of populations true structures of mass mobilisation and participation: education, the elimination of illiteracy, projects of social support and alternative economy. Such is the – long – way of a possible political, economic and identity liberation. Nor should one fail to express, with force and conviction, one's opposition to all the torturer regimes that want to legitimise their state terrorism through religion. This under the pretext that the Qur'ān asserts that one must obey "... *those in authority among you*" (Qur'ān, 4:59) while forgetting that the Prophet (peace be upon him) said: "In truth, obedience is only in that which is good." It is high time now to shake the passivities and acceptations in order to engage ourselves – even at the risk of our lives – in changing the world. Muḥammad (peace be upon him) reminded us that in the order of faith acting precedes passive regret: "If anyone of you sees what is displeasing to God let him act against it with his hands; if this is not possible, let him act against it with his tongue; and if this is not possible, let it be with his heart, and this is the minimum of faith." We should better remember these words.

Appendix III

The Western view on Islam is forged by a long history

One can never say enough about how the present perception that Westerners have regarding Islam is nourished and forged by old images that are anchored in people's memories. It is as if these images have formed a landscape in which are inserted all recent events; this as if to confirm old fears. If one adds, as one notices today, the permanent portrayal by the media of a "militant Islam", then the conclusions shower us with as many more proofs: the exotic Muslim has a rigid and stubborn practice and any discourse is either pre-emptory or perfidious.

The religion of the Arabs

It is impossible to enumerate all the commentaries which, from the beginning, have perceived Islam as the religion of the Arabs; crude, inhabitants of the desert who mix love of pleasure with an intransigence of custom. An exotic universe of the remote East in which was born a religion that learnedly married all the constitutive elements of its compost of origin. Nor is it possible to enumerate all the chroniclers, historians and writers who tried to outdo one another in finding qualifying terms to describe the world of Islam; where the will of war intermingles with ignorance, lust and fatalism. The genius of "Mahomet" is to have known how to derive benefit from these characteristics in order to triumph against his adversaries. We find nowadays these same motives expressed in a more or less explicit manner in a great number of books and articles. And one has always some difficulty in making others understand that one cannot reduce Islam to this alleged "faith of the Arabs", or to the instinct of conquest and domination. It is as if one has difficulty in the West – and despite all the good-will of some – abandoning these old ideas which have fed, throughout history, the difficult encounters between these two civilisations.

Crusade and colonisation

The Crusades remain – in people's consciences – one of the most decisive historical moments in the encounter between the Christianism of the West and the Islam of the East. The "Mahometans" and the Saracens are perceived, therefore, as rough warriors who derive their strength from the Qur'ānic message which, for the most part, is summed up in the offer of paradise to any fighter who is killed in conquest for the sake of God. The Crusades are, therefore, understood as the most sure means of defeating the religion of the "false prophet" and of ceasing his expansion. This perception continued until the eighteenth century. Thus, we find Chateaubriand asserting in his *Mémoires d'outre-tombe*: "The crusades were not follies, as they were affected to be called, neither in their principle nor in their result... The crusades, by weakening the Mahometan hordes in the centre of Asia itself, have made us avoid becoming the prey of the Turks and Arabs." The fact is clear and it is from such remote epoch that are born Western portrayals of *jihād*. This very Islamic notion was perceived as the counterpart in Islam of what the Crusade is in Christianity, and thus, it was translated as "holy war".

This is the first shift of meaning and we shall see that such shifts have been numerous during the course of history. This consists in short in applying to the other civilisation an interpretation that has readability only in a given cultural sphere. This is exactly what happened when there was an attempt to determine the content of the notion of *jihād*. The latter had to gather and confirm all that has already been said about Mahomet and of his conquests "sword in hand" (Gobineau). And if it were possible to admit that the Crusades were not the most glorious action of Christian history, it is assiduously asserted that the Christians of today have fortunately gone beyond these "mistakes". The latter want peace, the horizon of the Biblical message of love.

Such is not the case of the Muslims who always call for *jihād*; and this proves that "the holy war" is a component of their conquering faith. Yet, one should be reminded that the Crusades were not the doing of Muslims and, therefore, it is appropriate to clarify that this notion of *jihād* – literally effort – has not at all, in the religious and cultural Islamic referent, the sense it was given. It is part of a larger vision of human effort in order to achieve, as much on the personal level as on social and political levels, a balance that guarantees justice.

The colonisation period had to have in the same manner its share of inherited portrayals. And the least of these is not that which defines the relation between civilisations by the angle of the rapport of force. "Backward" nations are to be subjected and divided according to the terms of Lawrence of Arabia. The objective is clear, and if there are some *mujāhidīn* (the same root as *jihād*), leading a rearguard fight against civilisation, then to exterminate them would be "just and reasonable".

Absolute otherness

One has fortunately in the West gone beyond such bumptious and over-simplified kinds of discourse. Yet, it remains that certain well-anchored perceptions have difficulty disappearing from people's mentalities. These two major events in the historical encounter between Islam and the West give the impression that there was nothing but war and confrontation. Many are those Western intellectuals who lean on this conflictual inheritance. They refer to the absolute otherness of Islam to the extent of forgetting the Muslim contribution in the edification of Western civilisation.

To say nowadays that the same civilisation has no other sources except the Graeco-Roman or Judaeo-Christian is tantamount to asserting a half truth. It is also tantamount to forgetting the considerable contributions the Muslims in Spain made in the development of sciences, philosophy and mathematics in Europe and the world. Their contribution is one of the decisive factors, which brought about the Renaissance, humanism and the liberation of the reasoning faculty. One cannot insist too much on the fact that the liberation undertaken, over here, against the clerical order – a manifestation of religious fact – has been advocated, over there, in the name of a faith in God built and nourished by scientific reason which makes it accede to the understanding of the created universe, the universe of signs (*āyāt*). Applied reason is one of the ways of remembrance (*dhikr*) of the presence of God.

Religion and civilisation

One tends to either note the differences and conflicts, or to erase them without any further ado. According to the former, there is nothing but wars of religion; to the latter, it is but a question of two different revelations which, nonetheless, retain the same essence and on which the same terminologies can be freely applied.

Thus Islam, just like Christianism, is a "religion" in the sense that the faithful acknowledge the existence of a Creator to Whom he is linked by an ensemble of ritual acts. It is furthermore a question of the well-defined domain of the individual's life, an individual who has his points of reference and specific organisation: dogmas, clerical hierarchy, etc. Yet, it is undoubtedly here that lies the greatest misunderstanding of the West towards Islam. For if it is true that Islam does indeed cover the ritual domain – and that it is therefore a question of religion – it is nonetheless clear that one cannot find within it a clerical organisation (the *Shī'ite* case is specific) and that the only dogma – strictly speaking – is that of the unicity of God (*tawhīd*). Whoever studies the vast domain of Islamic studies, will find that there is a distinction in jurisprudence (*fiqh*) between that which is related to worship (*'ibādāt*) and that which is related to social affairs (*mu'āmalāt*). If worship (prayer, fasting, *zakāt* and pilgrimage) is not subject to modification, the same is not true with regard to the legislation which is related to social implication. For the latter, when derived from its point of reference of the Qur'ān and the *Sunna* of the Prophet (peace be upon him), is in keeping with the place and time.

Thus, the limit between the religious fact and the social fact does not correspond to that which Christianism, in its basis and history, has determined. One can easily be convinced of this today by observing that the religious datum is narrowly linked to daily existence in Muslim countries where Islam is both a religion and a way of life, civilisation and culture.

It is not possible, therefore, to grasp Islam with the sole Christian or Jewish religious points of reference. It is appropriate to understand the specific dimension, "the logic" one might say, of a Revelation encompassing all the domains of life in which there is no contradiction between the intimacy of faith and engagement in the city. One which makes of congregational prayer a necessarily and imperatively social act.

The profane and the sacred

One finds these same distinctions when one tackles the domain of the profane and the sacred. In effect, the history of Christianity reveals that it was at the moment when civil society freed itself from religious power — and restricted the sacred to the private domain — that it was able to accede to freedom of belief and conscience. Since the Renaissance, the fight of the Jews and Protestants for their survival has consisted in liberating the public space from religious exclusivism and its hierarchy.

The profane space, which became the space of laicity, is thus perceived at the reading of the history of the Christian West as the necessary guarantee of liberty. Furthermore, this liberty has been won in terms of a fight led against the dominant religions.

This history though is, precisely, that of the West. One cannot apply its conclusions to all civilisations when they do not even have the same referent or history. For in the Islamic horizon the aforesaid terms lose all their scientific and explanatory pertinence. Here, one must make an intellectual conversion because the difference between the "profane" and the "sacred" is very specific. Any action, no matter how profane it may look in appearance, but which is nourished by the remembrance of God is sacred. This from daily hygiene to the sexual act, and from prayer to fasting.

Thus the sacred resides in the profane, and the profane in the sacred through the sole remembrance of the Presence that, far from any religious hierarchy, allows one to keep the link with Being and the Revelation which is the point of reference. The norm here is the heart and not the Church.

A laic theocracy?

These fundamental differences between Christianity and Islam, as well as the particularities of their respective histories, have been pointed out by some Orientalists who found some difficulty in applying the tools of analysis as they stood that are particular to the history of Christianity. Thus, Louis Gardet, trying to explain the specificity of the Islamic society, spoke of "laic and egalitarian theocracy". This is an ambiguous expression, and consequently incomprehensible since it associates two historically opposing models. It is, however, interesting because it reveals the impossibility of translating, by using the same words, realities that are so different.

Certainly, Muslim society has as a fundamental point of reference the Qur'ān and the *Sunna* of the Prophet (peace be upon him) from which it derives the spirit of its social organisation but it has no clergy and it posits as a principle of its viability the necessity of a rational, juridical research, the application of the law, social participation (election, representation, etc.). Therefore, it is not a theocracy.

In fact, it matches up, as we have indicated, a considerable number of presuppositions of Western laicity (in addition to recognising liberty of conscience, religion and belief), but it never empties or cuts itself off from the general finalities of its religious and ethical point of reference. Therefore, it is, not strictly speaking, laic.

Faith and commitment

It seems clear that Islam, as religion and civilisation, is not easily grasped by reference to known categories in the West. The phenomenon is indeed more complex than it may seem at first. It is appropriate to bear this in mind in order to avoid disputes which may have sense only because one has not taken time to define the terms used.

In the same fashion, one must go beyond the old prejudices in order to try to understand Islam and Muslims in the positive assertion of their identity. The latter do not inevitably use the same terms, haunted by the same historical points of reference, and they have not put aside from their social action the religious referent which remains a component of their personality. They inevitably disturb Western categories and, *a fortiori*, they scare others with their determination to note down their differences, and even to claim their rejection.

But this fear should not engender the hasty, and often definitive judgements that we encounter today. This because Western society has drifted so much away from its Judaeo-Christian tradition that it finds it astonishing that there are still people practising their religion. And if the latter's practice is visible then they are swiftly identified as extremists. In the same manner, any discourse that is not inscribed within Western points of reference with its terminological apparatus is, straightaway, considered as an "enemy of universal values". In relation to which a shift sometimes operates: the words serve as norms more than meanings or true content.

It is a difficult encounter between civilisations. A long history made of conflicts, wars, collaborations or submissions to mark memories, and influence minds daily. Yet, one should go beyond immediate reactions in order to proceed further ahead in reflection and understand what the Muslims mean when they call for giving life to a society that responds to their faith and aspiration. This is not against the West because not everything that is not done as in the West (or according to their interests) is not necessarily done against the West. For Muslims, injunction surpasses the given of a conflict. The Qur'ān says: "*Surely God bids to do justice...*" (Qur'ān. 16:90), and such is the Muslims' right and duty.

Appendix IV

The question of woman in the mirror of Revelation

There is no doubt that the question which today raises most polemics around Islam is that of woman, her treatment and her situation in Muslim society. There is an accumulation of many texts which try to prove that Islam, by essence or accident, relegates woman to the rank of inferior being who is sacrificed in the name of a Divine Revelation that is impeccable because it is definitive.

Often the proof of this is found in one or two Qur'ānic verses or such and such a saying of Muḥammad (peace be upon him) which by their content confirm these considerations. Such is the case of verse 34 of *Sūra al-Nisā'* which stipulates that a man can beat his wife. Do we not find here a clear formulation of the status of woman? Furthermore, our interlocutors would be right to reproach the Muslims of having as a defence nothing but the refrain of the embarrassed: "you are taking the verse out of its context", without going further in the argument. This, in effect, is insufficient.

An appropriate response therefore requires some development. Let us try here to point out some of the elements that would in themselves best give a better knowledge of Islam on the subject.

To read the Qur'ān?

For one who is Muslim, the reading of the Qur'ān is edifying. It is a Reminder of the Divine Presence, as it is the Text of initiation for living in order to espouse the horizons of creation. It is the Sign, the Meaning and the Way. This "reader" (Qur'ān literally means "reading") knows (or should know), however, that his manner of opening up to the Text, and or entering in to the intimacy of its revelation is right away of the order of the recognition, and, strictly speaking, of worship (*ta'abbud*) of the Creator. In the same manner, he knows – because of the very nature of his reading – that he cannot derive, by means of the sole formulation of one or several verses read at such place of the Text, teachings or rules of a juridical, social or political order. Finally, he also knows that an understanding of the spirit of the Revelation on the subject of rights and duties, social, political or economic organisation requires a different reading and approach. It is, therefore, a question of reminding oneself that the Qur'ān was revealed over a span of 23 years; that there was the Makkan period and the Madinan period; that some verses precede others; that some prohibitions were revealed gradually (wine and *ribā* for example); that, finally, the absoluteness of the Revealed Message is subject to an interpretation that takes into consideration the historical moment – and therefore relative – that gives it meaning.

In short, as we can see, the approach of the Qur'ān is not simple for the one who wishes to understand the meaning of the Message. On the level of right, a good reading requires numerous types of knowledge which are the speciality, in Islam, of experts and scholars (*'ulamā'*) who are alone, without exercising a sacerdoce or a clerical function, capable of issuing juridical opinions.

It is, hence, not sufficient to cite a passage from the Qur'ān in order that one definitively demonstrates everything. Furthermore, one should know how the text in question is inserted in the Revelation and its history. Such is the necessary path that one must take in order to understand the meaning. And this is what we should frequently remind non-Muslim readers of when they stigmatise a formulation which shocks them by its apparent brutality. Some Muslim readers resort to the same, and in the same way for that matter, when they rely on a verse to justify a behaviour or a saying whose outlines are a little disturbing.

It is by keeping these considerations in mind that one can tackle the question which concerns us here. In effect, the question treating the situation of woman in Islam requires a reading of the Qur'ān that is necessarily precise, meticulous and sharp.

Woman and Revelation

The first revelations of the Qur'ān in Makka are all marked by a call for man to acknowledge the unique God, Creator of the heavens and earth. All of them, so to speak, have an eschatological scope, and references to the end of the world and Judgement Day are therefore permanent. This is quite logical since the new Revelation, in opposition to polytheist belief and some customs, aims at provoking an inward conversion which gives birth to a new faith and a new outlook. The Revelation is therefore straightaway adapted in order to be understood and will thus continue, year after year, guiding and accompanying men and women towards the understanding of Islam, considered by Muslims as the last revealed religion.

The Arab societies of Makka were patriarchal. A woman was little considered and did not have, strictly speaking, any real social status. In times of shortages, the Arabs of the pre-Islamic era had the custom of burying baby girls alive in order to get rid of those "surplus mouths". Hence, it is to the players of this society that the Message is first addressed, as it is against the inhumanity of their murderous habits that the Qur'ān is inscribed beginning from the first months of the Prophetic mission. *Sūra al-Takwīr*, amidst the scenery of the end of time has the following: "*When the sun shall be darkened...*" and then warns: "*When the buried infant shall be asked for what sin she was slain...*" (Qur'ān, 81:1, 8–9).

This was straightaway understood, following the example of Khadija who was the first person to adhere to the new faith, as identifying that the Revelation was indiscriminately addressed to both men and women and that, in fact, it was engaging people in a profound reform of society and its organisation.

For many years, the Revelations came in succession in order to mature the first believers and allow them, every day further, to distance themselves, to "uproot", so to speak, from their old habits and reflexes. Only a few months before migration, the

criticism of the comportment of Arab polytheists towards women
came as definitive:

> ... and when any of them is given the good tidings of a girl, his
> face is darkened and he chokes inwardly, as he hides himself from the
> people because of the evil of the good tidings that have been given
> unto him, whether he shall preserve it in humiliation, or trample it
> into the dust. Ah, evil is that they judge! (Qur'ān, 16:58–9)

This was the first stage in the pedagogy of the Qur'ānic
message. Through Revelation and the example of the Prophet
(peace be upon him), the first Muslims learned to reform
themselves. Soon, with migration, they reached a decisive stage
in their "religious education".

The women of Madina

The first Treaty ('Aqaba) that Muḥammad (peace be upon
him) concluded with the first converts of Yathrib (Madina) is
significant. One of the five clauses stipulate that the Muslims
should not kill their children. Furthermore, during the second
treaty, women were part of the delegation who engaged in the
defence of the Prophet and Islam.

The Madinan society was entirely different from the Makkan.
Women there enjoyed a social role that was indeed very
important and some clans were organised according to
matriarchal principles. The new immigrants were very quickly
disturbed by the way the women of the Anṣār (the women of
Madina) did things. Present in public life, they also asserted
themselves in the private domain. 'Umar ibn al-Khaṭṭāb (the
second successor to Muḥammad – peace be upon him)
maintained that before migration (Hijra): "We used to impose
ourselves on women and when we went to the Anṣār where the
women imposed themselves in their clans, our women began
taking the habit of the Anṣārī women..." (Bukhārī and Muslim),
and he regretted that his wife dared to answer him back when
he summoned her, and retorted that he had to support the life
example of the Prophet.

Thus, life in Madina was the second decisive stage in the assertion of the status of women in Islamic society. The Qur'ānic Revelations mention women as much as men in all that was related to ordinances and recommendations:

> ... 'I waste not the labour of any that labours among you, be you male or female...' (Qur'ān, 3:195)

Society was organising itself and women played an absorbing part in communal life. The revelation of *Sūra al-Nisā'* (the Women) determined some of the intangible rights of women. In a clear fashion and after having acknowledged for her an identical status as that of man on the religious plane, she found therein a clear formulation of her juridical personality on the familial and social plane. We realise that being the case that the Qur'ān has led man to understand both the fundamental equality and the necessary complementarity of man and woman.

The familial space

The family is the basic nucleus from which is built the Islamic society. All the Qur'ānic texts and the traditions of the Prophet (peace be upon him) convince us of this. In this domain, as in that of the recognition of the status of woman that we have indicated, it took many years to reform the customs of the epoch. In Makka especially, but also in Madina, there remained a considerable number of ill-treated women. After intervening against the murder of baby girls, the Qur'ān determined men's mode of behaviour in case it happened that the women neglected or betrayed them:

> And those you fear may be rebellious admonish; banish them to their couches, and beat them. (Qur'ān, 4:34)

Many have seen in this verse the proof that man had all the rights, among which is that of beating his spouse. Yet, to look closely – and in taking into account our previous remarks – one will realise that there is nothing of the sort. All the commentators, and this from very early on, have pointed out the fact that there was in this verse a precise command which, by its very nature, had a pedagogical function for men who are inclined to immediately use their hands (this verse was revealed after a woman had complained to the Prophet (peace be upon him) that she had been slapped by her husband – cf. Ṭabarī).

In effect, it is first a question of exhorting (waʿaẓa) one's spouse (and not admonishing her according to the translation of Masson or Chouraqui) through reminding her of the verses of the Qur'ān, as maintained by Muslim exegetes (cf. Ibn Kathīr and Qurṭubī). It is only when she persists in her attitude of refusal that it is appropriate to "move away from her in bed" which was interpreted as clearly manifesting the will to avoid any emotional rapport. If none of this works, then, and only then, is it allowed to "beat" her. All the commentators of the Qur'ān, from the most early ones (Ṭabarī) to the most recent have clarified that it is a question of going through the aforementioned stages. If nothing works, then it is a question, as Ibn ʿAbbās says in an interpretation which goes back to the time of the Prophet (peace be upon him), of using a symbolical blow with the help of a siwāk twig.

The theme from here on becomes very clear. In addressing the Arabs, it was clarified that all the ways had to be used before expressing one's bad temper. This is to be the last instance and, in its non-violence, it is the only violence allowed. The way of dialogue and concretisation with one's spouse is that which corresponds to the spirit emanating from the Revelation. Moreover, the teaching did not stop at this verse and its interpretation. This because the example of the Prophet (peace be upon him) more than anything else, was by itself enough to express the ideal comportment.

The living Qur'ān

The first Muslims lived for more than two decades in contact with the continuous Revelation. It led them from the roughest way of life to the exactness of mediation, delicacy and humility which the Qur'ān vivified in them:

... Turn not thy cheek away from men in scorn, and walk not in the earth exultantly; God loves not any man proud and boastful. Be modest in thy walk, and lower thy voice; the most hideous of voices is the ass's. (Qur'ān, 31:18–19)

They had, finally, drawn close to the essence of the Qur'ānic Message, in its dimension and profundity; they finally drew close to the model:

You have had a good example in God's Messenger for whosoever hopes for God and the Last Day (Qur'ān, 33:21)

And when his wife 'Ā'isha was asked about the character of Muḥammad (peace be upon him) she responded: "His character was the Qur'ān." He was its personification, the first and the best interpreter. Yet, never did the Prophet (peace be upon him) raise his hand to any of his wives; all the testimonies show him as attentive and respectful to the person and the personality of the women who surrounded him. The same 'Ā'isha was asked one day about what the Prophet (peace be upon him) did at home (in terms of chores); she responded that: "He was at the service of his family, he moreover sewed his clothes and repaired his shoes."

As a pedagogue with his Companions, he taught them Islam through example. This without rushing to attack customs but always with the concern of succeeding in communicating the essence of Islam. Once he was invited to eat; he asked his interlocutor "with her?" pointing to his wife 'Ā'isha. The man said "No", therefore the Prophet (peace be upon him) apologised for not being able to accept the invitation. The same situation happened again, and once again the invitation was declined. Upon the third encounter, the man finally understood and responded by confirming that the invitation included 'Ā'isha; the Prophet (peace be upon him) accepted to have dinner accompanied by his wife.

The Prophetic mission was coming to its end. The revelation of the verse, "*Today I have perfected your religion for you...*" (Qur'ān, 5:3) was a sign and an indication. From that moment on, everything of the meaning and spirit of the Message was given. Hence, the Prophet, during the "farewell pilgrimage", did not fail to remind men of the fundamental principles of Islam. To the 140 thousand faithful who were present, and only a few weeks before his death, he exhorted his community: "O people! Your women have a right on you as you also have a right on them." Then, after repeating the aforementioned Qur'ānic theme, he added: "Treat women with kindness! Have fear of God in relation to women and make sure to want good for them." Turning towards God, he supplicated: "Have I conveyed the Message?"; all the faithful responded "Yes", and the Prophet (peace be upon him) said: "O God, be witness!" These were his last public words concerning women which responded to the meaning of the last revealed verse regarding the life of a couple:

> And of His signs is that He created for you, of yourselves, spouses, that you might repose in them, and He has set between you love and mercy. Surely in that are signs for people who consider. (Qur'ān, 30:21)

Hence, through the Qur'ān and the example of the Messenger, which are the two sources of reference in Islam, is laid out the true status of the Muslim woman in her relation with man.

True daily existence

As we can clearly see, referring to a verse of the Qur'ān without inserting it into the historical unfolding of the Revelations separates the text from its educational dimension. One takes as an absolute that which, in itself, is but a stage leading to a broader appreciation of the Prophetic mission.

It remains that one should not blind oneself. In many Muslim countries today, women live in very difficult conditions. But the responsibility is entirely that of the Muslims. The future, their future, will be a result of their capacity to re-animate the living source of the Revelation in their hearts, families and societies. This because, when all is said and done, man or woman, the best among human beings is the one who is more pious.

Index